The Psychology
of Conservatism

The Psychology of Conservatism

edited by

GLENN D. WILSON

Department of Psychology,
Institute of Psychiatry,
De Crespigny Park,
Denmark Hill, London.

ACADEMIC PRESS
London · New York

A subsidiary of Harcourt Brace Jovanovich, Publishers

ACADEMIC PRESS INC. (LONDON) LTD.
24/28 Oval Road,
London NW1

United States Edition published by
ACADEMIC PRESS INC.
111 Fifth Avenue
New York, New York 10003

Copyright — 1973 by
ACADEMIC PRESS INC. (LONDON) LTD.

HM
271

.P77

Library of Congress Catalog Card Number: 72–7705
ISBN: 0 12 757950 8

PRINTED IN GREAT BRITAIN BY
COX & WYMAN LTD., LONDON, FAKENHAM AND READING

Contributors

CHRISTOPHER BAGLEY, *Centre for Social Research, Sussex University, England*

ROGER BOSHIER, *Centre for Continuing Education, University of Auckland, New Zealand*

GEORGE B. KISH, *Department of Psychology, Roanoke College, Salem, Virginia, U.S.A.*

FRANCIS J. LILLIE, *Queen Elizabeth II Hospital, Welwyn Garden City, England*

DAVID K. B. NIAS, *Institute of Psychiatry, University of London, England*

JOHN R. PATTERSON, *Department of Psychology, University of Otago, New Zealand*

JOHN J. RAY, *School of Sociology, University of New South Wales, Australia*

ROBERT A. C. STEWART, *Department of Education, Massey University, New Zealand*

ALAN C. WEBSTER, *Department of Education, Massey University, N.Z.*

GLENN D. WILSON, *Institute of Psychiatry, University of London, England*

Foreword

At one time, the measurement of attitudes was almost synonymous with social psychology. Thurstone had shown how attitude statements could be scaled, to provide proper measuring instruments; Likert had introduced his novel form of questioning; Bogardus had made use of his "social distance scale" to investigate racial prejudice; and most social psychologists were intent on employing these various devices in substantive researches. Later on appeared theoretical notions like the "Authoritarian Personality", "Dogmatism" and "Machiavellism", together with the appropriate scales to measure these hypothetical entities, while in this country a general model of social attitude structure was being developed around the two concepts of radicalism-conservatism and tough-mindedness versus tender-mindedness. In recent years there has been something of a lull in this field; social psychologists have gone off in other directions, while important questions, such as the relationship between the various concepts mentioned above, have remained largely unanswered. This seems a pity; attitude measurement is not the be-all and end-all of social psychology, but it is a very important part of it, and in particular it has advanced much farther than many other parts.

Dr. Wilson and his co-authors therefore fill a very real need when they put before us now a new book on Conservatism, together with a new method of measuring this concept, and much detailed experimental work to indicate the degree to which a person's standing on the continuum from conservative to liberal pervades his general behaviour and attitudes—even including his sense of humour and his aesthetic values! They spice their account with well-taken criticisms of such sacred cows as the "authoritarian personality" and the concept of dogmatism, and add, for good measure, theoretical portions dealing with the psychological and political meaning of conservatism. Quite rightly they stress that they are concerned with a psychological, not a political concept; people may be politically pro-labour, but psychologically conservative (like many trade-union leaders), or politically conservative, but psychologically liberal (like many middle-class people). This is an important distinction, and much confusion has arisen from a failure to heed it.

The appearance of this book may revive interest in proper attitude measurement, as opposed to the Gallup-Poll type of questioning; it is the latter which to most people represents "attitude measurement". Yet Gallup-Poll testing has many disadvantages. It may be compared to the efforts of a man instructed to find out facts about the height of Englishmen; he selects a stick and goes out to find a random sample. Each person chosen for his sample is then put up against the stick, and marked down as "Yes—taller", "No—smaller", or "Don't know—just about the same". He then reports his findings in percentage form—30% Yes, 69% No, and 10% Don't know. This might make a minimum of sense if we knew the actual height of the stick, but we don't usually know that in Gallup polling—even slight variations in the question produce marked variation in the results. Obviously there is a better method; use a proper yardstick and measure each person's height to the nearest quarter-inch. Considering that proper scales are now available for attitude measurement, or can easily be constructed for areas not hitherto covered, it is very odd that Gallup polling has continued along its old-fashioned path, without taking notice of these developments. Perhaps the public, reading its favourite paper, is thought incapable of understanding anything but percentages; one may take leave to doubt such an underestimate of the intelligence of the general public which has for many years managed perfectly well the much more complicated business of working out odds on the football pools, or making sense out of knitting patterns. Proper scales can answer questions which Gallup cannot even begin to put; this book may serve as an appetizer, showing the many different areas in which further research of great interest might be conducted.

The major advance claimed by the authors of this book is the format of their questionnaire; instead of asking respondents to agree or disagree with lengthy statements about religion, the Jews, capital punishment or God, they simply ask for reactions to the words themselves, on the hypothesis that the first "feeling" reaction to such terms would be at least equally diagnostic as a more cognitive, considered judgment—and free of all the misunderstandings which can be mediated by questions, however carefully framed these might be. This is certainly an important new development, which has the additional advantages of speed and easy scoring; it is reassuring that the major results, in so far as they are comparable, do not deviate too much from those reported by earlier investigators.

Readers who are themselves social psychologists will of course pay much attention to the technical details of *eigenvalues* and oblique rotations; many readers will be more interested in the general conclusions, and the thoughts these may suggest about the nature of political organizations, the differences and similarities between East and West, and the implications the results may have for the future of our democratic institutions. How dearly one would like to carry out such studies in the U.S.S.R., or in the new China of Chairman Mao! Until this is possible, we will have to make do with studies carried out in Western countries exclusively; "The Psychology of Conservatism" is an excellent introduction to a large and important field of research which is of interest not only to experts, but also to any thinking man and woman.

H. J. EYSENCK
February 1973

Contents

Part I. CONCEPT

1. The Concept of Conservatism

GLENN D. WILSON

2. Conservatism, Authoritarianism and Related Variables a Review and Empirical Study

JOHN J. RAY

3. The Need for a New Approach to Attitude Measurement

GLENN D. WILSON AND DAVID K. B. NIAS

4. Development and Evaluation of the C-Scale

GLENN D. WILSON

5. The Factor Structure of the C-Scale

GLENN D. WILSON

6. Measurement and Structure of Children's Attitudes

DAVID K. B. NIAS

7. Religion, Racialism and Conservatism

GLENN D. WILSON AND CHRISTOPHER BAGLEY

12. The Temperamental Basis of Attitudes

GLENN D. WILSON

13. Stimulus-Seeking and Conservatism

GEORGE B. KISH

14. Conservatism Within Families:
A Study of the Generation Gap

ROGER BOSHIER

15. Conservatism, Psychiatry and Mental Distress

FRANCIS J. LILLIE

16. Attitudes to the Common Market:
A Case Study in Conservatism

DAVID K. B. NIAS

17. A Dynamic Theory of Conservatism

GLENN D. WILSON

Part I

CONCEPT

B

The Concept of Conservatism

GLENN D. WILSON

Institute of Psychiatry, University of London

Introduction

This book overlaps two major areas of psychology: social psychology, and personality. On the one hand it is about attitudes: their measurement, factorial structure, origins and functions. On the other, it is about a particular characteristic or "dimension" of personality that is inferred on the basis of the organization of such attitudes. "Conservatism" is conceived as a general factor underlying the entire field of social attitudes, much the same as intelligence is conceived as a general factor which partly determines abilities in different areas. This general factor is manifested as a largely positive pattern of group intercorrelations amongst different attitude areas, and is presumed to reflect a dimension of personality similar to that which has previously been described in the semi-scientific literature in terms of a variety of labels such as "fascism", "authoritarianism", "rigidity", and "dogmatism".

The term "conservatism" is preferred not only because it provides the best overall description of the factor concerned, but also because it is relatively free of derogatory value-tone. Most people would quite reasonably take exception to being described as "fascist", "authoritarian" or "dogmatic", whatever their actual orientation, but would probably be happy to admit to being "conservative" if they were, in fact, positioned towards this end of the spectrum. Likewise, the term "liberal" is usually perfectly acceptable to individuals located towards the other end of the dimension. (The terms "liberal" and "conservative" may, however, tend to have a mild negative connotation to individuals at the opposite pole.)

An example may serve to show how a relatively non-evaluative term is more generally acceptable. In threatening to close the schools of Georgia rather than comply with Government plans for racial integration, Governor Maddox was quoted as follows:

> School desegregation is part of the Communist plot to overthrow this country. They are destroying America through sex education and not letting teachers pray and read the Bible. (*Guardian*, 25. 7. 79.)

Those who agree with this statement might call Maddox morally sound, forthright, enlightened, and patriotic; those who disagree might call him fascist, authoritarian, bigoted, or even paranoid. Everybody, regardless of his own orientation, would agree that he is conservative.

Because the terms conservative and liberal happen, in Britain, to correspond to the names of major political parties, it may be necessary to point out that we are not particularly concerned with the prediction of voting behaviour or with politico-economic conservatism (although these areas may later be found to have some relevance). The term conservatism is used in the broader, more literal, sense of resistance to change and the tendency to prefer safe, traditional and conventional forms of institutions and behaviour. To a large extent voting behaviour and political opinions are presumed to reflect habit, social class, and personal expediency rather than any characteristic of personality. Thus, when political opinions are involved in what follows, they are of interest only in so far as they throw light on a more fundamental personality characteristic which is presumed to vary considerably amongst supporters of each of the major political parties. On the other hand, followers of certain minor political parties, such as the National Front, may well be fairly homogenous with respect to this dimension. In any case, the question of conservative–liberal personality differences amongst supporters of various political parties is an empirical one that is easily investigated once suitable methods of measurement have been developed.

The meaning of the dimension as it will be used here is probably best illustrated by considering the position of certain organizations in relation to it. In the U.S. the Ku Klux Klan and the John Birch Society are widely recognized as conservative organizations, as are the National Front, the Gideons, and the Monday Club in Britain, even though the major aims and interests of these groups are far from completely overlapping. Some groups that are generally agreed to be relatively liberal might include the Humanist Society, the acting profession, social scientists, and the "Samaritans".

II. The "Ideal" Conservative

We may now list some of the attitude clusters which would be expected to characterize the extreme or "ideal" conservative, while acknowledging that very few organizations or individuals will correspond to this picture in every detail. (For purposes of illustration the views of one individual who does approximate to this ideal are shown in Fig. 1.) The following description is based largely on the popularly held image or "stereotype" of the typical conservative. The extent to which this picture is valid will be investigated in the later chapters, in which empirical evidence is presented and evaluated.

A. RELIGIOUS FUNDAMENTALISM

Religion has long been recognized as a conservative force in society, i.e. as an institution resistant to progressive change. Thus the Roman Catholic Church and the more puritan of Protestant denominations have been at the forefront of protests against a great many new ideas and trends in social behaviour, from the heliocentric theory of the universe and evolution theory to birth control and stage nudity. However, since it must be recognized that not all religious persons and organizations are characteristically resistant to change (some of them are actually the products of change themselves), it seems reasonable to suggest that the ideal conservative will adhere to religion of a dogmatic and fundamental kind, e.g. believing in the absolute authority of the established church and the literal truth of the Bible, including such notions as miracles and Divine retribution. Incidentally, it may be that religious beliefs of this kind are today found more commonly among laymen or members of the congregation than among theologians and clergy. Also, it hardly needs to be mentioned that the religion need not be Christianity; it may be any established religion or even a prevailing ideology such as Maoism.

Reprinted with permission from the Brighton and Hove Herald

The colonel pleads for drastic action

I was taking a summer stroll along Hove seafront when I perceived two lewd youngsters in a compromising position on the beach. I could not bring myself to go over to reprimand them and there was not a police officer in sight.

I felt my only recourse was to air my views in public through your columns. I have been a regular visitor to your lovely town since I was a lad—65 years ago—and I have never seen anything so shocking. What made it worse was that I was with my widowed sister, a ratepayer of this town, whom I was not able to shield from this disgusting spectacle.

Isn't it time all decent people got together to put a stop to this orgy of sex and drug-taking which our young people are encouraged to indulge themselves in by our permissive society'?

Of course, there are many good youngsters in our community—witness the Boy Scouts and Girl Guides—and these undesirable elements constitute only a minority. But this scourge on our towns will grow like a cancer and unless the very fabric of our society is to be completely eroded by these subversive, Communist inspired louts, everything that we of the older generation fought in two World Wars for —democracy, Christian morals, decency, respect for authority and unselfish service to others— will have been in vain.

I suggest Compulsory National Service for all young people aged between 16 and 24. A good dose of discipline never did anybody any harm. And if these pseudo intellectuals persist in wearing long hair and throwing all standards of hygiene to the four winds, we should give them a dose of their own Red medicine by interning them in correction camps.

It may sound drastic but these are drastic times; we are fighting for the very survival of our way of life. When I was a junior subaltern in the trenches many years ago now we found internment very effective in dealing with these subversive blighters.

I urge all like-minded people to campaign for a ban on pop-music— not only is it an infernal row but it is used by these subversive elements in our society to plant their foreign ideas in our young people's minds. Then we should mount a concerted campaign to get people back in the churches. Without God all hope is lost.

And we should deport all foreigners who are doing our society no good — students, jazz musicians and (yes, I am not afraid to say it) disgruntled coloured

folk who don't apreci- the upsurge and only Royal Family who go
ate what we British have stiffer penalties and the about their task without
done for them. return of capital punish- complaint.
The time will come ment will act as a
when decent people deterrent. I think young *Name and Address*
cannot walk the streets people could do no *Supplied*
without fear of being worse than follow the
molested. Crime is on example of our own

FIG. 1

Letter to a provincial English newspaper illustrating many of the
characteristic views of the "ideal" conservative.

B. PRO-ESTABLISHMENT POLITICS

Another widely accepted characteristic of the ideal conservative is his commitment to political organizations which favour maintenance of the *satus quo*, if necessary, by the use of force and strict censorship. In Western countries this would mean "right-wing" extremism, e.g. the National Front in Britain, the "Colonels' regime" in Greece. In present day Czechoslovakia, conservative individuals would be just as clearly aligned with the "left-wing", i.e. pro-Russian. Such political commitments might be tapped with items relating to patriotism, nationalism, and fear of corruption by foreign influences (xenophobia) or internal dissent and anarchy. Note that this is not the same as political Conservatism in the sense of favouring *laissez-faire* economics rather than nationalization of industry and legislation aimed at the equal distribution of wealth and protection of the weak.

C. INSISTENCE ON STRICT RULES AND PUNISHMENTS

Perhaps related to the above, is the tendency for the conservative to favour strict regulation of individual behaviour, either for the social or Divine good, or for its own sake, by rules, laws, etc., and a tendency to respond in a harshly punitive way towards violations of these laws (i.e. stress on "law and order"). In addition, he will tend to be resistant to any proposed changes in the moral or legal codes, viewing them as God-given, fixed and immutable. Thus the conservative will tend to favour the use of corporal and capital punishment, and firm action of police, magistrates, judges, school prefects, and authorities generally. This characteristic is, of course, central to the concept of the "authoritarian personality" (Adorno *et al.* 1950). These authors note that respect for authority is manifested in extreme deference to persons higher in the "pecking order" as well as the insistence on obedience from those below.

D. MILITARISM

A tendency to favour the maintenance of military strength, and participation in military conflicts, justified or rationalized on grounds of defending the nation or its values, is also characteristic of the conservative. This is, of course, really an "international" extension of the patriotic, nationalistic fervour, the fear of corruption by foreign influences, and the insistence on "law and order".

E. ETHNOCENTRISM AND INTOLERANCE OF MINORITY GROUPS

Also widely recognized as typical of the "conservative" person and closely related to the above characteristics, is the tendency to prefer people of one's own kind, and to be suspicious, fearful, even hateful, of people who are different in any way (race, religion, dress, length of hair, etc.). Thus the ideal conservative resists the upgrading of Negro status in the U.S.A., would restrict immigration from any cultural group which is noticeably different from his own, and feels threatened by deviant sub-cultures such as hippies, homosexuals, etc., whether or not they represent any real danger to him.

F. PREFERENCE FOR THE CONVENTIONAL IN ART, CLOTHING, INSTITUTIONS, ETC.

Remembering that conservatism is broadly defined as "resistance to change", it follows that the conservative ought to prefer what is familiar, traditional, and conventional in behaviour generally, including art, music, literature, clothing, and social institutions. Modern art forms, fashions, fads, etc., will therefore be expected to evoke a reaction which is disproportionately unfavourable, i.e. more negative than can be satisfactorily explained in terms of rational objections to these changes. Thus certain kinds of art and music may be seen as "eroding the moral fibre of the young", and changes in clothing fashions may be said to promote promiscuity, anarchy, etc.

G. ANTI-HEDONISTIC OUTLOOK AND RESTRICTION OF SEXUAL BEHAVIOUR

A tendency to regard pleasure as necessarily bad or "sinful" is also widely accepted as typifying the conservative "syndrome". This applies particularly to sex, but also to food, drugs, dancing, entertainment, and leisure generally. Thus the conservative favours the strict censorship of literature and entertainment, clothing that is sexually non-arousing, and reservation of sexual activity for the purpose of reproduction of the species within marriage. Any sexual behaviour which is participated in purely for the sake of pleasure is classified as undesirable, e.g. use of contraceptives, homosexuality, perversions, masturbation. Similarly, entertainment for entertainment's sake (comics, horror films, etc.) is thought to be undesirable, while austere books with formal or religious content are favoured.

H. OPPOSITION TO SCIENTIFIC PROGRESS

Another well recognized aspect of "ideal" conservatism is the refusal to accept "new-fangled" ideas. Many issues come to mind throughout history: the heliocentric theory of the universe and evolution theory were mentioned above in connection with religious opposition; there is also anaesthesia, vaccination, blood transfusion, fluoridation and space travel. Not all resistance to technological development, however, can be attributed solely to conservatism. Some fears may have a rational basis and be partly or entirely legitimate, e.g. nuclear bombs, pollution of the environment. (Note here a distinction between conservatism and *conservation*.) Extreme conservatism is characterized by *non-rational* objections to scientific discoveries, e.g. that a scientific finding does not accord with ancient writings.

I. SUPERSTITION

Perhaps related to religious fundamentalism and the dislike for science is the tendency to be superstitious and fatalistic—to believe that one's destiny is not within one's own control, and that one is a victim of supernatural forces (cf. the internal–external control dimension; Rotter, 1966). Conservatives, then, are inclined to be convinced of the efficacy of fortunes, horoscopes, and "patent cures", and fearful of "omens" that are traditionally supposed to portend bad luck or doom.

III. Organization of Attitudes

Although the above characteristics have been listed as separate areas, it should be remembered that many of them intuitively and logically overlap, so the list is based on arbitrary divisions. In fact, the stereotype of the conservative personality assumes that there is some connection between them such that possessing one such characteristic raises the probabilities that the others will also apply. This, of course, is a hypothesis which is subject to empirical confirmation or disconfirmation, and it is one of the aims of this book to investigate the extent to which these attitude areas are intercorrelated.

Figure 2 illustrates the way in which the various attitude clusters may be organized to form a general conservatism (C) factor. This is highly diagrammatic because: (a) We have not yet examined the empirical evidence concerning the manner in which these clusters relate to each other, and (b) while the angles between the vectors can be used to represent the degree of commonality it is possible to do this only within two dimensions, while the "true" picture would involve many more. The diagram does,

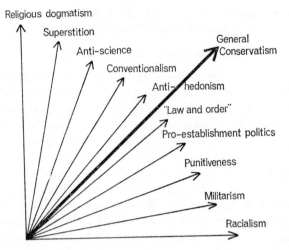

Fig. 2. Diagram to illustrate possible arrangement of attitude clusters
to form a general conservatism factor.

however, serve to illustrate the present conceptualization of conservatism
as a kind of average of all these vectors (mathematically, the single factor
which absorbs maximum variance from the intercorrelation matrix).

Two other points to note about Fig. 2. (a) It is really only half the picture;
the liberal end of the dimension would presumably show a similar pattern.
(b) It shows that there is no necessity for every pair of attributes to overlap (intercorrelate) for the hypothesis of a general conservatism factor to
be confirmed. For example, religious dogmatism and racial prejudice can
theoretically be totally independent and yet both still be useful measures
of conservatism.

This example recalls the important distinction implied at the beginning
of the chapter between social attitudes *per se* and personality characteristics
inferred on the basis of attitude configurations. There would be little value
in the discovery that belief in God was correlated with a favourable attitude
towards the Church since the overlap in content is logical and self-evident.
Far more interesting are the cases of overlap between apparently unrelated
or even incompatible attitudes and beliefs, for these suggest the role of
more fundamental underlying personality dynamics. Katherine White-
horn, writing in the *Observer* (30. 11. 69) cites a letter written to the Conservative M.P. Mr Duncan Sandys, which, agreeing with his stand on
abortion, went on for several pages about the sanctity of human life, and
ended "P.S. I'm with you on hanging too". In this case it might be supposed that the argument concerning "sanctity of life" was some kind of
secondary rationalization adopted in order to bolster and justify an attitude towards the abortion issue which derived primarily from a generally

conservative personality disposition. With reference to the letter which comprises Fig. 1., we might ask about the logic of the connection between the colonel's stress on "unselfish service to others" and his suggestion that coloured people should be deported because they "don't appreciate what we British have done for them".

This point about the distinction between attitude content and personality dimensions will be taken up in greater detail in later chapters. Suffice it to say at this stage that conceptual schemes and attitudes scales that are concerned only with locating subjects within specific content areas such as racialism, religion, sexual freedom, law and punishment, etc., may be expected to prove of limited usefulness compared to systems that deal with the organization of social attitudes across broader content areas.

IV. The Distribution of Conservatism

Another question that may be introduced here is that of the shape of the distribution of the population along the liberal–conservative dimension of social attitudes. Figure 3 illustrates three different hypotheses: (a) There

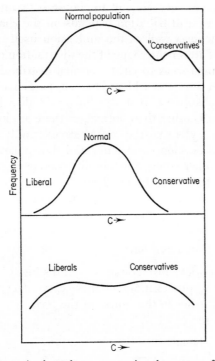

FIG. 3. Three alternative hypotheses concerning the nature of conservatism as indicated by its distribution in the population.
(a) Pathological syndrome; (b) Normal distribution; (c) Polarized normal distribution

may be a small group of extreme conservatives who are clearly separated off from the normal population in terms of the clustering of conservative attitudes in different areas, and who may therefore be described as abnormal in the statistical or even pathological sense. Such a hypothesis is implicit in the work of Adorno, *et al.*: "authoritarianism" is conceived as a kind of *pathological syndrome* like psychopathy or schizophrenia. (b) A currently more popular viewpoint, is that of a liberal–conservative dimension which is *normally distributed* like height or extraversion–introversion, or at least ought to be if the measuring instrument was ideal. This would probably approximate more closely to the viewpoints of Rokeach (1960) and Eysenck (1954). (c) A third possibility and one that has not been explicitly considered previously, is that of a *polarized normal distribution*, i.e. a distribution which is symmetrical and might have been normal were it not for certain processes which operate to "push people off the fence and into one camp or the other" or which tend to sharpen small differences between them (contrast effects or "reactions"). Such processes could give rise to several different possible distributions: bipolar, rectangular, or a bell-shape more widely spread than the classical normal curve.

In practice it proves very difficult to choose between these hypotheses because the shape of a distribution depends on the characteristics of the measuring instrument as well as the dimension itself. Some researchers might argue that whatever the shape of the distribution of raw scores, they should be transformed so as to yield a normal distribution. It is our contention that this procedure is seldom justified, particularly when there are possible reasons to suppose that the "natural" distribution across the variable in question is other than normal, as there are in the present case.

One such possibility is that the conservative attitude constellation (like liberalism) tends to develop consistency and thus polarization, because it functions like any other concept to simplify the environment, in this case by providing a stable set of values and rules for conduct, thereby reducing the need for the individual to evaluate the details of a new situation in order to decide upon an appropriate course of action.

V. Four Views of Conservatism

We now turn to a brief consideration of four distinguishable though overlapping current conceptualizations of the nature of conservatism. These will be developed further in the course of the text.

The four views are:

(a) Resistance to change
(b) "Playing safe"
(c) The "generation gap"
(d) Internalization of "parental" prohibitions

They should be regarded as complementary viewpoints rather than conflicting theories.

A. CONSERVATISM AS RESISTANCE TO CHANGE

Literal definitions of the word "conservatism" stress three aspects (1) preference for *existing* institutions i.e. resistance to change, (2) preference for *traditional* institutions, and (3) the disposition towards being *moderate* and *cautious*. By combining these three components, it can be deduced that the conservative will resist change except when the proposed change is perceived to be in a traditional direction or such as to increase the security of the individual or his society.

In fact, it is possible to distinguish three types of social change assuming that social trends are predictable on the basis of historical experience and consideration of the implications of scientific and technological developments. These may be called:

(i) *Progressive changes*, which project recognized trends and which are made appropriate by technological advances and other changing social conditions, e.g. penal reform, Britain's change to decimal currency and metric measurements.

(ii) *Reactionary changes*, which amount to a return to an earlier state of affairs or reversal of a well recognized social trend, e.g. reinstatement of the death penalty, abolition of the contraceptive pill.

(iii) *Neutral changes*, which are unrelated to major trends but may reflect a desire for novelty or "change for the sake of change", e.g. clothing fashions, styles of art.

It is hypothesized that conservatism is characterized by the tendency to resist change which corresponds to the progressive and neutral types, but to favour either maintenance of the status quo or change in a reactionary direction. In corollary, liberals would be expected to resist reactionary change, to support progressive change and at least tolerate neutral change.

B. CONSERVATISM AS "PLAYING SAFE"

The third part of the definition of conservatism given above, that of cautiousness, may be regarded as subsuming the other two aspects. Thus resistance to change and the preference for traditional institutions and behaviour are seen as being two aspects of a general preference for "playing safe" and avoiding risks. In this view, the conservative individual is prone to feel threatened and to experience insecurity in a complex and unfamiliar environment, and is therefore intolerant of change because it increases the complexity of the experiential world, i.e. the world is seen as falling apart (see Chapter 17).

C. Conservatism as a Quantification of the "Generation Gap"

The parallel drawn earlier between intelligence as a general factor in the field of human abilities and conservatism as a general factor in social attitudes may be taken a little further. It will be recalled that early I.Q. tests based their measure of intelligence on the concept of *mental age*. This meant that knowing the relationship of average test performance to chronological age, the score of a given individual could be expressed as the age at which this performance would be achieved on the average.

Similarly, given the information that raw conservatism scores increase markedly in adulthood as a function of age (see Chapter 4), it would be possible to assign to an individual an *attitude age* score, meaning that his attitudes are most like those of the average person of a given age. Although this is somewhat outmoded as a psychometric technique and will not, in fact, be adopted here, it does illustrate the possible approach to conservatism as that of a quantification of the recently much-published concept of the "generation gap", either in terms of individual scores or between-group differences.

D. Conservatism as Internalization of "Parental" Prohibitions

Finally, one other current interpretation of the liberal–conservative dimension is that of an index of the extent to which "parental" prohibitions have been internalized so as to become a stable (perhaps inflexible) framework within which social phenomena and behaviour are evaluated (i.e. a measure of "conscience" or "superego strength"). Clearly, the exact structure of the individual conscience will depend upon the particular parents, peer groups, and other social institutions to which one is exposed, as well as personality characteristics that determine differential susceptibility to these influences. Nevertheless, it may be assumed that there is a fair amount of consensus as regards the kind of behaviour that should be considered "right" or "socially desirable" in the context of "middle-class respectability", and conservatism may be viewed as a quantification of the extent to which this normative value-pattern has been absorbed. We should not, therefore, be surprised to discover that conservatism is related to measures of "conformity" and "social desirability".

VI. A Brief Outline of the Book

The next chapter will consider in some detail the relationship between conservatism, authoritarianism, dogmatism, and other apparently similar variables such as tolerance and ethnocentrism. In particular, it will be asked whether there are any grounds for distinguishing the latter concepts from conservatism other than in terms of the breadth of their scope.

Chapter 3 criticizes conventional approaches to the measurement of conservatism, and Chapter 4 describes the development of a new scale (the C Scale) specifically designed to circumvent the deficiencies of the previous measures, followed by an evaluation of the extent to which this has been achieved. Chapter 5 deals with the factorial structure of the C-Scale in several European countries both for the light that this throws on the question of the organization of social attitudes in general, and for the purpose of developing a method for scoring subfactors in the scale.

Chapter 6 describes the development of a children's version of the C Scale, including investigation of its reliability, validity and factor structure, and a study of the relationships between personality and children's attitudes.

Chapters 7–16 present the results of several important research studies dealing with the relationship of conservatism to a variety of different behaviours (e.g. superstition, aesthetic judgments, humour preferences, stimulus-seeking, mental disorder) and demographic variables (e.g. religious affiliation, personality), while Chapter 17 is an attempt to integrate these empirical findings within a dynamic theory of conservatism.

References

Adorno, T. W., Frenkel-Brunswik, E., Levinson, D. J. and Sanford, R. N. (1950). "The Authoritarian Personality". Harper, New York.
Eysenck, H. J. (1954). "The Psychology of Politics." Routledge and Kegan Paul, London.
Rokeach, M. (1960). "The Open and Closed Mind." Basic Books, New York.
Rotter, J. B. (1966). Generalized expectancies for internal versus external control of reinforcement. *Psychol. Monogr.*, **80** (Whole No. 609).

2

Conservatism, Authoritarianism, and Related Variables: A Review and Empirical Study*

JOHN J. RAY

University of New South Wales, Australia

I. Introduction

A. AIM

In this chapter the hypothesis that many important social attitudes can be ordered on one bipolar dimension will be investigated. In particular, an

*The assistance and co-operation of the Department of the Army in the empirical research reported here is gratefully acknowledged.

attempt will be made to answer the question as to whether there is any ground for distinguishing the construct of "authoritarianism", as measured by the California "F"-Scale, from the traditional notion of "conservatism". This question will be investigated (a) at the conceptual level, (b) in a review of previous empirical studies, and (c) in a new specially designed empirical study.

B. THE EXISTENTIAL QUESTION

The most fundamental question which may be asked in the area would be: "Is there anything there for the words to denote? Do authoritarianism and conservatism actually exist?" Certainly, a vast number of authors seem to believe that they do. Among the many scales that have claimed to tap such a dimension are the "PEC"-Scale of Adorno *et al.* (1950), the PEC-Scale of Peabody (1961), the conservatism scale of Ekman and Kuennapas (1963), the Tulane Factors of liberalism–conservatism (Kerr, 1955), the conservatism scale of McClosky (1958), the "R" scale of Eysenck (1954) and the PEC-Scale of Anderson and Western (1967). Authoritarianism too has been more frequently scaled than might at first be supposed. There is the Rokeach "D"-Scale (1960), the "D"-Scale of Anderson and Western (1967), the Eysenck "T"-Scale (1944 and 1954), the "F"-Scale of Adorno *et al.* (1950), the "TFI"-Scale of Levinson and Huffman (1955), the Stereopathy scales of Stern, *et al.* (1956), the "J" type of Jaensch (1938) and the "A", "AA" and "BF" Scales by Ray (1971, 1972 a, b).

It need not, of course, be claimed that either authoritarianism or conservatism are unidimensional, but it would be expected that a cluster of oblique dimensions would be found that have something in common that justifies use of these names as general rubrics. The Tulane factors of liberalism–conservatism (Kerr, 1955) are five in number, and there is also no shortage of claims that authoritarianism is multidimensional (O'Neill and Levinson, 1954; Camillieri, 1959; Krug, 1961).

C. PROCEDURES OF DEFINITION

Once a research worker has come to believe that there is some consistency in the expressed attitudes that he wishes to scale, there are two major ways he may proceed. These will be called "conceptual" and "factorial" definition (these words describe *operations* of defining, not categories of definition). The first is the approach strongly favoured by Christie (1956); the second is identified by him as "typically Eysenckian". Each method may produce more than one consistent solution. For example, factorial definition of intelligence is of several types but few psychologists would want to claim as a consequence that the variable "intelligence" does not exist.

Conceptual definition is of the type employed by Adorno *et al.* and Rokeach. A construct from some source is developed theoretically, and items are written that have relevance to the construct. The set of items is then scaled by various procedures according to the taste of the authors. The second approach (e.g. Eysenck, 1954) is to use factor analysis on the intercorrelations of a large and hopefully random set of items. The factors that emerge are then "interpreted" in terms of constructs possessed by the researcher.

Both approaches, then, require theorizing in terms of constructs. The difference is that the latter method is *ad hoc* whereas in the former, hypotheses are subjected to empirical test. While the former may be methodologically preferable, the decision on what items to include in a factor analytic study is often such as to make the two approaches not greatly different. Studies that employ both tend to gain the strengths of both without necessarily adding weaknesses. If several variables are scaled in one factorial study, their relationships may still be compared providing orthogonality was not stipulated for the factor solution.

A point that *should* not need to be made is that if it is desired to present proof that two variables (e.g. conservatism and authoritarianism) are essentially related, the procedures employed must not be such as to make the finding a necessary artifact. And yet, this was precisely what Adorno *et al.* did. They *required* the F- and PEC-Scales to correlate.

"In form 60 the PEC-Scale was shortened to fourteen items and numerous changes made in content and wording ... Two items which worked relatively well in form 78, numbers twenty-seven (Rebellious Ideas) and sixty-one (Security is Bad) were placed in the form 60 F-scale because they seemed on theoretical grounds to fit better there. Several new items have been added. Item thirteen (The American Way) was taken from the form 78 E-scale ... (p. 163).

Apparently items were freely circulated among the various scales in the study by these authors. An item at one time said to measure authoritarianism is said a little later to measure conservatism, etc. To find that items correlated well with other items said to measure conservatism and then to put those items in the F-Scale makes the subsequent finding of a correlation between the two scales tautological. The average correlation (circa +0·5) is in fact surprisingly low—possibly because of the restricted range in socio-economic status of their respondents.

Eysenck may be said to have made a similar type of error, but in the opposite direction. By stipulating an orthogonal factor solution he required his R and T factors *not* to correlate. Both authors were apparently interested primarily in demonstrating that their position was one to which certain data can be fitted.

II. Some "Conceptual" Definitions

A definitional resource that seems to have been unjustifiably neglected is the Oxford English Dictionary. Its definitions are exhaustive, its historical scope unrivalled and its quotations both extensive and authoritative. It is on the great range of materials collected in this work under the heading "liberal", "liberalism", "conservative" and "conservatism" that the "conceptual definition" of liberalism–conservatism to be given below is built. ("Liberal–conservative" is preferred to "radical–conservative" because "radical" is sometimes used of any belief strongly held or held in the extreme. Thus we hear of the "radical Right.")

A. CONSERVATISM AS ANTI-INNOVATION

The common element that stands out most in the definitions of the Oxford Dictionary under the headings listed is preference or rejection of innovation and new things generally. A liberal prefers the new and a conservative the old. Thus John Stuart Mill is quoted as saying: "A Liberal is he who looks forward for his principles of government; the Tory looks backward". It is this which explains why the radicalism of today becomes the conservatism of tomorrow. Once that to which the belief refers has become accepted and ceases to be an innovation, it is no longer a proper object for liberal agitation and will eventually come to be defended by conservatives. This explains the usefulness of such test items as: "The highest form of government is democracy and the highest form of democracy is a government run by those who are most intelligent" (from Rokeach's D-Scale). Because democracy has become so normative the conservative must defend it, but knowledge of an early *élitist* era in government still with us in various forms leads the conservative also to defend *élitist* ideals. The apparent contradiction is in fact a simple defence of the status quo as we actually have it.

Liberalism is not, however, entirely content-free. Liberal thinkers in fact appear to have *guided* society's evolution rather than passively accept any innovation or new idea that comes along. Nor does the conservative appear to accept *any* feature of society that becomes normative. The second highest item on Ekman and Kuennapas' (1963) ratio scale of conservatism is "Only those with formal education in the problems of society should be allowed to vote". This is not normative and does in fact appear to be opposed to a norm.

B. STRUCTURE VERSUS CONTENT

The distinction that seems needed to resolve the apparent contradiction above might be called the difference between "structure" and "content".

This is a different distinction to that used by Rokeach. Structure is used here to denote the most general and lasting feature of an attitude system and "content" the specific themes which may be discussed among people (or tapped by test items) at any one point in time.

The content of liberalism appears to be egalitarianism and desire for personal freedom (after all "liberal" is derived from the Latin *"liber"* meaning "free", and *"liberalis"* meaning "pertaining to a free man"). Note the following definitions from the Oxford Dictionary:

4. Free from narrow prejudice; openminded, candid.
5. Of political opinions; favourable to constitutional changes and legal or administrative reforms tending in the direction of freedom or democracy, Hence used as the designation of the party holding such opinions, in England or other states; opposed to Conservative.

A quote from H. M. Williams is given dated 1801, attributing to conservatives:

The extinction of every vestige of freedom, and of every liberal idea with which they are associated.

A quote from the Pall Mall Gazette dated 1884 is given which says:

Conservative and Liberal, as we ordinarily use the terms, are distinctions having reference to a particular practical struggle, the gradual substitution of government by the whole body of the people for government by privileged classes.

So far, then, we have seen that a liberal attitude has the structure of preferring new things, change or innovation and the content of desiring that change be in an egalitarian and libertarian direction. If a conservative attitude has the structure of preferring the status quo and established ways of doing things, what is its content? Is it simply opposition to liberal ideas and rejection of libertarianism, egalitarianism, etc? Kerlinger (1967) would predict not. He claims, in fact, that the issues which concern liberals would be matters of indifference to conservatives, i.e. that liberalism and conservatism are orthogonal—which contrasts with the usual view that they are opposites. There is a way to reconcile the opposing claims of Kerlinger and other writers who claim that liberalism and conservatism are negatively related. Perhaps Kerlinger is right because the content of liberal and conservative attitudes is unrelated, and perhaps more conventional theorists are right in that the structure of liberal and conservative attitudes is opposed.

McClosky (1958) notes that the content of conservative attitudes is surprisingly clear right throughout the time period he samples. Unlike the Oxford Dictionary, his summary gives most weight to the content of conservative beliefs. It deserves to be quoted in full:

(1) Man is a creature of appetite and will, "governed more by emotion than by reason" (Kirk), in whom "wickedness, unreason, and the urge to violence lurk always behind the curtain of civilized behaviour" (Rossitar). He is a fallen creature, doomed to imperfection, and inclined to license and anarchy.

(2) Society is ruled by "divine intent" (Kirk) and made legitimate by Providence and prescription. Religion "is the foundation of civil society" (Huntington) and is man's ultimate defence against his own evil impulses.

(3) Society is organic, plural, inordinately complex, the product of a long and painful evolution, embodying the accumulated wisdom of previous historical ages. There is a presumption in favour of whatever has survived the ordeal of history, and of any institution that has been tried and found to work.

(4) Man's traditional inheritance is rich, grand, endlessly proliferated and mysterious, deserving of veneration, and not to be cast away lightly in favor of the narrow uniformity preached by "sophisters and calculators (Burke)." Theory is to be distrusted since reason, which gives rise to theory, is a deceptive, shallow, and limited instrument.

(5) Change must therefore be resisted and the injunction heeded that "Unless it is necessary to change it is necessary not to change" (Hearnshaw). Innovation "is a devouring conflagration more often than it is a torch of progress" (Kirk).

(6) Men are naturally unequal, and society requires "orders and classes" for the good of all. All efforts at levelling are futile and lead to despair (Kirk and Rossiter), for they violate the natural hierarchy and frustrate man's "longing for leadership". The superior classes must be allowed to differentiate themselves and to have a hand in the direction of the state, balancing the numerical superiority of the inferior classes.

(7) Order, authority and community are the primary defence against the impulse to violence and anarchy. The superiority of duties over rights and the need to strengthen the stabilizing institutions of society, especially the church, the family, and, above all, private property.

Conservatives, then, believe man is not naturally good, are superstitious, and prefer hierarchical social structures. They think highly of order, authority and duty.

The prominence in conservative beliefs of preference for hierarchical social structures is clearly contradictory to the liberal's preference for equality. In the other respects listed, however, there is no obvious opposition to liberal beliefs. Thus the historical evidence does allow the possibility that there is more orthogonality between the content of liberal and conservative beliefs than might at first be supposed, and Kerlinger's (1967) argument becomes feasible.

C. CONSERVATISM VERSUS REACTIONISM

A liberal attitude, then, is one that states a preference for innovation in an egalitarian or humanitarian direction whereas a conservative thinks we are egalitarian enough already and change might be dangerous. As "progress" is, within limits, normative in our culture, the conservative may believe in a certain (slow) rate of change towards greater humanitarianism, etc., whereas the liberal will want a faster rate of change than is normative. In this context we also have a basis for a distinction between conservatives and "reactionaries". A reactionary wants a negative change back to a former state. Liberalism, conservatism, and reactionism form a clear continium, then, and it is therefore not surprising to find the reactionary desire for a return to more *élitist* government in such a high position on the ratio scale of Ekman and Kuennapas (1963). Regrettably, authors of attitude scales have tended to ignore the distinction between reactionary and conservative. It may well turn out that reactionaries have the same traits as conservatives, but this cannot be established until the two are first separated. As the quote given in the Oxford Dictionary dated 1862 says: "Let not one presume to identify conservatism with reaction."

D. CONSERVATISM AND AUTHORITARIANISM

By now it must be clear that the picture of the typical conservative which has so far emerged bears startling resemblances to the "authoritarianism" of Adorno *et al.* (1950). The "rigidity" of the authoritarian and the "oposition to innovation" of the conservative are wholly identifiable. The stress on the importance of duty and the desire for a hierarchical social structure are also identical. Adorno *et al.* do not provide us with much idea of what the opposite to authoritarianism might be, but in view of our finding that the liberal believes in egalitarianism and individual liberty, the definition of "authoritarianism" given in the Oxford Dictionary is interesting: "Favourable to the principle of authority as opposed to that of individual freedom." An example dated 1884 is: "A lover of liberty, not an authoritarian." Thus it is not surprising that Adorno *et al.* felt that the F- and PEC-Scales must correlate; it is almost impossible to distinguish the two concepts. *The only distinction that appears tenable is to say that "authoritarian" is a rather more particular concept than "conservative" as far as content is concerned.*

It is not of course clear that the F-Scale does measure authoritarianism in this classic sense. In spite of the title of their book, Adorno *et al.* (1950) usually refer to the syndrome tapped by their scale as "pre-fascist". Be this as it may, a great deal of research (Kirscht and Dillehay, 1967) on "the new anthropological type" purportedly discovered by these authors has used the F-Scale as the categorizing instrument and it has become widely accepted that this "type" is properly called "authoritarian". Given the residual doubt about whether the F-Scale does measure authoritarianism in the classic sense, the contention that the "authoritarian" (as familiar to the psychologist) is none other than the old fashioned conservative, must be supported by reference to empirical studies in the literature.

III. Review of Empirical Evidence

A. AUTHORITARIANISM AND CONSERVATISM

From the beginning, Adorno *et al.* (1950) acknowledged that conservatism and "pre-fascism" were inevitably interrelated. The inevitability of this relationship was, however, widely questioned (Shils, 1954). An important reason for dissent was that any radical or "left-wing" regimes on the world scene were also held to display markedly authoritarian characteristics (Smith, 1967). Thus the concept of an "authoritarianism of the left" achieved some currency (Brown, 1964). The most constructive attacks on the claim of an invariant relation between authoritarianism and conservatism have been made by Rokeach (1960) and Eysenck (1954). Other major studies to be considered are: Kerlinger (1967), Lipset (1960), McClosky (1958) and Martin and Westie (1959).

B. ATTITUDES AND PERSONALITY

Before further work is considered, however, an attempt to differentiate "personality" and "attitude" scales is in order. The work of Adorno *et al.* (1950) implied that there is such a distinction. Their work, in fact, primarily dealt with a personality "type"—the "authoritarian." Their F-Scale, however, was quite clearly like a conventional attitude scale rather than a personality inventory. As a consequence the distinction between attitude and personality might seem blurred. To confuse the two, however, is to ignore a major assertion of the California work—that in their "pre-fascist" attitude scale they have an *indirect* instrument which can be used to detect authoritarians only because people with authoritarian personalities characteristically happen to hold pre-fascist attitudes.

If their work implies that there is a distinction between personality and attitude statements it is clearly of some importance to have some definition of the difference. The definition used here is that personality items ask the respondent to rate, describe or assess himself or his own behaviour. An attitude item asks his opinion on something in the world outside himself. The distinction preferred by Eysenck (1954) is that attitudes have particularity, i.e. they have a particular "object" such as "the church", "children", or simply "them", whereas personality statements refer to a general predisposition to behave—largely regardless of object. Whichever definition is adopted, some such distinction is important to the following consideration of work by both Rokeach (1960) and Eysenck (1954).

C. ROKEACH'S DOGMATISM

Rokeach adopts the view that it is more important to consider the "structure" of attitudes as distinct from "content". By "structure" he appears to mean the rigidity with which attitudes are held. The particular structural feature that Rokeach considers to be evident in those attitudes previously characterized as "authoritarian" he has named "dogmatism" and his D-Scale was designed to tap this. Although Rokeach's D-Scale shows consistently high correlations with the F-Scale (Rokeach, 1956; Peabody, 1966) it has also been shown *not* to discriminate between communistic respondents and fascistic respondents—which the F-Scale, of course, was designed to do. Rokeach thus is able to claim that dogmatism is orthogonal to liberalism–conservatism and that the F-Scale is probably a confused measure of both factors. Both the F- and D-Scales however, suffer from similar problems of response set, which could account for much of the correlation between them (Peabody, 1961).

It should be noted that, in spite of his claim to measure structure rather than content, Rokeach does not use items that appear generically different from those of previous authors. The D-Scale, looks very much like the F-Scale or Eysenck's R-Scale. The one major difference is that Rokeach does include some personality items (whichever criterion one adopts). It would in any case be rather difficult to maintain a distinction between a personality variable and Rokeach's "structural" variable. If, as Rokeach says, structure is independent of attitude content, it does not seem to belong to the realm of attitude measurement at all—but is certainly comprehensive as a part of personality. Some examples of these obvious "personality" items are: "Once I get wound up in a heated discussion I just can't stop", and "I'd like it if I could find someone who would tell me how to solve my personal problems". On the other hand, self reference in many D-Scale items is often disguised, e.g. "It is only natural for a person to be rather fearful of the future" is probably little more than a palatable version of "I am afraid of the future".

For all that, there are sufficient indisputable attitude items in the D-Scale for us to ask whether there is not some purely attitudinal dimension that is orthogonal to liberalism–conservatism. Using their Australian revision of the D-Scale on a large group of students, Anderson and Western (1967) found a correlation with their liberalism scale of ·00. An unpublished study by the present author, however, throws some doubt on the invariance of this relationship. In that study a significant interaction was shown with social class on Eysenck R-Scale scores. Rokeach D-Scale scores were in fact highly related to Eysenck R-Scale scores for the lower class respondents but, as in Anderson and Western's finding, the two were unrelated for upper class respondents. Other reports that D-Scale scores and conservatism are related have been made by Direnzo (1968) and Kirtley and Harkness (1969). It is evident that Rokeach's work does not represent clear proof that there are two orthogonal dimensions in general social attitudes.

D. Eysenck's R and T Factors

In spite of Rokeach's attacks on the (prior) work of Eysenck (Rokeach and Hanley, 1956 a, b), the main divergence between the two authors is in methodology rather than theory. From a large pool of "social attitude" statements, Eysenck was able to extract two orthogonal factors which he named "Tough–tender Mindedness" "T" and "Radicalism–Conservatism" "R". He shows that his T-Scale has similar characteristics to the F-Scale in validation studies. The T-Scale is superior to the F-Scale in being fairly well counterbalanced for response bias (ten "tender" and twelve "tough" items). The R-Scale is completely balanced and also extensively validated.

Eysenck claims that the F-Scale is oblique to both his R and T factors. Schematically, then, Eysenck is able to resolve the problem of "left" versus "right" authoritarianism. The Fascist is identified as a tough-minded conservative and the Communist a toughminded radical. This schematic solution is supported by some empirical data (Eysenck, 1954) and the major political parties of Great Britain also are assigned positions in this two-factor space. Their main difference lies along the R–C continuum with the T dimension of little importance. A difficulty with Eysenck's two factor solution is that no single item comes near to uniquely defining either end of Eysenck's T-factor, i.e. there is not one item loading highly on the T factor that does not also load highly on the R factor. This could be cured by a 45° rotation but Eysenck points out that this would deprive the dimensions of much of their explanatory attractiveness.

Eysenck, however, does *not* claim that his T-factor is a dimension of social attitudes in its own right. In fact, he makes the radical claim that there is only *one* fundamental dimension of social attitudes, i.e. radicalism–conservatism. He argues (like Rokeach) that the T-factor is just a projection on to the attitude level of a personality variable ("extraversion" in Eysenck's work, "dogmatism" in Rokeach's). This projection takes different forms in the case of radicals and conservatives, which explains why the T factor is not uniquely defined by any one item. Once this point is comprehended, most of the attacks by Eysenck's critics (Rokeach and Hanley, 1956, a, b; Christie, 1956) lose their point. Rather than attack the "purity" of the T-Scale or Eysenck's arithmetic, they might do better to investigate his claim that both "radical–tough" and "conservative–tough" statements correlate with extraversion. Eysenck's work does at least have the virtue of keeping the personality and attitude levels separate (unlike Rokeach), which makes such a test possible in his case. In any event, note that all the attacks made have been on Eysenck's T-Scale. His findings with respect to the R-Scale have not yet been challenged.

In examining Eysenck's claim that there is only one fundamental dimension of social attitudes "R" it is profitable to inspect the items defining that dimension as given by him (Eysenck, 1954). It contains such items as: "The Japanese are by nature a cruel people", "Coloured people are innately inferior to white people", "War is inherent in human nature" and "Crimes of violence should be punished by flogging". All these items are again strongly reminiscent of the "authoritarian" syndrome described by Adorno *et al.* (1950). Rather surprisingly, therefore, Eysenck quotes research by Coulter to show that there is no significant relation between the F- and R-Scales. Some possible reasons for this result might be acquiescence bias in the F-Scale, differences in scoring procedures, or peculiarity of the sample (43 Communists, 43 Fascists and 83 British Soldiers).

Eysenck's assertion that there is only one dimension of social attitudes is certainly unusual in the literature. By contrast, Kerr (1955) reports that even conservatism scores in two slightly different areas (political and economic) are unrelated. In their survey of Australian student attitudes, Anderson and Western (1967) find six intercorrelated factors and one orthogonal politico–economic factor. The difference is at least partly accountable for in terms of the different factor-analytic methods popular in Britain and the U.S.A. Eysenck (1954) reports a British analysis of the original F-Scale data from the California study which "showed a strong general factor throughout". By contrast, Camillieri (1959) and Krug (1961) in the U.S.A. had no difficulty in finding six or seven factors in the F-Scale.

E. KERLINGER'S "CRITERIAL REFERENTS"

Kerlinger (1967) provides some reconciliation of the opposing camps by taking out second order factors from a range of attitude items. As a result of both theoretical considerations and extensive empirical evidence, he comes out in favour of there being only one fundamental parameter of social attitudes—which he names liberalism–conservatism. He does, however, take the novel position that liberalism and conservatism are orthogonal! While he agrees that all attitudes can be grouped into the broad categories of "favourable to innovation" versus "preference for established institutions and procedures", it is implicit in his theory of "criterial referents" that endorsement of "conservative" statements is not predictive of rejection of "liberal" statements. This is also a part of Peabody's (1961 and 1966) position and, if true, makes futile the attempt to construct balanced scales.

Thus, rather than deplore the one-way wording of the F-Scale, Kerlinger deplores the attempt to construct any other sort of scale. He takes the extreme position that no attitude variable is naturally bipolar and to introduce bipolarity is to introduce artificiality. Acquiescent response set does remain a problem but Kerlinger would prefer to remove its influence by partial correlation with a separate acquiescence measure. This was the procedure apparently employed by Campbell *et al.* (1960) in their extensive work with McClosky's conservatism scale. The trouble with this method, of course, is that partial correlation cannot restore discriminating power that is not there. This, perhaps, is one reason why McClosky's scale showed a negligible relation to political party choice.

Methodological considerations aside, the evidence of Kerlinger does indicate two well defined orthogonal second order factors—one containing assertions of liberal ideals and the other containing assertions of conservative ideals. On the other hand, we have Eysenck's analysis showing negative correlations between liberal and conservative items. This discrepancy may be accounted for by the samples or items used, or genuine differences between the U.S.A. and Britain. There is some evidence for differences in attitude structure between Australia and the U.S.A. Anderson and Western (1967) and Kerr (1955) both used student samples and both used non-balanced liberalism scales. Yet Kerr in the U.S.A. found economic and political liberalism to be uncorrelated, whereas Western in Australia found them so highly correlated as to make it impossible to retain separate scales.

F. Social versus Economic Conservatism (Lipset)

Although the pattern that exists in social attitudes is unclear, Kerlinger and Eysenck both seem convinced that a liberal–conservative differential is in some sense fundamental. This position is shared by Lipset (1960) who equates conservatism and authoritarianism as both describing "working class ideology". He presents a wide variety of sociological evidence to show that conservative beliefs and preference for authoritarian social structures are characteristic of the working classes—having as their common cause intellectual, social and economic deprivation, Lipset finds it important, however, to distinguish liberalism in general from liberalism in the one area that most clearly distinguishes the working classes from "them", i.e. economic liberalism. He produces evidence to show that while conservatism generally increases down the social scale (as do F-Scale scores; Brown, 1964), *economic* conservatism moves in the opposite direction— being greatest among those who have most to lose from change, i.e. the upper classes. For Lipset the problem of "left wing authoritarianism" on the international scene does not arise. He regards it as a natural consequence of the proletarian base that has, through revolution, given rise to such regimes. For him, middle class authoritarianism or "fascism" is a more difficult problem. He calls this authoritarianism of the centre, identifies it as less thoroughgoing than authoritarianism of the left, and claims that it is only in exceptionally disorganized and deprived circumstances

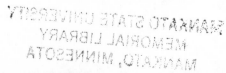

that middle class people turn to authoritarian political and social institutions. Lipset, then, attributes the "radical" nature of working class political movements solely to economic motives; where these are not involved, the workers are naturally the most conservative.

The fact that many people must have some conflict between their economic interests and their general social attitudes makes it again more understandable why conservatism scales such as McClosky's show little relation to political party choice (Campbell *et al.* 1960). Parties presumably are less free to be inconsistent than are people. For all that, it is a notable confirmation of Lipset's contention that the lower class based Australian Labour Party was historically the strongest supporter of the White Australia Policy. As the studies to be mentioned subsequently show, ethnocentrism is a reliable correlate of conservatism. (The role of the F-Scale as an indirect measure of ethnocentrism, of course, is well known.)

Eysenck's finding that high scores on the R-scale (predominantly a measure on non-economic radicalism) correlate with left wing party preference is not as damaging to Lipset's position as might at first appear. As Lipset points out, this is an era of "Consensus Politics" and the two major parties that are characteristic of the English speaking world tend to separate only on minor details of emphasis. This being so, it is possible that the discriminating power of the scale was contributed entirely by the "economic radicalism" items.

We now have, incidentally, a perfect triad: Anderson and Western claim political and economic liberalism are positively correlated, Kerr claims they are orthogonal, and Lipset claims they are negatively correlated. As Lipset used evidence from far more normal samples than the other two, and quotes a wide, international range of studies, we might be inclined to favour his interpretation. Almost all his data are sociological however, and the one piece of questionnaire evidence that he quotes for the negative correlation between political and economic conservatism is based on responses to three items of the California PEC-Scale by students at the "American University" in Lebanon. Better psychological data are obviously needed.

G. THE POLITICAL CONSERVATIVE (MCCLOSKY)

Support for Lipset's equation of conservatism and authoritarianism is, however, forthcoming from the study of conservatism by McClosky (1958). A political scientist, McClosky started out with the very sophisticated and historically based definition of conservatism quoted earlier. Basing himself on materials drawn from writers as diverse in time as Edmund Burke and American "New Conservatives", McClosky was able to write items expressing sentiments which undoubtedly are typical of conservative ideology. The

resulting scale, together with several clinical-type scales, was then administered to a large and fairly general sample of the population of an American
city. When his high conservative scorers were compared with others, the
pattern of traits that appeared characteristic for them might almost have
been a transcript of "authoritarian" characteristics from Adorno *et al.*
(1950)—although McClosky appears to have been little influenced by that
study. The conservatives were high on: hostility, paranoid tendency, contempt for weakness, ego defense, rigidity, obsessive traits and intolerance
of human frailty. Conservative beliefs were most frequent "among the uninformed, the poorly educated, and so far as we can determine, the less
intelligent" (p. 35). Identification of conservatism with authoritarianism
was of course a central tenet of Adorno *et al.* (1950). This independent
confirmation of their work does do something to rebut the attacks on that
assumption. Regrettably, however, McClosky's scale has a response set
problem identical to that of the F-Scale. The critics still have room to
assert that it is "the acquiescent personality" that is being described. If
they choose to do so, however, Rorer (1965) has argued that the burden of
proof is at least partly on them.

Given McClosky's results and the original reliable correlation between
the F- and PEC-Scale reported by Adorno *et al.* (1950), it is not really
clear how one is to interpret Peabody's (1961) finding that these scales do
not correlate at all. He did use balanced versions of the two scales but
before one hastens to a response set interpretation of the original results,
let it be remembered that the PEC-Scale was partly balanced from the
beginning.

H. Martin and Westie's "Tolerant Personality"

The final major independent study in this area is "The Tolerant Personality" by Martin and Westie (1959). Their study is notable in that it
seems relatively free of the methodological doubts that have plagued the
other studies reported here. They used a sophisticated measure of tolerance
in which a "tolerant" response was *not* simply rejection of an ethnocentric
item. Thus neither "response set" nor "criterial referent" (Kerlinger, 1967)
criticisms can be levelled against it. Like McClosky, they also administered a large range of other questionnaires to their respondents—differing
only in that they were specifically chosen to allow examination of the hypotheses in Adorno *et al.* (1950). As with McClosky, the pattern found might
well have been a transcript from "The Authoritarian Personality". The intolerant were more: nationalistic, intolerant of ambiguity, superstitious,
threat-oriented, authoritarian, religious, child-punitive, distrustful of politicians and venerative of their mothers. They were less interested in politics, of lower social class and less educated.

The sample was an almost random one obtained by house to house calls. There was, however, the inevitable limitation of such methods that a large number of the people contacted (two out of three) failed to co-operate fully. It might also be questioned whether the results for one American city could be generalized to other cities, states or countries.

I. SUMMARY

In the field of general social attitude measurement there is some evidence for the pre-eminent importance of one underlying conservatism *cum* authoritarianism dimension. The studies of Adorno *et al.* (1950), Lipset (1960), Martin and Westie (1956) and McClosky (1958) point to the identity of authoritarian and conservative attitudes, while the work of Lipset (1950), Eysenck (1954), and Kerlinger (1967) point to this as being the one fundamental dimension that there is. At issue with the first point is the finding of Peabody (1961) that conservatism and authoritarianism are unrelated. At issue with the second, are a number of studies that have found several orthogonal factors in this area (e.g. Ferguson, 1941; Kerr 1955; Anderson and Western, 1967). There is also Kerlinger's unusual qualification that, although conservatism and liberalism are opposed, liberal and conservative tests are unrelated. Lipset too has a qualification about economic conservatism, but this has had no appreciable support from the psychological literature.

IV. Some New Empirical Evidence

A. AIM

In the present study a deliberate attempt was made to fit a unifactor model to empirical data that is reasonably free of the usual doubts about sample adequacy and representativeness of scale items.

B. METHOD

A questionnaire consisting of items from the F-Scale, the Eysenck R-Scale, an ethnocentrism E-Scale and the D-Scale was administered to a group of 474 Australian regular army conscripts. This battery (henceforth known as the F.R.E.D. battery) included the Eysenck R-Scale (sixteen items) and the Australian D-Scale revision (nine items) by Anderson and Western (1967) in their entirety. The E-Scale consisted of the ten "strongest" items of the Beswick and Hills (1969) Australian Ethnocentrism Scale (selected on the basis of the item analyses provided by the authors). From the F-Scale, only those ten items having the most direct reference to authoritarianism in the classical sense were selected. The items expressing superstition, projection, etc., were omitted (cf. Prothro and Melikian, 1953; French and Ernest, 1955). Thus the scales and constructs represented in this study are the ones that have been most discussed in the field of social attitude measurement.

The sample chosen was unusually representative. In Australia, conscripts are chosen randomly on the basis of a birth date procedure from the entire male 20-year-old population. Eligibility is not influenced by area of residence and noncitizens are equally liable with Australian nationals. Students may have their eligibility deferred but may not be exempt. The questionnaire was administered on the first day of the October 1968 intake at No. 3 Training Battalion, Singleton, New South Wales. Perhaps the most useful feature of this sample is the absence of any "volunteer effect" such as occurs in door-to-door samples.

C. ANALYSIS

Out of 474 protocols returned, seventy were discarded due to various defects such as partial incompleteness, zigzag response set, etc. The 404 left for analysis were coded for computer processing and tested for single-factorness by the procedure of Morrison et al. (1967). This program is a modification of the Lawley maximum likelihood procedure which seeks the maximum amount of variance explainable by a single factor and provides a chi square test for the residual. While this program has been especially written to test the sort of model being examined here, it does have two defects common to all maximum likelihood methods: 1. As Nunnally (1967) points out, the maximum likelihood method produces more and more significant factors as N is increased. If N is large enough, the number of significant factors approaches the number of variables. 2. The basic data for the maximum likelihood procedures are principal components—and principal components, as a method of analysis, is biased towards multiple factor solutions. While there is no easy cure for the latter defect, a rough correction for the first has been tentatively suggested by Law (1967). He proposes that the chi square value obtained be divided by the number of hundreds in the sample. (The examples of the program's use given in the manual by its authors are with a sample where N = 100). In spite of the above limitations, however, this was the best program available for the task.

For any test of single-factorness an important theoretical requirement is that all scales included should be of approximately equal length. Otherwise at least part of the single-factorness observed may be said to have been obtained by overrepresenting one scale. It may be seen that the scales of nine, ten, ten and sixteen items approach this ideal fairly closely, especially when it is realized that the sixteen item R-Scale was expected on the basis of Anderson and Western's (1967) recent Australian study to be resolvable into two eight item scales—one containing the "political" and "economic" items and the other the "social" and "moral" items.

D. RESULTS

The Lawley chi square value produced was 3717·84 with d.f. of 945. This corresponds to a Z of 22·7 and a highly significant departure from single-factorness is at first indicated. If Law's (1967) correction is applied however, chi square is reduced to 929·46 and Z becomes 0·3 which indicates no significant departure from single-factorness.

The "coefficient alpha" reliability of the entire forty-five items was 0·72. This is comparable with the internal consistency coefficients usually observed in groups of items deliberately written to tap only one concept. The first eight eigenvalues were 5·4, 2·7, 2·3, 1·99, 1·73, 1·51, 1·49 and 1·34. Note that the "natural break" occurs after the first eigenvalue. By this criterion as well then, single-factorness (unidimensionality) in F.R.E.D. is indicated.

V. Conclusion

The result of the above study may be seen to confirm our findings from the literature review concerning the appropriateness and usefulness of a single factor account of the social attitude domain. The social attitude items of the F-, R-, E- and D-Scales are all orderable along a single dimension, best called liberalism–conservatism. Neither conceptually nor empirically does there appear to be any ground for distinguishing authoritarianism and conservatism—except that the former may be regarded as a somewhat more particular case of the latter.

References

Adorno, T. W., Frenkel-Brunswik, E., Levinson, J. and Sanford, R. N. (1950). "The Authoritarian Personality". Science Editions, Wiley, New York.

Anderson, D. S. and Western, J. S. (1967). An inventory to measure students' attitudes. *University of Queensland Papers*, Vol. 1 No. 3. University of Queensland Press, St. Lucia, Brisbane.

Beswick, D. G. and Hills, M. D. (1969). An Australian ethnocentrism scale. *Aust. J. Psychol.* **21**, 211–226.

Block, J. (1965). "The Challenge of Response Sets." Appleton-Century-Crofts. New York.

Brown, R. (1964). "Social Psychology." Free Press, New York.

Camillieri, S. F. (1959). A factor analysis of the F scale. *Social forces*, **37**, 316–323.

Campbell, A., Converse, P. E., Miller, W. E. and Stokes, D. E. (1960). "The American Voter." Wiley, New York.

Christie, R. and Jahoda, Marie. (eds) (1954). "Studies in the Scope and Method of the Authoritarian Personality." Free Press, Glencoe, Illinois.

Christie, R. (1956). Some abuses of psychology. *Psychol. Bull.* **53**, 439–451.

Direnzo, G. J. (1968). Dogmatism and presidential preferences in the 1964 elections. *Psychol. Rep.* **22**, 1197–1202.

Ekman, G. and Kuennapas, T. (1963). Scales of conservatism. *Percept. mot. Skills.* **16**, 329–334.

Eysenck, H. J. (1944). General social attitudes. *J. Soc. Psychol.* **19**.

Eysenck, H. J. (1954). "The Psychology of Politics." Routledge, London.

Ferguson, L. (1941). The stability of the primary social attitudes: I. Religionism and humanitarianism. *J. Psychol.* **12**, 283–288.

Fishbein, M. (1967). A consideration of beliefs and their role in attitude measurement. *In* "Readings in Attitude Theory and Measurement". (Fishbein, M., ed.). Wiley, New York.

French, Elizabeth and Ernest, R. R. (1955). The relation between authoritarianism and acceptance of military ideology. *J. Pers.* **24**, 181–191.

Jaensch, E. R. (1938). "Der Gegentypus." Barth, Leipzig.

Kaiser, H. F. (1968). A measure of the average intercorrelation. *Educ. psych. Meas.* **28**, 245–247.

Kerlinger, F. N. (1967). Social attitudes and their criterial referents: A structural theory. *Psychol. Rev.* **74**, 110–122.

Kerr, W. A. (1955). "Tulane Factors of Liberalism–Conservatism (manual)." Psychometric Affiliates, Chicago.

Krug, R. (1961). An analysis of the F scale: I. Item factor analysis. *J. soc. Psych.* **53**, 285–391.

Kirscht, J. P. and Dillehay, R. C. (1967). "Dimensions of Authoritarianism: A Review of Research and Theory." University of Kentucky Press, Lexington.

Kirtley, D. and Harkness, R. (1969). Some personality and attitude correlates of dogmatism. *Psychol. Rep.* **24**, 851–854.

Law, H. G. (1967). The measurement of theological belief. Unpublished B.A. thesis, University of Queensland.

Levinson, D. J. and Huffman, P. E. (1955). Traditional family ideology and its relation to personality. *J. Pers.* **23**, 251–278.

Lipset, S. M. (1960). "Political Man." Doubleday, New York.

Martin, J. G. and Westie, F. R. (1959). The tolerant personality. *Amer. Sociol. Rev.* **24**, 521–828.

McClosky, H. (1958). Conservatism and personality. *Am. pol. Sci. Rev.* **52**, 27–45.

Morrison, D. G., Campbell, D. T. and Wolins, L. A. (1967). Fortran IV program for evaluating internal consistency single-factoredness in sets of multilevel attitude items. *Educ. Psychol. Meas.*, **27**, 201.

Nunnally, J. C. (1967). "Psychometric Theory." McGraw-Hill, New York.

O'Neill, W. M. and Levinson, D. J. (1954). A factorial exploration of authoritarianism and some of its ideological correlates. *J. Pers.*, **22**, 449–463.

Peabody, D. (1961). Attitude content and agreement set in scales of authoritarianism, dogmatism, anti-semitism and economic conservatism. *J. abnorm. soc. Psychol.*, **63**, 1–12.

Peabody, D. (1966). Authoritarianism scales and response bias. *Psychol. Bull.* **65**, 11–23.

Prothro, E. T. and Melikian, L. (1953). The California public opinion scale in an authoritarian culture. *Public Opinion Quarterly*, **17**, 353–362.

Ray, J. J. (1971). An "attitude to authority" scale. *Aust. Psychologist*, **7**, 31–50.

Ray, J. J. (1972 in press). Non-ethnocentric authoritarianism. *A.N.Z. J. Sociol.*

Ray, J. J. (1972, in press). A new balanced F scale—and its relation to social class. *Aust. Psychol.*

Rokeach, M. (1956). A factorial study of dogmatism and related concepts. *J. abnorm. soc. psych.* **53**, 356–350.

Rokeach, M. and Hanley, C. (1956). Eysenck's tender-mindedness dimension: A critique. *Psychol. Bull.* **43**, 169–176.

Rokeach, M. and Hanley, C. (1956). Care and carelessness in psychology. *Psychol. Bull.* **53**, 183–86(b).

Rokeach, M. (1960). "The Open and Closed Mind." Basic Books, New York.

Rorer, L. G. (1965). The great response-style myth. *Psych. Bull.* **63**, 129–156.

Shils, E. A. (1954). Authoritarianism: Right and left. *In* Studies in the Scope and Method of "the Authoritarian Personality". (Christie, R. and Jahoda, M., eds.). Free Press, Glencoe, Illinois.

Smith, M. B. (1967). Foreword in: Kirscht, J. P. and Dillehay, R. C. "Dimensions of Authoritarianism: A Review of Research and Theory". University of Kentucky Press, Lexington.

Stern, G. G. (1956). Stein, M. I. and Bloom, B. S. "Methods in Personality Assessment." Free Press, Glencoe, Illinois.

Part II

MEASUREMENT AND STRUCTURE

3 | The Need for a New Approach to Attitude Measurement*

GLENN D. WILSON and DAVID K. B. NIAS

Institute of Psychiatry, University of London

I. Introduction

Any science is built upon measurement, and before we can fruitfully embark upon a scientific study of conservatism it is necessary to establish an agreed and satisfactory operational definition of the dimension. Unfortunately, the tests which have been used in the past to measure conservatism and the related concepts discussed in the previous chapter have fallen short of the mark in a number of respects. Most of what follows will be directed at the California F-Scale (Adorno *et al.*, 1950) and the Dogmatism Scale (Rokeach, 1960) since these are still the most frequently cited attitude measures, particularly in the American literature, but the relevance of these criticisms to the majority of other scales will be apparent.

---

*This chapter is based in part upon arguments introduced elsewhere (Nias and Wilson, 1971; Wilson and Nias, 1972).

II. Acquiescence

A. The Problem

Both the F-Scale and the D-Scale key all of their items in one direction; agreement with any statement is taken to imply authoritarianism or dogmatism respectively. Numerous critics have pointed out that test scores derived in this way may also reflect a tendency for the respondent to agree with any opinion statement (acquiesce) regardless of the meaning or content of that statement. There is, in fact, a great deal of empirical evidence to show that these attitude scales are strongly contaminated by acquiescence effects (e.g. Peabody, 1966), and what is worse, the unidirectional keying system means that response due to item content is inextricably confounded with acquiescence response; in other words, it is impossible to assess the degree to which this bias has occurred.

B. Attempts to Counterbalance

What seemed an obvious way to deal with the problem of acquiescence was the construction of a parallel set of items matched in terms of content but worded the opposite way, i.e. so that a negative response is scored authoritarian, dogmatic, etc. In this way it was expected that the effects due to acquiescence response style would balance out, leaving a measure of pure authoritarianism or whatever. Unfortunately, it did not turn out to be as easy as this. When various efforts were made to "counterbalance" the F-Scale it was discovered that the original and reversed items were correlated very poorly, if at all (see Table I), which meant that when acquiescence bias was balanced out there was virtually nothing left that could be called authoritarianism.

Some attempts were made to shrug off this "double agreement" phenomenon, e.g. the argument that acquiescence is an inherent part of authoritarianism, or Rokeach's suggestion that subjects may be telling the truth in the first instance and lying in the second. Such counter-arguments have in turn been countered by Peabody (1966) and Rundquist (1966) and do not merit further discussion here.

C. The Forced-Choice "Solution"

A more desperate attempt to cope with the problem of acquiescence was the construction of forced-choice versions of the F-Scale, in which the original and reversed items were paired together and the subject asked to decide which he agreed with more (e.g. Berkowitz and Wolkon, 1964). This of course, was a way of evading the problem rather than examining it, and since the F+ and F− items are uncorrelated it is difficult to imagine what

TABLE I

Some Obtained Reliabilities of the F Scale*
(From Berkowitz and Wolkon, 1964)

| Reliabilities | Studies Reported by Chapman and Bock | | | | | | | | Mogar | | OPD Study |
	a†	b†	c†	d	e‡	f	g	h	i**	j**	k‡
F+	0·69	0·53	0·71	0·52	—	—	0·60	0·69§	0·67	—	0·71
F−	0·41	0·41	0·42	0·43	0·77	—	0·42	—	0·61	0·59	0·40
Correlation of F+ and F−	0·17	−0·1	0·29	0·05	−0·35	0·17	0·19	0·25	0·18	−0·14	−0·16

*Chapman and Campbell's reversals used in columns a, b, and c; Christie's reversals used in Columns d, f, g, and k; Jackson and Messick's reversals used in columns e and j; Bass' reversals used in column i; Levitt's reversals used in column h.
† Kuder-Richardson 'Formula 20' reliabilities.
‡ Corrected split half reliabilities (Spearman–Brown).
§ Correlation with other positive items.
** Retest reliability.

meaning can obtain in the choice between them. In fact, scores derived in this way tended to correlate more with F+ than F— but were of lower, and generally quite unacceptable, reliability. A practical objection to this approach is that the items became more cumbersome than they were in the original F-Scale.

The incredible thing is that in spite of all, the popularity of the F and D Scales has continued to grow, perhaps demonstrating the truth of the maxim that "there is no such thing as bad publicity".

III. The Causes of Acquiescence

A. ITEM CONTEXT

The outstanding feature of the attempts to deal with acquiescence response bias outlined above is their common failure to show interest in the causes of acquiescence. It will be argued here that the main reasons why traditional attitude scales have proved unsatisfactory can be traced to the *format of the items* of which they are composed, and the *response alternatives* attached to these items.

It is appropriate at this point to cite a fascinating study of the Manifest Anxiety Scale by Kimble and Posnick (1967), the relevance of which will become clear later. These authors constructed a new personality questionnaire parallel to the M.A.S. in style of wording, emotional intensity and social acceptability, but devoid of anxiety content. This was done by devising a new series of items to match those in the original scale.

> e.g. I am a very nervous person.
> I am a very envious person.
>
> My hands and feet are usually warm enough.
> My plans and goals are usually clear enough.

Using two samples of undergraduate students, Kimble and Posnick found that their new non-anxiety test, which we might name the "Manifest Nonsense Scale", was correlated with the Manifest Anxiety Scale 0·84 and 0·74 respectively. Considering that the reliability of the M.A.S. is hardly any higher than this, it can now be seriously doubted that the test has anything to do with anxiety at all. Certainly, this is a striking demonstration of the extent to which the *context* of items in traditional personality and attitude scales can determine responses regardless of the actual *content*.

When one comes to consider in detail the structure of items such as those in the F-Scale, it becomes apparent that they have many characteristics which particularly lend themselves to contextual interference. These items can be analysed into at least three major classes of components:

(1) *The referent.* The intended subject or central content of an attitude item, usually a person, group, institution, or issue, e.g. President Nixon, birth control, the Jews, homosexuals, smoking pot.

(2) *Quantitative terms.* Words which give an impression of frequency, degree, probability, or extremity, e.g. never, seldom, always, often, everybody, a great deal, probably, possibly, certainly.

(3) *Evaluation.* The persuasive direction of the statement. The subject is represented as desirable or undesirable, true or untrue, e.g. X is a bad thing, Y should be done, Z is false.

An example from the F-Scale: "Science has its place, but there are many important things that can never possibly be understood by the human mind". In this case, the central content or "referent" is "science", the terms "many", "never", and "possibly" are quantitative and the general evaluative tone is in the negative direction, i.e. agreement with the statement implies a negative attitude towards science.

It might be possible to isolate more than these three elements, but this is not necessary for purposes of illustrating the present point. It is our argument that all three of these components in the statement are partial determinants of the response, whereas the investigator should only be interested in the response to the first of them (the referent). Thus, the other two components can only serve to confuse the issue. Furthermore, even if he were interested in the other two components (e.g. individual differences in perceived frequency implied by the word "seldom") he would be likewise unable to investigate them because of the confounding due to other elements.

We may now expand in slightly greater detail on some of the particular characteristics of traditional attitude scale items which are hypothesized to be primarily responsible for the confounding of response to content with response to context.

B. Ambiguity

One major criticism which can be levelled at traditional statement-form items is their tendency to be "double-barrelled", and sometimes even multi-barrelled. That is to say, the items contain several logically discriminable aspects. Therefore, response to them must necessarily follow some process of assigning emphasis on the part of the subject, which may be quite arbitrary and variable from one person to another. Consider the following item from the F-Scale: "What the youth needs most is strict discipline, rugged determination, and the will to work and fight for family and country". If this item was intended to tap attitudes towards youth (probably the most central referent), how could it possibly do so without confounding by attitudes towards discipline, determination, work, family, country, and fighting? There may indeed be some degree of overlap amongst these various attitude areas, but they are by no means logically identical and the inclusion of them all within a single item makes it impossible to test their degree of relationship empirically. Furthermore, if subjective emphasis was placed at the quantitative term "most", then the item may fail in its intent if the above values are held to be very important by authoritarian respondents but second-ranked to some other virtue (e.g. chastity)—in which case they might be compelled to disagree with the statement.

This may seem like going into unnecessary detail concerning a single item but it must be remembered that most of the items in the F-Scale and other traditional attitude scales can be criticized on similar grounds, and at the moment we are trying to indicate some of the likely reasons why such tests have not proved valid measures of the dimensions that they were supposed to be concerned with.

Peabody (1966) put forward a strong argument that the double-agreement phenomenon results from ambiguity of items, suggesting that the M.M.P.I. is less susceptible to this effect because its items are shorter (containing fewer words on average) than attitude scales, and are therefore presumably less ambiguous. McBride and Moran (1967) found that double-agreement on the F, D, and Anti-Semitism scales correlated 0·88, 0·83, and 0·65 respectively with the independently rated ambiguity of their items. This may be taken as very strong evidence that traditional scales are subject to acquiescence effects at least partly because their items are ambiguous.

C. MULTI-NEGATIVE GRAMMAR

Another likely reason why attitude scales have been influenced by acquiescence to such an extent may be the logical difficulties arising from their grammatical structure, particularly double-negative and multi-negative combinations, e.g. "There is *hardly anything* lower than a person who *does not* feel great love, gratitude, and respect for his parents." (From the F-Scale; italics ours). This is already in the form of a double-negative statement; if the respondent chooses to disagree we go into a triple-negative phase, with the logic running something like this: "It *is not* true that there *is not* (hardly) anything lower than a person who *does not* love, etc." While it may not be beyond the capacity of a skilled logician to think through multi-negative grammar such as this, it must be supposed that many people are confused by items of this kind and give responses which are either meaningless, acquiescent, or the reverse of that which they intended. The problem is even more apparent when attempts are made to reverse F-Scale items logically, e.g. "Homosexuals are hardly better than criminals and ought to be punished." Two attempts at reversing this item are as follows: 1. "Homosexuals *are not* criminals and should *not be* punished" (Bass 1955). 2. "*It's nobody's* business if someone *is* a homosexual as long as he *doesn't* harm other people." (Christie *et al.*, 1958). In both cases the grammatical construction of the statement is extremely clumsy, and by the time the valence of the response alternatives is also taken into account the algebraic sign-adding processes that are necessary for a logical response are getting very complex, and no doubt beyond the capacity of the average respondent.

D. EVALUATIVE WORDING

We now come to what is probably the most salient though little recognized fault with traditional questionnaires, and that is the highly evaluative, directional or "pushy" nature of their items. What is wrong with this? Quite simply that the response is strongly suggested by the manner in which the statement is worded, so that respondents who are either submissive by temperament or lacking intelligence enough to understand the exact logic of the statement will be inclined to acquiesce. Thus, to a large extent what is being measured is the tendency to agree with strongly worded statements no matter how ignorant or illogical they be. Such an interpretation is supported not only by the double agreement phenomenon, but also by the finding that F-Scale scores are correlated (negatively) with intelligence to as great a degree as can be expected considering the (lack of) reliability of the two measures involved (Berkowitz and Wolkon, 1964).

"Leading questions" which strongly suggest a particular answer are not permissible as a form of cross-examination in the law courts of civilized countries, and there is no reason to suppose that they have any greater validity in the context of a supposedly scientific attitude scale. The technique is reminiscent of the way in which a Czechoslovak newspaper was able to claim that the majority of Czechs viewed the Russian invasion of their country as justified. They were questioned on a section of "the Party's analysis of the 1968 reform era" which said: "The entry of allied troops into Czechoslovakia . . . prevented (fratricidal) bloodshed and was therefore the requisite and only justified solution." (*The Times*, 23. 4. 71). From closer to home, we may cite the example of a Bishop's angry complaint that a certain TV company was cutting its allocation for religious broadcasting as a result of a survey which discovered that a majority of people agreed with the statement: "I do not want to have religion pushed down my throat."

It is easy to laugh at questions such as these without realizing how close they are to the kind of items that are employed in the most frequently used attitude questionnaires.

The argument up to this point may be summarized by the following quotation from Wilson and Patterson (1970):

Traditional social attitude questionnaires are composed of items that are formulated as lengthy and detailed statements of opinion with which the respondent is required to indicate some amount of agreement or disagreement. This item format is based upon the implicit assumption that respondents would be unable to express an opinion unless provided with a fully specified context. It is our contention however, that *items presented in the form of detailed propositional statements can never provide a satisfactory basis for the measurement of attitudes.* Rather than clarify an issue, they tend to create in the respondent conflict between rating the idiosyncrasies of the particular statement presented, versus the more general issue which he suspects the tester is broaching. Because they are wordy and elaborate, often requiring multi-negative thinking of a complex order, they may not be fully understood, and meaningless or acquiescent responses are the result. The tendency towards acquiescence bias is further aggravated by the directional (i.e. leading or "pushy") nature of the items. Finally, ambiguity is increased because item meaning is dependent upon the point in the statement at which emphasis is arbitrarily placed by the respondent.

E. ACQUIESCENCE VERSUS AGREEMENT

The foregoing may clarify the distinction between acquiescence bias and agreement response set. Agreement is simply saying "yes" for any of a variety of extraneous reasons (e.g. a position preference favouring "yes", or believing it looks more tolerant or positive to say "yes"); acquiescence is the tendency to "submit" to a suggestion. Thus, while acquiescence effects may give rise to agreement response set, it is also possible to acquiesce with a "no" response, e.g. in reply to the question "You don't really approve of abortion, do you?". It follows that a measure of acquiescence based on a simple "yes"-count may be quite spurious.

IV. Direction and Extremity of Response

Finally, the traditional attitude questionnaires may be criticised on the grounds of the irrationality of their scoring systems, which confound the two variables of direction and extremity of response. These scales usually permit responses to be made according to a bipolar Likert scale with five, six, or seven alternatives, e.g. strongly agree, partly agree, indifferent, partly disagree, strongly disagree. The usual scoring procedure is to assign arbitrary weights to these levels of agreement and disagreement and then summate over the items in the test. This gives a composite score in which direction and extremity are irrevocably confounded.

As it turns out, little damage is apparently done by this procedure, since two-point and multi-point answer formats attached to the same scale give near perfect correlations (e.g. Komorita, 1963). However, the evidence which is available does suggest that "the intensity with which a statement is accepted or rejected may be a quasi-variable . . . in fact, nothing more than an imperfect indicator of direction" (Ehrlich, 1968). At the very least, the use of multi-alternative response formats must be viewed as uneconomical, and contributing unnecessarily to the general confusion which invalidates traditional attitude scales.

V. Summary

In this chapter we have attempted to show that the scales that have been used most frequently in the past to measure conservatism and related personality and attitude dimensions (e.g. authoritarianism) are unsatisfactory on a number of counts. Acquiescence response bias is seen as a source of error so powerful that counterbalancing is an ineffective way of dealing with it. It is argued that acquiescence can be traced to some characteristics of the items that have typically been employed—particularly ambiguity, multi-negative grammar, and direction of wording. It is also suggested that obtaining an attitude intensity score by summating over a number of items that are individually scored according to a multi-point scale is a dubious procedure that contributes to the general lack of validity of previous attitude measures.

We may also express our argument against traditional attitude scales by saying that those responsible for their construction have made two fundamental errors:

(i) They have attempted to incorporate their own theoretical position (with respect to the relationship between personality and attitude structure) into the actual wording of the questionnaire items employed to investigate that theory.

(ii) They have attempted to scale attitude intensity both within and across items at the same time.

The complex problems to which these errors have given rise would seem to necessitate a completely new approach. The development of a new measure of conservatism, specifically designed to circumvent the deficiencies of previous measures, is described in the next chapter.

References

Adorno, T. W., Frenkel-Brunswik, E., Levinson, D. J. and Sanford, R. N. (1950). "The Authoritarian Personality". Harper, New York.

Bass, B. M. (1955). Authoritarianism or acquiescence? *J. abnorm. soc. Psychol.* **51**, 616–623.

Berkowitz, N. H. and Wolkon, G. H. (1964). A forced choice form of the F-Scale —free of acquiescent response set. *Sociometry*, **27**, 54–65.

Christie, R., Havel, J. and Seidenberg, B. (1958). Is the F Scale irreversible? *J. abnorm. soc. Psychol.* **56**, 143–159.

Ehrlich, H. J. (1968). Is intensity a spurious variable in attitude measurement? *Psychol. Rep.* **22**, 373–374.

Kimble, G. A. and Posnick, G. M. (1967). Anxiety? *J. Personality soc. Psychol.* **7**, 108–110.

Komorita, S. S. (1963). Attitude content, intensity, and the neutral point on a Likert scale. *J. soc. Psychol.* **61**, 327–334.

McBride, L. and Moran, G. (1967). Double agreement as a function of item ambiguity and susceptibility to demand implications of the psychological situation. *J. Personality soc. Psychol.*, **6**, 115–118.

Nias, D. K. B. and Wilson, G. D. (1971). A new approach to the measurement of conservatism. Proceedings of the XVIIth International Congress of Applied Psychology, Liège, Belgium.

Peabody, D. (1966). Authoritarianism scales and response bias. *Psychol. Bull.* **65**, 11–23.

Rokeach, M. (1960). "The Open and Closed Mind." Basic Books, New York.

Rundquist, E. A. (1966). Item and response characteristics in attitude and personality measurement: a reaction to L. G. Rorer's "The great response-style myth". *Psychol. Bull.* **66**, 166–177.

Wilson, G. D. and Nias D. K. B. (1972). Measurement of social attitudes: a new approach. *Percept. mot. Skills.* **35**, 827–834.

Wilson, G. D. and Patterson, J. R. (1970). "Manual for the Conservatism Scale." N.F.E.R., Windsor, England.

4

Development and Evaluation of the C-Scale

GLENN D. WILSON

Institute of Psychiatry, University of London

I. Introduction

The Conservatism Scale was developed by Wilson and Patterson (1968) in an effort to answer the criticisms of previous tests outlined in the previous chapter. Beginning with the assumption that most of the difficulties encountered with traditional attitude questionnaires could be traced to the format of their items, it was argued that the central processes occurring when persons respond to these items can be analysed into two sequential stages:

(1) An immediate, emotional response to the central, controversial issue embodied in the statement (the referent).

(ii) Suspension of judgment while the qualificatory and justificatory details of the statement are examined.

During the second of these stages, various inhibiting and perturbing cognitive factors were presumed to operate.

> The respondent begins to develop a sense of responsibility and commitment—the feeling that a considered, rational judgment is expected of him since the question is so "carefully" worded. He also becomes more concerned about the motives of the tester in asking the question; catches are suspected and his initial reaction, is adjusted in the direction of social desirability. In short, his eventual response becomes more a function of cognitive processes than affective.

Wilson and Patterson went on to suggest that it is the first (affective) stage which we should seek to measure, since it is the evaluative nature of attitudes which distinguishes them as intervening variables. (Recognition of this fact was probably what led to the assumption that heavily evaluative items were needed in the first place in order to measure attitudes.) Although recent research had indicated the possibility of observing emotional responses to attitude statements by direct recording of physiological changes (McGuire, 1969), for practical purposes these techniques were regarded as far too cumbersome to replace the questionnaire.

The solution proposed then, was to abandon the evaluative propositional form of item and instead present a list of brief labels or catch-phrases representing various familiar and controversial issues. For example, the item from Eysenck's Social Attitudes Inventory, "Unrestricted freedom of discussion on every topic in the press, in literature, on the stage, etc." was replaced by "Censorship" (Yes, ?, or No). Similarly, an item from Stacey and Green's (1968) questionnaire, "If the rich were made to share their wealth then everybody would be a lot happier, including the rich who have more money than is good for them anyway" was reduced to "Socialism".

It was assumed that in the course of informal discussion and argument concerning these issues, the respondent would already have placed himself in relation to the perceived spectrum of opinion prevailing in the general population. He would "know where he stood" on the issue, and have no difficulty in indicating his "position" immediately in terms of simple response alternatives.

Note, this new item format differs from the old in that the *evaluation occurs only in the response*, not in the items as well. That is, the basic formula, "X is a good/bad thing" (agree or disagree) is substituted by the simpler formula, "X" (good or bad). Because the item is reduced to attitude *content* or *referent* alone, we might expect that contamination due to *context* (grammatical confusion, ambiguity, task conflict, acquiescence, etc.) will be brought to a minimum.

II. Construction

Development of the C-Scale began with the list of characteristics of the ideal conservative given in Chapter 1. These may be summarized as follows:

(1) Religious dogmatism.
(2) Right-wing political orientation (in Western society).
(3) Insistence on strict rules and punishments.
(4) Ethnocentrism, and intolerance of minority groups.
(5) Preference for conventional art, clothing, and institutions.
(6) Anti-hedonistic outlook (the tendency to regard pleasure, particularly sexual, as necessarily bad).
(7) Superstition, and resistance to scientific progress.

Next, large pools of items were chosen intuitively as being likely discriminators of these characteristics, and their performance examined in a series of upper-lower third difference item-analyses. Finally, fifty items were selected, half for which affirmative responses would be scored in the conservative direction and half for which negative responses would be scored in the conservative direction (thus balancing for any response category biases that might appear). These fifty items were chosen on the basis of the following criteria: (1) positive correlation with whole-test scores, (2) power to discriminate, i.e. divide the population so that a reasonable percentage of responses fall into each category, (3) ease of understanding, (4) avoidance of redundancy in meaning, (5) roughly even representation of the attitude areas listed above, (6) expected ability to maintain validity over several years and to withstand cultural transplantation. The exact wording of items was decided upon only after careful consideration of the different ways in which people might perceive them, and the general approach was to satisfy all intuitive, logical, and construct criteria before proceeding with detailed empirical evaluations. It was felt that the premature use of "blind" statistical techniques such as factor analysis could result in an instrument that would be psychologically sterile.

To complete the layout of the test, the fifty items were randomly ordered within the restriction of an alternating pattern of affirmatively and negatively scored items (Table I). The response alternatives were kept to a minimum in accordance with the comments made previously about the confounding of direction and extremeness of response. It was, however, felt necessary to include a "?" category because many respondents experience considerable annoyance if forced to make a dichotomous choice. Also, there is considerable evidence that neutral responses represent valid and consistent attitude positions which should not be ignored or

TABLE I

The Conservatism Scale: Instructions, items and format.*

Which of the Following do you Favour or Believe in?
(Circle "Yes" or "No". If absolutely uncertain, circle "?". There are no right or wrong answers; do not discuss; just give your first reaction. Answer all items).

1 death penalty	Yes	?	No	26 computer music	Yes	?	No
2 evolution theory	Yes	?	No	27 chastity	Yes	?	No
3 school uniforms	Yes	?	No	28 fluoridation	Yes	?	No
4 striptease shows	Yes	?	No	29 royalty	Yes	?	No
5 Sabbath observance	Yes	?	No	30 women judges	Yes	?	No
6 beatniks	Yes	?	No	31 conventional clothing	Yes	?	No
7 patriotism	Yes	?	No	32 teenage drivers	Yes	?	No
8 modern art	Yes	?	No	33 apartheid	Yes	?	No
9 self-denial	Yes	?	No	34 nudist camps	Yes	?	No
10 working mothers	Yes	?	No	35 church authority	Yes	?	No
11 horoscopes	Yes	?	No	36 disarmament	Yes	?	No
12 birth control	Yes	?	No	37 censorship	Yes	?	No
13 military drill	Yes	?	No	38 white lies	Yes	?	No
14 co-education	Yes	?	No	39 birching	Yes	?	No
15 Divine law	Yes	?	No	40 mixed marriage	Yes	?	No
16 socialism	Yes	?	No	41 strict rules	Yes	?	No
17 white superiority	Yes	?	No	42 jazz	Yes	?	No
18 cousin marriage	Yes	?	No	43 straitjackets	Yes	?	No
19 moral training	Yes	?	No	44 casual living	Yes	?	No
20 suicide	Yes	?	No	45 learning Latin	Yes	?	No
21 chaperones	Yes	?	No	46 divorce	Yes	?	No
22 legalized abortion	Yes	?	No	47 inborn conscience	Yes	?	No
23 empire-building	Yes	?	No	48 coloured immigration	Yes	?	No
24 student pranks	Yes	?	No	49 Bible truth	Yes	?	No
25 licensing laws	Yes	?	No	50 pyjama parties	Yes	?	No

*N.B. This test is under strict copyright and must not be reproduced. It is available to qualified users from the N.F.E.R. Publishing Co., Thames Ave., Windsor, England.

assigned to one of the polar positions (e.g. Caffrey and Capel, 1968). It was intended that in the present case the "?" category could be used to mean "not understood", "neutral", or "indifferent", and for any of these responses it seems reasonable to give them an intermediate score. The instructions were also kept very short and simple in order to minimize confusion.

III. Administration and Scoring

The scale was designed to be entirely self-contained. The brief instructions at the top of the test form were regarded as quite sufficient and not to be altered or elaborated in any way. If asked for advice by respondents, testers were permitted only to emphasize an appropriate section of the instructions, e.g. drawing attention to the availability of the "?" response if a yes–no decision could not be made for any reason. Respondents were not permitted to consult other persons or written material, not even a dictionary. Encouraging respondents to work quickly was regarded as permissible since in our rationale first reactions are theoretically the best.

As noted above, the items were ordered such that an individual falling at either the liberal or conservative pole would produce an alternating pattern of responses. This pattern was seldom observed except by very extreme respondents (partly because subjective randomness tends towards alteration), and even when it was noticed it apparently had no appreciable effect upon subsequent responses.

The advantage of the alternating pattern is that no key is required for scoring. Each "Yes" to an odd-numbered item, and each "No" to an even-numbered item was scored two. Queries, omissions, and other ambiguous responses were scored one. Thus each item was effectively rated on a three-point Likert-type scale (liberal response $= 0$, ambiguous response $= 1$, and conservative response $= 2$). The range of possible scores was thus 0 to 100 (the higher the more conservative), and if any one of the three response alternatives should happen to have been used throughout, an intermediate score of fifty would have resulted.

IV. Standardization

Means and standard deviations for various groups are shown in Table II. Students and professionals tend to come out as the most liberal of the major occupational groups, while housewives and businessmen are among the most conservative. Skilled and unskilled workers, and clerks, generally tend to fall somewhere in between. Although it has previously been suggested (Wilson and Patterson, 1968) that little error would result from treating scores on the scale as natural T-scores, i.e. having a mean of fifty and S.D. of ten, there is such variability between different groups that an overall population average cannot be regarded as very meaningful.

C-scores have been found to correlate quite considerably with age (Wilson and Patterson, 1970), the coefficients so far reported ranging from 0·23 to 0·61, depending mainly upon the amount of variability in the sample. Therefore, where comparisons across different age groups are contemplated it will be necessary either to partial out the effect of age or use age-standardized scores. The regression of C-scores upon age for an occupational quota sample of 360 New Zealanders is shown in Fig. 1. It will be noted that females score consistently higher than males, the difference increasing slightly as a function of age. This difference is of certain theoretical interest, but is very small and may be disregarded for most practical purposes.

TABLE II

Performance of various groups on the C-Scale

Group	N	M	S.D.	Source
University students (U.K.)	50	25·33	13.00	Wilson (1970)
University students (Netherlands)*	50	26·10	11·11	Bagley (Unpublished)
University students (W. Germany)†	133	26·20	10·46	Schneider (Unpublished)
University students (N.Z.)	107	32·57	10·36	Wilson and Patterson (1968)
University students (U.S.A.)	100	42·21	11·31	Caffrey (Unpublished)
University students (U.S.A.)	149	46·00	8·8	Kish (Unpublished)
College of Education, students (U.K.)	298	36·07	10·50	Nias (Unpublished)
College of Education, women (U.K.)	82	43·10	11·78	Nias et al. (1971)
Adult Education, students (N.Z.)	357	43·10	14·72	Boshier (Unpublished)
Secondary school pupils (N.Z.)	133	44·64	11·63	Wilson and Patterson (1968)
Schoolgirls (State school, U.K.)	85	36·86	10·19	Insel and Wilson (1971)
Schoolgirls (Catholic school, U.K.)	100	51·99	11·30	Insel and Wilson (1971)
Professionals (N.Z.)	53	43·76	11·24	Wilson and Patterson (1968)
Businessmen (N.Z.)	30	58·40	10·59	Wilson and Patterson (1968)
Professionals and businessmen (U.K.)	50	33·82	18·60	Wilson (1970)
Professionals and businessmen (Netherlands)	50	43·50	14·14	Bagley (Unpublished)
Clerical workers (U.K.)	50	43·52	16·40	Wilson (1970)
Clerical workers (U.K.)	22	40·96	17·03	Di Scipio (Unpublished)
Clerical workers (Netherlands)	50	42·60	12·28	Bagley (Unpublished)
Clerical workers (N.Z.)	30	52·85	11·12	Wilson and Patterson (1968)
Laboratory technicians (N.Z.)	22	42·08	10·85	Wilson and Patterson (1968)
Trade apprentices (U.K.)	187	39·65	8·54	Wilson (Unpublished)
Skilled workers (U.K.)	50	45·43	12·93	Wilson (1970)
Skilled workers (Netherlands)	50	48·84	10·03	Bagley (Unpublished)
Unskilled workers (N.Z.)	45	47·24	10·45	Wilson and Patterson (1968)
Full-time pop musicians (U.K.)	76	31·83	10·83	Maclean (Unpublished)
Housewives (N.Z.)	44	60·98	12·02	Wilson and Patterson (1968)
Occupational quota sample (N.Z.)	360	49·72	11·34	Wilson and Patterson (1968)
Heterogeneous males (U.K.)	200	36·81	17·24	Wilson (1970)
Heterogeneous males (Netherlands)	200	40·06	13·66	Bagley (Unpublished)
Parents of college students (U.S.A.)	41	61·00	7·00	Kish (Unpublished)

*Dutch translation by Dr A. Hoogvelt.
†German translation by Dr U. Frith.

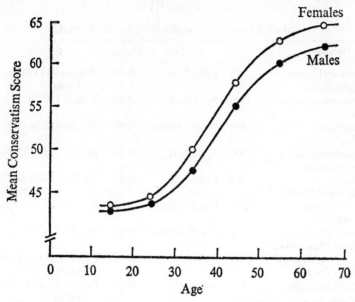

FIG. 1. The relationships of C-scores to age and sex, based on a quota sample of 360. New Zealanders (From Wilson and Patterson 1968).

It cannot be said yet whether the increase in conservatism with age is longitudinal (increasing over time within individuals) or cross-sectional (a constant difference between generations), but it may be hypothesized that both tendencies are probably involved.

V. Internal Consistency

Table III summarizes the evidence which is currently available concerning the internal consistency of the C-Scale. The split-half coefficients were calculated in each case by correlating scores on the first twenty-five items with scores on the second twenty-five and correcting for attenuation with the Spearman-Brown "Prophecy Formula". The coefficient alpha is a similar statistic, except that it represents the average of all possible split-half coefficients rather than one particular, possibly unrepresentative, comparison of split halves. The obtained internal consistency coefficients are generally very high; certainly higher than those reported for previous attitude scales.

The one exceptional finding is that of Ray (1971) who reports an alpha coefficient as low as 0·63 using a sample of 276 Australian army conscripts. There is no obvious explanation for this. Ray suggests that it may have occurred because his sample was heterogeneous, the recruits being selected by a "random ballot procedure". But heterogeneous samples would be

TABLE III

Internal consistency coefficients for the C-Scale

Sample	N	Method	Coeff.	Source
Occupational quota sample (N.Z.)	244	Split-half	0·94	Wilson and Patterson (1968)
Heterogeneous males (U.K.)	200	Split-half	0·93	Wilson (1970)
Heterogeneous males (U.K.)	200	Coeff. Alpha	0·91	Wilson (1970)
Heterogeneous males (Netherlands)	200	Split-half	0·89	Bagley *et al* (1970)
Schoolgirls (U.K. aged 12–16)	185	Split-half	0·84	Insel and Wilson (1971)
Army conscripts (Australia)	276	Coeff. Alpha	0·63	Ray (1971)
First-year psychology students (Australia)	262	Coeff. Alpha	0·83	Ray (1971)
First-year psychology students (N.Z.)	183	Split-half	0·94	Cloud and Vaughan (1969)
University students (Germany)	272	Split-half	0·86	Schneider and Minkmar (1972)

expected to yield *higher* consistency coefficients, not lower. (Since correlations are based upon common variance, they are restricted by the amount of variance that is available in the situation). In any case, his sample was actually *more* homogeneous than those employed in many of the other studies reported in the sense that it was drawn only from 20-year-old males. A more promising clue is perhaps to be found in the peculiar motivational conditions surrounding the administration of the scale, including the fact that the recruits were tested by "uniformed Army psychologists". The effects of such conditions of administration on scale performance might make an interesting study in its own right.

Using the same statistical method for calculating internal consistency with a group of 262 first-year psychology students (also a fairly homogeneous group) Ray found the rather more acceptable alpha coefficient of 0·83. All the other coefficients reported have been higher still, especially those based on truly heterogeneous samples, which are uniformly in the region of 0·9 and above.

VI. Unidimensionality

Also relevant to the question of internal consistency are results pertaining to the principal components factor structure of the scale. It will be recalled that the scale was developed on the assumption that all areas of social attitudes: religious, political, artistic, moral, scientific, etc., would be to some extent intercorrelated, forming a general factor of considerable importance. While this hypothesis was to some degree supported in the course of simple items analyses during the process of scale construction, a principal components analysis on a fresh sample would provide a more direct test.

Such a study was reported by Wilson (1970) using a sample of 200 males from the London area, heterogeneous with respect to age and occupation.

TABLE IV

Means, S.D.s., item-whole correlations, and unrotated factor loadings for the Conservatism Scale (From Wilson, 1970)

Item	Mean	S.D.	Item × Whole	I	II	III	IV
1. Death penalty	0·93	0·97	0·62	0·65	0·27	0·22	0·06
2. Evolution theory	0·41	0·72	0·30	0·31	0·23	−0·15	−0·15
3. School uniforms	0·94	0·97	0·49	0·47	−0·31	0·26	0·15
4. Striptease shows	0·64	0·83	0·36	0·32	−0·32	−0·49	0·15
5. Sabbath observance	0·61	0·86	0·49	0·51	−0·28	0·05	−0·32
6. Beatniks	1·23	0·89	0·68	0·69	0·01	−0·17	0·19
7. Patriotism	1·16	0·93	0·50	0·52	0·04	0·41	−0·02
8. Modern art	0·73	0·89	0·53	0·56	0·18	−0·13	0·19
9. Self-denial	1·01	0·92	0·21	0·16	−0·33	0·07	−0·26
10. Working mothers	0·80	0·90	0·28	0·28	0·22	−0·28	0·14
11. Horoscopes	0·45	0·77	0·12	0·10	0·27	0·20	−0·27
12. Birth control	0·19	0·56	0·31	0·31	0·16	−0·30	−0·53
13. Military drill	1·00	0·97	0·62	0·64	−0·04	0·41	0·06
14. Co-education	0·23	0·57	0·31	0·32	0·22	−0·22	0·05
15. Divine law	0·84	0·86	0·54	0·54	−0·25	−0·00	−0·22
16. Socialism	0·82	0·89	0·42	0·43	0·16	0·15	0·04
17. White superiority	0·42	0·76	0·36	0·38	0·50	−0·00	−0·04
18. Cousin marriage	0·77	0·85	0·39	0·38	−0·25	0·04	0·06
19. Moral training	1·51	0·79	0·42	0·42	−0·27	0·22	0·05
20. Suicide	1·38	0·86	0·39	0·38	−0·29	0·03	0·05
21 Chaperones	0·32	0·64	0·32	0·32	−0·04	−0·14	0·20
22. Legalized abortion	0·42	0·77	0·38	0·36	0·00	−0·37	−0·42
23. Empire-building	0·64	0·85	0·40	0·42	0·40	0·19	−0·14
24. Student pranks	1·00	0·92	0·24	0·20	−0·06	−0·19	0·22
25. Licensing laws	0·95	0·95	0·38	0·36	−0·25	−0·07	0·20
26. Computer music	1·02	0·90	0·45	0·46	−0·02	−0·15	0·31
27. Chastity	0·86	0·91	0·60	0·62	−0·29	−0·02	0·05
28. Fluoridation	0·62	0·76	0·24	0·22	0·16	−0·18	−0·10
29. Royalty	1·07	0·92	0·56	0·57	−0·06	0·29	−0·01
30. Women judges	0·56	0·82	0·37	0·37	0·24	−0·43	−0·20

Item	Mean	S.D.	Item × Whole	Factors I	II	III	IV
31. Conventional clothes	1·13	0·91	0·56	0·58	−0·07	0·14	0·08
32. Teenage drivers	0·38	0·73	0·30	0·28	0·16	−0·02	0·07
33. Apartheid	0·44	0·69	0·40	0·42	0·49	−0·05	−0·07
34. Nudist camps	0·46	0·74	0·36	0·34	−0·27	−0·42	0·13
35. Church authority	0·49	0·76	0·48	0·46	−0·26	0·07	−0·53
36. Disarmament	0·71	0·91	0·51	0·54	0·28	0·08	−0·01
37. Censorship	0·63	0·87	0·45	0·46	−0·09	0·08	0·10
38. White lies	0·40	0·74	0·18	0·13	−0·31	−0·21	−0·20
39. Birching	0·77	0·95	0·52	0·54	0·20	0·39	−0·02
40. Mixed marriage	0·67	0·90	0·59	0·60	0·27	−0·21	0·23
41. Strict rules	0·63	0·84	0·48	0·47	−0·25	0·17	0·06
42. Jazz	0·43	0·76	0·39	0·38	0·21	−0·20	0·12
43. Straitjackets	0·67	0·83	0·34	0·35	0·22	0·14	0·08
44. Casual living	0·55	0·81	0·30	0·26	−0·40	0·02	0·39
45. Learning Latin	0·90	0·89	−0·01	−0·09	−0·35	0·24	−0·29
46. Divorce	0·35	0·70	0·34	0·33	0·13	−0·46	−0·36
47. Inborn conscience	1·16	0·86	0·35	0·34	−0·31	0·23	0·01
48. Coloured immigration	1·00	0·91	0·60	0·64	0·39	0·00	0·19
49. Bible truth	0·80	0·86	0·57	0·58	−0·16	0·02	−0·40
50. Pyjama parties	0·77	0·85	0·30	0·27	−0·33	−0·43	0·34
			Latent root	9·33	3·25	2·71	2·32
			% Variance	18·67	6·49	5·42	4·64

Table IV shows loadings on the first four principal components emerging from this analysis, as well as mean scores for each item, standard deviations, and item-whole correlations. Several features of these results suggest the predominance of a general factor in the scale (i.e. unidimensionality). Firstly, although fifteen factors gave latent roots of greater than unity, the "natural break" in their progressively decreasing magnitudes occurs conspicuously between the first and second factors. Secondly, the item-whole correlations are nearly all positive and are almost identical to the loadings on the first principal component.

Wilson also compared the strength of the general factor in attitudes with that of the well-established general factor in the field of abilities (intelligence), using a fairly analogous factor-analytic study of the W.A.I.S. by Saunders (1959). The latent roots of the first four unrotated factors in the W.A.I.S. were 3·92, 1·78, 1·40, and 0·74, which when converted into alpha coefficients gave values of 0·77, 0·46, 0·30, and 0·37 respectively. The alpha coefficient for the first factor in the C-Scale came to 0·91, and it was calculated that it would take the first *three* factors from the W.A.I.S. to give reliability equivalent to this. While there may have been certain reasons why these two factor analytic studies do not permit precise comparison, e.g. sample homogeneity, this finding may be interpreted as indicating that the concept of "general attitude" (C) is at least as legitimate as that of "general intelligence" (g).

It may be recognized at this point that internal consistency and uni-dimensionality *per se* are not necessary or even always favourable attributes of a psychometric test. For example, either could be readily inflated by incorporating a large number of virtually identical items. Therefore, in order to fully evaluate the present findings it is necessary to look at the actual content of the items which load highest and lowest on the general factor underlying the C-Scale.

The highest loadings are on Beatniks (0·69), Death penalty (0·65), Coloured immigration (0·64), Military drill (0·64), Chastity (0·62), Mixed marriage (0·60), Bible truth (0·58), Conventional clothing (0·58), Royalty (0·57), Modern art (0·56), Divine law (0·54), and Disarmament (0·54). Many other items also load substantially on the general factor but there are two important things to note about these top twelve: (a) They are widely representative of the different attitude content areas represented in the scale, and indeed, could be regarded as covering all major areas of social controversy (sex, race, religion, law and politics). (b) They are approximately evenly divided as to direction of scoring (seven "Yes"-conservative items and five "No"-conservative items), which may be taken as suggestive evidence that the previously insistent problem of direction-of-wording effects has been largely eliminated by the new item format adopted in this test.

Similarly, if we examine the items which have comparatively slight load-ings on the general factor: Learning Latin (−0·09), Horoscopes (0·10), White lies (0·13), Self-denial (0·16), Student pranks (0·20), Fluoridation (0·22), Casual living (0·26), Pyjama parties (0·27), we find that they do not represent any readily identifiable content area within social attitudes but differ from the high loading items only in terms of the specificity and salience of their referent (the low loading items being less salient and more specific). Again, they include both "Yes" and "No"-scored items. In any case, all the items in the scale load positively on the general factor with the single exception of Learning Latin, which comes out as a "passenger item" in this particular analysis.

Thus the evidence not only supports the interpretation of the C-Scale as predominantly unidimensional in content; to the extent that the test is an adequate sample of the universe of social attitudes it may be asserted that a very important general factor (conservatism) underlies that field.

Such a conclusion is confirmed by the results of replications of this study in other European cultures: New Zealand and the Netherlands

(Bagley *et al.*, 1970), South Africa (Wilson and Shutte, 1973) and Germany (Schneider and Minkmar, 1972). In each of these countries principal components analysis of the C-Scale yielded a strong general factor, most adequately described as "conservatism", which accounted for a much greater proportion of variance than any of the subsequent factors. Schneider and Minkmar also reported that the first principal component loadings correlated 0·98 with item-whole correlations, a result which they interpreted as further evidence for the overwhelming importance of the general (C) factor. All this is not to say that no further information can be gained from the examination of group factors and oblique solutions; these will be considered in some detail in Chapter 5.

One final point: C-scores obtained by simple summation using equal weights on all items have been found to correlate almost perfectly with scores calculated on a weighting system based on general factor loadings (e.g. 0·98, Bagley, 1970). This means that little is to be gained by adopting a factor-scoring system, at least as far as the conservatism dimension is concerned.

VII. Stability

Although internal consistency coefficients are often regarded as an index of reliability, the coefficient of stability as defined by the test-retest correlation is in some ways a more important statistic because it indicates the extent to which results using the measure are repeatable from one occasion to another. The only real limitation of this statistic is that it is necessary to assume that the subjects themselves do not change differentially on the dimension in question between the two testing oacasions, i.e. that any change which is recorded is a function of instrument error rather than a "true" shift in the phenomena under investigation.

Nias *et al.* (1971) studied the stability of the C-Scale under different conditions of anonymity and identification. Four groups of female students from a college of education were tested twice with an interval of twelve weeks. Group 1 were asked to give their names on the first occasion of testing and to remain anonymous on the second occasion. (The two sets of answer sheets were later linked using a code system.) For Group 2 the procedure was reversed; they were asked to withhold their names on the first testing occasion but provide them on the second. Group 3 were asked to give their names on both occasions, and Group 4 remained anonymous on both occasions. Table V shows the mean C-scores for each group on the two occasions of testing. Reliabilities were computed using product-moment correlations.

The test-retest reliability for the total sample was 0·89, which compares very favourably with those reported for other scales. The difference between

TABLE V

Means, standard deviations and reliabilities for the four groups
(From Nias, Wilson and Woodbridge, 1971)

Group	N	Test	Retest	Reliability
		Mean (and S.D.)		
1. Named-Anonymous	28	45·1 (12·2)	42·4 (13·4)	0·94
2. Anonymous-Named	25	42·2 (11·2)	41·3 (10·6)	0·82
3. Named	15	39·3 (10·9)	38·3 (11·4)	0·84
4. Anonymous	14	44·8 (12·7)	43·5 (14·0)	0·90
Total	82	43·1 (11·8)	41·5 (12·2)	0·89

the reliabilities for the four subgroups was not significant ($\chi^2 = 4·5$, df = 3). C-scores were slightly lower on retesting, the overall mean change of 1·6 being statistically significant (t = 2·4, df = 81, p < 0·05). This change towards liberalism may, of course, be attributable either to the effects of retesting or to a change in attitudes for the group over the twelve weeks; the present data do not enable us to say which is the case.

This study also provided an opportunity to investigate the possibility that scores obtained on the scale when completed anonymously would differ from those obtained under the identification condition, e.g. because one end of the scale or the other might be perceived as more socially desirable. Thus Nias *et al.* combined the scores for the Named condition from Groups 1 and 3 and compared the mean with that for the Anonymous condition from Groups 2 and 4. The two means obtained in this way were the same at 43·1. Another comparison was made by combining the scores for Groups 1 and 2 so as to form a "cross-over" design; the mean under the Named condition was 43·2 and under the anonymous condition 42·3. This difference was not significant either (F = 1·4, df = 1, 51). Thus these results indicate that there was little or no difference in social desirability between conservative and liberal responses for this sample. There is, however, strong evidence that differences on the conservatism dimension may be antecedent to differences in willingness to identify oneself (Patterson and Wilson, 1969).

One other study of the test-retest reliability of the C-Scale has been reported—that of Schneider and Minkmar (1972). Using a forty-item German version of the scale, they tested a group of twenty-eight psychology students twice across a four-week interval and obtained a stability coefficient of 0·94. Taken together, these two studies indicate a very satisfactory level of stability for the C-Scale, which may be attributed to the new item format.

VIII. Freedom from Acquiescence

In the early part of the chapter it was argued that the new item format adopted in the C-Scale should have the effect of reducing the influence of acquiescence response bias so that it would be possible to obtain a measure based on attitude *content* without the contamination of item *context*. Is there any empirical evidence to indicate that this aim has been realized?

Cloud and Vaughan (1969) addressed themselves to this question in a study that was designed (a) to determine the extent to which acquiescence responding occurs in the C-Scale, and (b) the extent to which it is controlled for by the balanced keying. They used the same items as those in the original C-Scale but randomized the order of presentation in case any respondents should "perceive the drift and meaning" which they suspected might cause them to revert to an alternating response style. The sample consisted of 183 students enrolled in an introductory psychology course.

Besides the standard C-score, several other scores were calculated for each subject: A *style score* (S) was obtained following formulae recommended by Messick (1961) for use with personality and attitude scales:

$$C_o = \frac{R_a}{N_a} + \frac{R_b}{N_b} - 1$$

$$S = \frac{\dfrac{R_a}{N_a} - \dfrac{R_b}{N_b}}{1 - |1C_o|}$$

where R_a is the number of items keyed *a* that are marked *a* by the respondent, R_b is the number of items keyed *b* and marked *b*, and N_a and N_b are the number of items keyed *a* and *b* respectively. (To avoid confusion with the conservatism score Messick's *content* score was designated Co.) The only modification introduced into the Messick formula was the subtraction of those items answered "?" from N_a and N_b; i.e. these items were treated according to the procedure appropriate for omitted items in scales where a choice is forced between "Yes" and "No", since the basic formula referred only to items marked by the respondent in one direction or the other. Combining Messick's formulae for C_o and S, and introducing the above subtractions gave the following definition of S:

$$S = \frac{\dfrac{R_a}{N_a - R_{a'}} - \dfrac{R_b}{N_b - R_{b'}}}{1 - \left[\dfrac{R_a}{N_a - R_{a'}} + \dfrac{R_b}{N_b - R_{b'}} - 1\right]}$$

where the subscripts a and b could be interpreted as conservative and liberal respectively, and hence $R_{a'}$ and $R_{b'}$ were the numbers of conservative and liberal items answered "?". For correlational purposes Cloud and Vaughan used a linear transformation of S, converting it from a range of -1 to $+1$ to a range of 0 to 100, but not otherwise affecting it.

A somewhat simpler *Yeasaying score* (Y) was also obtained, counting two for items answered "Yes" and one for items answered "?" (the latter again to cancel out the effect of "omitted" items). The difference between the two measures of response style is that S is based on a discrepancy between subscales rather than on the absolute number of "Yes" responses. Finally, two other subscores were obtained by combining elements obtained for S, such that $S_a = 2R_a + R_{a'}$ and $S_b = 2R_b + R_{b'}$.

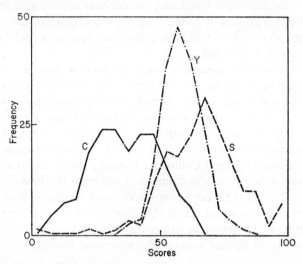

FIG. 2. Frequency distributions of Content (C), Style (S), and Yeasaying (Y) Scores on the Conservatism Scale (N = 183). (From Cloud and Vaughan, 1970.)

The distributions of the three scores, C, S and Y are shown in Fig. 2. The fact that the means of both S and Y are clearly above 50 indicates that some amount of "yeasaying" (a more appropriate term than acquiescence in this context) has occurred. That this response style is much attenuated by comparison with the F-Scale, however, is indicated by the finding that the liberal and conservative subsections of the scale (S_a and S_b) were correlated 0·68. (The sign here was positive because all items were scored in the conservative direction according to the standard procedure.) This means that it should be possible for the balanced structure of the C-Scale to cancel out response style contamination so as to leave a very meaningful attitude content score. In fact, the product-moment correlation between C and S was found to $-0·134$ and that between C and Y was 0·225, leading Cloud and Vaughan to conclude that "the dimension of conservatism measured by this test is for all practical purposes acquiescence free".

IX. Comparison of Old and New Item Formats

In the Cloud and Vaughan study it was demonstrated (a) that the liberal and conservative scored items of the C-Scale are fairly well correlated in the predicted direction, and (b) that the remaining variance due to response style is satisfactorily cancelled by the balanced keying so as to provide a "pure" content measure of the liberal–conservative dimension. These findings may be contrasted with the large body of literature which indicates that previous attitude scales are unsatisfactory in both respects. While Cloud and Vaughan have produced results that are consistent with the Wilson–Patterson argument concerning the importance of item format in determining the extent to which acquiescence occurs, a more direct test of this hypothesis is available.

Ray (1970) made a comparative study of the two types of item format, with particular reference to the correlations between liberal and conservative items. To one group of 474 Australian Army conscripts (selected randomly by a birth-date ballot procedure from the whole 20-year-old male population) he administered a battery of attitude tests comprising items of the conventional directional-statement format. This consisted of ten of the "strongest" items from the California F-Scale, the sixteen-item Eysenck R (radicalism) scale, ten of the strongest items from the Beswick and Hills (1969) Australian E (Ethnocentrism) scale, and Anderson and Western's (1967) Australian version of the D (Dogmatism) scale. To a second comparable group of 111 Army conscripts Ray administered the C-Scale along with seventy-six additional items in the new short format.

TABLE VI

Reliabilities of liberal and conservative subscales, and the correlations between these subscales compared for conventional and short item formats.
(From results of Ray, 1970)

| | Reliability (Coeff. alpha) | | |
	"Liberal" items	"Conservative" items	^{r}L × C
Old item format	0·53	0·80	0·099
New item format	0·74	0·78	−0·639

The results are summarized in Table VI. The most striking finding is that while the internal consistency of liberal and conservative subscales do not differ markedly, *the two halves are uncorrelated with the old format but substantially correlated in the predicted direction with the new format.* (Here the sign is negative because liberal items were not reverse scored.) These results are in clear accord with the literature concerning attempts to reverse traditional scales (e.g. Berkowitz and Wolkon, 1964). Given the large N involved the correlation of 0·099 between liberal and conservative items in the old format is actually in the "wrong" direction ($p < 0.05$). Also, the correlation of -0.639 for these two types of items in the C-Scale format is in close accord with that of $(-)0.68$ found in the Cloud and Vaughan study. Together, these findings confirm that balanced keying of conventional attitude scales simply cancels response bias to leave virtually nothing meaningful, but that the balancing of items in the C-Scale format yields a highly satisfactory attitude content score.

X. Social Desirability

How do the two item formats compare in terms of susceptibility to social desirability responding? Orpen (1971) administered the C-Scale together with a specially constructed propositional scale covering the same content areas to several large samples of South African high-school students. The influence of social desirability was assessed four ways: (a) correlations with the Crowne–Marlow Scale, (b) correlations between endorsement frequency and social desirability ratings of the individual items, (c) differences between scores under anonymous and "faking" conditions, and (d) completion of the two scales under "real life" conditions that had been shown to "demand" liberal and conservative replies respectively. Only in the case of the second indicator was there no significant difference between the two scales; on each of the other indicators the C-Scale was significantly less susceptible than the propositional equivalent. Orpen concludes that "the catch-phrase questionnaire measure of conservatism is markedly less susceptible to social desirability than is the propositional measure, despite the fact that the two measures only really differ in item format".

XI. Validity

The question of validity is considerably more complex than the readers of most test manuals are led to believe. In psychometrics there is generally no perfect criterion against which to evaluate a test, and therefore there can be no such thing as a single "validity coefficient" for a given test. The present author tends towards the opinion that "all validity is contruct validity", i.e. that it is based upon an understanding of the meaning of test scores which develops slowly as empirical data concerning their relationships with other kinds of behaviour are accumulated.

Perhaps the best kind of construct validation involves the testing of *a priori* hypotheses concerning the nature of the dimension which the test purports to measure. Thus the earlier findings that C-Scale scores increase monotonically with age and are slightly higher for females than for males

D

are consistent with what is known about the construct of conservatism and may therefore be taken as partial evidence in support of the validity of the test. (As suggested in Chapter 1, the concept of the "generation gap" implies some notion, such as "attitude age", and the C-Scale appears well-suited to its quantification.) In fact, most of the empirical evidence so far presented (occupational group differences, internal consistency, etc.) contributes in some way to the overall picture of what C-scores mean, and may therefore be interpreted as partial validation. Likewise, the various findings to be reported in the rest of the book also contribute to the validation of the C-Scale. This section, however, will deal only with some selected studies that are conventionally considered to be especially concerned with the assessment of validity.

The "known groups" technique involves comparison of two or more groups that are widely recognized as representing fairly extreme positions on the continuum under study, and showing that their scores on the test are satisfactorily separated. Control must be exercised over any extraneous variables which might effect a spurious separation.

The first two such comparisons were made by Wilson and Patterson (1968) with pairs of groups that were essentially matched for age, sex balance and socio-economic status. The New Left Club and Junior National Party were socialist and conservative political groups respectively, both within a New Zealand university. The Gideons, an international society organized specifically for the purpose of placing Bibles in hotel rooms, was compared with a group consisting of physical and social

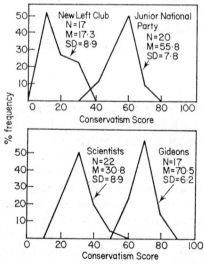

FIG. 3. Validation comparisons: the distribution of C-scores for four "known groups". (From Wilson and Patterson, 1968).

scientists, and medical practitioners. Figure 3 shows the distributions of C-scores for these groups, as well as means and standard deviations. To the extent that the pairs of groups differ on *a priori* construct grounds, it may be asserted that the C-Scale shows evidence of being a valid measure of conservatism.

In another study of this kind, Wilson and Lillie (1972) gave the C-Scale to a group of Salvation Army officer cadets and a group of Young Humanists. Again, the groups were roughly matched on the major demographic variables. Not only were the distributions of C-scores clearly separated with minimal overlap (Fig. 4), but it was also demonstrated that this

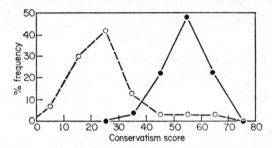

Fig. 4. Distributions of conservatism scores for Young Humanists and Salvation Army officer cadets. •, Humanists (N = 31, mean = 24·4, S.D. = 11·6), ○, Salvationists (N = 43, mean = 53·7, S.D. = 9·7). (From Wilson and Lillie, 1972.)

discrimination could not be accounted for by religious items alone. The Salvationists were not only more conservative in terms of religion, but were relatively more anti-hedonistic, punitive, militaristic, politically conservative, and conventional. This study is discussed in greater detail in Chapter 5. At this point it is sufficient to note that the results are consistent with the general factor hypothesis as well as confirming the discriminative validity of the C-Scale.

One other "known groups" study is that of Insel and Wilson (1971) who administered the original C-Scale plus a children's version of it (Chapter 6) to a sample of schoolgirls aged 12 to 16 years (100 from a Catholic convent school and 85 from a State secondary school. As expected, the results showed a great deal of overlap in the distributions, but both scales discriminated between the two schools at a very high level of significance.

A different method of assessing validity was adopted by Schneider and Minkmar (1972) in the evaluation of their German version of the C-Scale. After completing the scale, the group of 272 students were asked to rate themselves on two fairly global political scales: (1) A scale of political "position" running from "extreme left" to "extreme right", and (2) a scale of attitudes towards a left-wing student organization called the "Socialist German Student Union" (S.D.S.). This scale ranged from "strongly agree" to "strongly disagree". The correlation between total C-scores and the former criterion measure was 0·51 (p < 0·01) and with the latter 0·43 (p < 0·01). These correlations are about the magnitude that would have been predicted, remembering that the conservatism dimension as measured by the C-Scale is not supposed to be synonymous with the political 'left–right" continuum.

Schneider and Minkmar also compared the mean C-scores of different faculties and departments within the University of Saarland (Table VII). The ordering of means was generally in accord with *a priori* expectation, the students of social sciences being more liberal than those in physical sciences, law and economics. Analysis of variance showed these intergroup differences to be highly significant (F = 5·79, df = 5, p < 0·01).

TABLE VII

C-scores for different groups of German students
(From Schneider and Minkmar, 1972)

Faculty	N	Mean	S.D.
Mathematical and natural sciences	48	37·18	13·46
Medicine	63	37·07	12·90
Law and Economics	28	32·25	15·45
Education	56	36·98	13·99
Psychology	46	27·58	13·50
Sociology	31	26·22	13·51
Total	272	32·88	13·80

In view of the criticisms of previous tests of social attitudes outlined earlier, results relating to what is sometimes described as "concurrent validity" are perhaps not very meaningful. Certainly it is difficult to say in advance what magnitude of correlations with other tests should be regarded as favourable evidence concerning the present measure. Nevertheless, it may be of some interest to report the results of a study by W. B. Crano (private communication, 1969) who correlated the C-Scale with the California F-Scale, the Gough–Sanford Rigidity Scale and the Rokeach Dogmatism Scale using a sample of 100 students at Michigan State University (Table VIII).

TABLE VIII

Intercorrelations amongst four attitude scales. N = 100
U.S.A. students (After Crano, 1969)

	F-Scale	Rigidity	Dogmatism
C-Scale	0·68	0·51	0·39
F-Scale		0·64	0·60
Rigidity			0·46

At first sight the correlation of 0·68 between C and F seems embarrass-ingly high, since it suggests that the two tests have nearly 50 per cent in common. However, there are two possible explanations for this: (a) The most likely possibility is that with student groups (who are presumably above average in intelligence) the confusion arising from item context in traditional scales may be less severe, enabling the F-Scale to register some amount of "true" authoritarianism. (b) Alternatively, or additionally, if the F-Scale is in fact measuring a large proportion of acquiescence response bias, this variable may itself be correlated with conservatism. Such a hypothesis has been invoked in the past as an answer to criticisms of the F-Scale based on the double-agreement phenomenon but could not be tested because in the F-Scale acquiescence is confounded with "true" authoritarianism. Now that the C-Scale is available as an acquiescence-free measure of social attitudes it would be possible to test this hypothesis by correlating C-scores with acquiescence scores derived from "content free" tests.

XII. Economy

Finally, it hardly needs to be mentioned that the C-Scale is considerably more economical than previous measures in both cost and time. Experience tells that it seldom takes more than a few minutes to administer, and the response records can be scored in a few seconds without computers or keys, simply by scanning for departures from alternation. In view of the manifest simplicity and economy of the instrument, as well as the evidence reviewed above, the onus is now squarely upon proponents of traditional statement-form attitude scales to demonstrate that their approach has some measurable advantage. Otherwise, it must be regarded as obsolete.

XIII. Summary

It was argued in the previous chapter that most of the difficulties en-countered with traditional attitude scales such as the F- and D-Scales could be traced to the directional statement format of their items. There-fore, the C-Scale was designed with a short non-directional item format—catch-phrases representing controversial issues. Apart from its obvious advantage in economy, the new scale is shown to be internally consistent, predominantly unidimensional in content, stable, free of acquiescence response bias, less susceptible to the effects of social desirability response set, and highly satisfactory in terms of construct validity. Evidence so far available suggests that the C-Scale provides, possibly for the first time, a measure of attitude *content* which is free of the confounding effects of item *context*.

References

Anderson, D. S. and Western, J. S. (1967). An inventory to measure students' attitudes. Univ. Queensland Papers: Dept. of Govt. and History, 1, No. 3.

Bagley, C. R. (1970). Racial prejudice and the conservative personality. Pol. Stud. 18, 134–141.

Bagley, C. R., Wilson, G. D. and Boshier, R. (1970). The Conservatism Scale: A factor-structure comparison of English, Dutch, and New Zealand samples. J. soc. Psychol. 81, 267–268.

Berkowitz, N. H. and Wolkon, G. H. (1964). A forced-choice form of the F-Scale —free of acquiescence response set. Sociometry, 24, 54–56.

Beswick, D. G. and Hills, M. D. (1969). An Australian ethnocentrism scale. Aust. J. Psychol. 21, 211–226.

Caffrey, B. and Capel, W. C. (1968). The predictive value of neutral positions in opinion and attitude research. J. Psychol. 69, 145–154.

Cloud, J. and Vaughan, G. M. (1969). Using balanced scales to control acquiescence. Sociometry, 33, 193–202.

Insel, P. M. and Wilson, G. D. (1971). Measuring social attitudes in children. Brit. J. soc. clin. Psychol. 10, 84–86.

McGuire, W. J. (1969). The nature of attitudes and attitude research. In "Handbook of Social Psychology." (Lindzey, G. and Aronson, E. , eds, 2nd. edn. Vol. 3, Addison-Wesley, London.

Messick, S. (1961). Separate set and content scores for personality and attitude scales. Educ. psychol. Measur. 21, 915–923.

Nias, D. K. B., Wilson, G. D. and Woodbridge, J. M. (1971). Test-retest results on the Conservatism Scale completed under conditions of anonymity and identification. Brit. J. soc. clin. Psychol. 10, 282–283.

Orpen, C. (1971). The relative susceptibility of catch-phrase and propositional scales to social desirability. Psychol. Rep. 29, 487–495.

Patterson, J. R. and Wilson, G. D. (1969). Anonymity occupation and conservatism. J. soc. Psychol. 78, 263–266.

Ray, J. J. (1970). "Are liberalism and conservatism orthogonal?" Unpublished MSS. Macquarie Univ.

Ray. J. J. (1971). A new measure of conservatism: its limitations. Brit. J. soc. clin. Psychol. 10, 79–80.

Saunders, D. R. (1959). On the dimensionality of the W.A.I.S. battery for two groups of normal males. Educational Testing Service Res. Bull. RB—59–7.

Schneider, J. and Minkmar, H. (1972). Deutsche Neukonstruktion einer Konservatismus-Skala. Diagnostica, in press.

Stacey, B. G. and Green, R. T. The psychological bases of political allegiance among white-collar males. Brit. J. soc. clin. Psychol. 7, 45–60.

Wilson, G. D. (1970). Is there a general factor in social attitudes? Evidence from a factor-analysis of the Conservatism Scale. Brit. J. soc. clin. Psychol. 9, 101–107.

Wilson, G. D. and Lillie, F. J. (1972). Social attitudes of humanists and salvationists. Brit. J. socl. clin. Psychol. in press.

Wilson, G. D. and Patterson, J. R. (1968). A new measure of conservatism. Brit. J. soc. clin. Psychol. 7, 264–269.

Wilson, G. D. and Patterson, J. R. (1970). "Manual for the Conservatism Scale." N.F.E.R. Publishing Co., England, Windsor.

Wilson, G. D. and Shutte, P. (1973). The structure of social attitudes in South Africa. J. soc. Psychol. in press.

5 | The Factor Structure of the C-Scale

GLENN D. WILSON

Institute of Psychiatry, University of London

I. Introduction

In the last chapter it was noted briefly that principal components analysis of the C-Scale was in general support of the uni-dimensional hypothesis concerning the content of social attitudes. This conclusion was based upon the observation that the first principal component comprised a general factor which not only accounted for a much greater proportion of variance than any of the subsequent factors but was also widely representative of the various attitude content areas which make up the questionnaire.

While these findings may be taken as substantiating the primary rationale upon which development of the C-Scale was based, and as a general validation of the recommended scoring procedure, it remains very worthwhile to examine the factor structure of the scale in greater detail for several reasons:

(a) There may be other broad attitude dimensions in the scale, apart from conservatism, which are of psychological significance, e.g. Eysenck's Toughminded-Tenderminded (T) factor, which he found to be orthogonal to his Radical–Conservative (R) factor. If so, then the factor loadings can be used as the basis for developing an appropriate procedure for scoring them.

(b) The examination of rotated and higher-order factor solutions may provide a better understanding of the way in which attitudes are "naturally" organized. Methods not subject to the restraints of orthogonality would be expected to give an indication of the extent to which different attitude areas are correlated before the general factor variance is extracted, without recourse to an examination of the intercorrelations amongst all the individual items. Thus, for example, racialism may be more closely related to punitiveness than to anti-hedonism or religious fundamentalism. Information such as this may in turn have relevance to hypotheses concerning the origins and psychological significance of the general C-factor.

(c) The various sub-factors can be expected to provide a great deal of information about the way in which individual items are perceived by respondents. e.g. If "Mixed marriage" clusters with racial items it is presumably being interpreted by subjects as meaning inter-*race* marriage; if it loads with religious items then it is perhaps read as referring to inter-*denominational* marriage.

(d) Detailed factor analysis provides a good summary picture of the item content distribution in the questionnaire, i.e. it can be regarded as a kind of content analysis. For some purposes it may be useful to provide a procedure for scoring the various content areas of the scale (religion, sex, race, punitiveness, conventionalism, etc.) so that different individuals and groups can be compared on content profiles as well as general conservatism.

This chapter, then, is concerned with the different factor analytic approaches that have been used in connection with the C-Scale, beginning with an examination of the principal components (all of them, not just the first, general factor), then with the oblique first-order and higher-order promax solutions described in the literature. Where data are available, comparisons are made across different European cultures in order to see whether the factors which emerge are stable from one national group to another. Comparisons are also made with factor structures based on other tests, especially that of Eysenck, in order to determine the extent to which these solutions are compatible with previous findings. Finally, some procedures for scoring various sub-factors in the C-Scale are suggested.

II. Principal Components

A. An English Sample

A principal components analysis of the C-Scale reported by Wilson (1970) has already been referred to in the previous chapter, and the main results shown in Table IV, Chapter 4. The sample consisted of 200 males from the London area: 50 students, 50 professionals and businessmen, 50 white-collar workers (clerks, public servants, soldiers, etc.) and 50 blue-collar workers (mostly trade apprentices). This sample was not claimed to be random or representative of any particular population, merely heterogeneous with respect to occupation and age. The age range was 17 to 56 years, with a mean of 28 years. The C-Scale was administered and scored according to the standardized procedure (Chapter 4) and a principal components analysis conducted on the product-moment intercorrelations amongst the fifty scale items.

In the interpretation of the results shown in Table IV, Chapter 4, it is important to note that all of the items have been scored in the conservative direction, i.e. so that on the basis of the general factor hypothesis they would be expected to show a pattern of positive correlations one with another. (As noted in Chapter 4, this hypothesis has been very largely confirmed.)

The mean item scores are of some interest because they indicate the extent to which the population in this analysis is divided on the issue in question. A mean of 1·00 indicates that approximately 50 per cent of the sample gave the conservative response. Thus, for this sample of British males, "Death penalty" was favoured by about half of the respondents, while "Evolution theory" was favoured by more than three-quarters. The S.D.s are somewhat less interesting because they are constrained by the level of the mean and the number of "?" responses evoked by the item. The mean number of "?"'s per subject was 7·02.

Fifteen factors gave latent roots of greater than one, but only the first four have been listed in Table IV, Chapter 4; the rest were not so readily interpretable. Factor I has high loadings on items representing all the major attitudes areas included in the scale and is clearly the general (*conservatism*) factor. The extent to which the structure and content of this factor supports the hypothesis of a single-factor field in social attitudes has been considered previously.

Factor II has highest loadings on White superiority (0·50), Apartheid (0·49), Empire-building (0·40) and Coloured immigration (0·39), and may therefore be described as a specific *racialist* factor. In passing, it may be noted that even these top four items on the second factor, have, on average, higher loadings on the general C-factor than their own specific factor.

Factor III loads on Striptease shows (−0·49), Divorce (−0·46), Pyjama parties (−0·43), Women judges (−0·43), Nudist camps (−0·42), and appears to be concerned primarily with *sexual freedom*.

Factor IV loads on Church authority (−0·53), Birth control (−0·53), Legalized abortion (−0·42), and Bible truth (−0·40), and might be described as a *religious* factor, with particular emphasis on fundamentalist, perhaps Roman Catholic style religion.

Thus the evidence does suggest that after the general C-factor has been taken out, items relating to similar attitude content areas group together to form specific factors in a fairly predictable way.

B. CROSS-CULTURAL REPLICATION

The above analysis has since been replicated using roughly comparable samples of Dutch and New Zealand subjects (Bagley *et al.*, 1970). In this three-culture comparison, Wilson's English sample was compared with a similar sample of 200 males gathered in the Hague (using a Dutch translation of the C-Scale), and a sample of 357 adult-education students collected in Wellington, N.Z. The N.Z. sample differed from the other two in that it was rather more biased towards subjects with higher education, and it also contained some females whereas the others were all male.

Principal components analysis was conducted separately for each of these samples, and the results are shown in Table I. In each of the three cultures a strong general factor of conservatism emerged, accounting for 18·7, 15·3, and 14·0% of variance respectively. The main point to note about this factor is that in each culture the high loading items cover a wide range of attitude content areas. The factor is not dominated by any one content area, and there is no major content area which is consistently unrelated to the general factor such that it should be excluded from the test, or at least from the scoring of the C-factor. However, there are one or two individual items which show fairly consistently low loadings on the C-factor, and may therefore be described as "passenger items" as regards the standard scoring procedure. These are: Horoscopes (0·10, −0·02, 0·03), White lies (0·13, 0, 0·19), and Learning Latin (−0·09, 0·29, 0·07). If they have anything at all in common, it is not their content, but probably either their specificity of referent or their lack of salience compared to items such as Disarmament and Death penalty.

The second factor has consistently high positive loadings on *racialist* items (White superiority 0·50, 0·50, 0·35; Apartheid 0·49, 0·34, 0·47; Coloured immigration 0·39, 0·38, 0·40; Empire building 0·40, 0·35, 0·26). While this appears to be a specific racialist factor, it should be remembered again that these four items have higher average loadings on the C-factor than they do on this content factor. Incidentally, since Empire-building is not explicitly concerned with race, it is interesting to note that it loads relatively more highly on this factor in Britain and the Netherlands (the two countries with histories of imperialism) than it does in New Zealand (itself a colony of Britain).

Although this second principal component factor has highest loadings that are all positive and relevant to racial issues, it is really a bipolar factor

TABLE I

Loadings on the first four principal components of the C-Scale in England, The Netherlands and New Zealand
(From Wilson and Patterson, 1970)

	Factor I			Factor II			Factor III			Factor IV		
	E	N	NZ	E	N	NZ	E	N	NZ	E	N	NZ
1. Death penalty	65	33	32	27	04	28	22	01	26	06	09	06
2. Evolution theory	31	44	32	23	31	19	-14	05	-30	-05	-08	-20
3. School uniforms	47	21	41	-31	03	-04	-26	-07	27	15	-07	01
4. Striptease shows	32	42	45	-32	-07	-16	-49	-26	-20	15	34	20
5. Sabbath observance	51	43	49	-28	-26	-28	05	-21	-04	-32	-22	-34
6. Beatniks	69	61	53	01	15	08	-17	18	04	19	11	37
7. Patriotism	52	64	37	04	-04	-17	-41	-11	38	-02	-27	-20
8. Modern art	56	37	40	18	29	25	-23	14	-09	19	15	09
9. Self-denial	16	18	39	-33	-37	-28	07	-20	-06	-26	-10	-09
10. Working mothers	28	40	35	22	22	00	-28	-21	-22	14	20	06
11. Horoscopes	10	-02	03	27	28	23	20	-01	23	-27	-24	-24
12. Birth control	31	28	35	-16	16	06	-30	-16	-55	-53	-30	-21
13. Military drill	64	43	52	-04	-14	00	41	30	36	06	-10	-15
14. Co-education	32	18	22	22	57	31	-21	-02	-29	05	08	-12
15. Divine law	54	50	55	-25	-33	-22	-33	-00	-11	-22	-20	-24
16. Socialism	43	36	32	16	30	25	15	03	06	04	-18	03
17. White superiority	38	14	32	50	50	35	-00	-05	-09	04	-19	-25
18. Cousin marriage	38	40	41	-25	-14	-08	04	-09	09	06	10	07
19. Moral training	42	03	28	-27	-48	-37	22	04	22	05	-24	09
20. Suicide	38	55	40	-29	-01	-31	03	04	08	09	-09	18
21. Chaperones	32	12	32	-04	25	10	-14	-12	09	20	06	-10
22. Legalized abortion	36	46	34	00	15	-22	-37	-34	-50	-42	06	-10
23. Empire-building	42	43	38	40	35	26	19	-13	09	-14	-42	-32

	Factor I			Factor II			Factor III			Factor IV		
	E	N	NZ	E	N	NZ	E	N	NZ	E	N	NZ
24. Student pranks	20	−01	36	−06	22	16	−19	−05	−06	22	20	34
25. Licensing laws	36	22	33	−25	−13	−12	−07	19	26	20	−28	−08
26. Computer music	46	37	29	−02	−10	16	−15	28	03	31	25	38
27. Chastity	62	41	48	−29	−31	−38	−02	−37	−01	05	01	−02
28. Fluoridation	22	12	12	16	13	46	−18	−11	−10	−10	05	−01
29. Royalty	57	63	41	−06	−12	−18	29	10	26	−07	−22	−15
30. Women judges	37	08	18	24	13	38	−43	−24	−27	−20	−06	−04
31. Conventional clothes	58	37	37	37	−07	−17	14	13	26	08	37	26
32. Teenage drivers	28	42	13	16	05	40	−02	26	−03	07	10	15
33. Apartheid	42	23	22	49	34	47	−05	08	−11	−07	−14	−28
34. Nudist camps	34	48	48	−27	05	−04	−42	−40	−07	13	28	30
35. Church authority	46	47	54	−26	−03	−17	07	−37	−18	−53	−25	−27
36. Disarmament	54	43	33	28	20	31	08	24	19	−01	−14	−13
37. Censorship	46	35	45	−09	−42	−21	08	−06	02	10	−26	05
38. White lies	13	−00	19	−31	−06	−11	−21	−43	−24	−20	11	15
39. Birching	54	23	35	20	−04	29	39	22	37	−02	−18	−06
40. Mixed marriage	60	34	39	27	−05	31	−21	−07	07	23	13	18
41. Strict rules	47	51	39	−25	−04	03	17	19	21	06	−14	−00
42. Jazz	38	34	30	21	−14	19	−20	05	−28	12	45	−07
43. Straitjackets	35	00	04	22	08	04	14	17	22	08	09	−23
44. Casual living	26	15	43	−40	−40	−12	02	−10	01	39	35	17
45. Learning Latin	−09	29	07	−35	−25	−14	24	18	07	−29	−17	−06
46. Divorce	33	29	39	−13	08	−06	−46	−46	−52	−36	10	09
47. Inborn conscience	34	38	26	−31	−05	−14	23	16	24	01	−05	08
48. Coloured immigration	64	36	39	39	38	40	00	09	20	19	22	22
49. Bible truth	58	36	65	−16	−14	−21	02	−24	−09	−40	−29	−27
50. Pyjama parties	27	57	48	−33	−01	02	−43	−09	01	34	26	32

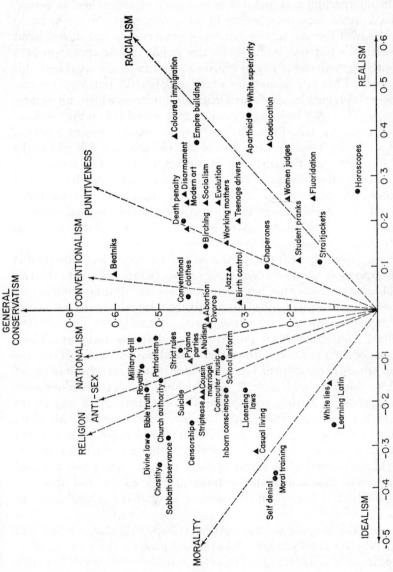

FIG. 1. Loading of C-Scale items on the first two principal component factors averaged over three cultures (England, Netherlands and New Zealand). Co-ordinates marked as circles represent positive loadings; triangles show negative loadings. The oblique subfactors of conservatism (– – –) are drawn by inspection to assist in the interpretation of the second principal component.

which opposes moral and religious items against racial and punitive ones. This can be seen clearly in Fig. 1 in which loadings on the first two principal components averaged over the three cultures are plotted against each other. In interperting this graph it is necessary to remember, as before, that all the items have been scored in the conservative direction, i.e. in accordance with the alternating pattern of conservative and liberal items upon which the test was built. While this might at first appear to be a kind of prejudgment of the way in which social attitudes are organized, this scoring method has two advantages which undoubtedly outweigh the disadvantages: (a) It enables one to spot instantly any items which run counter to the general C-factor hypothesis because they would fall on the "wrong" side of the second axis. (This did not happen in the present analysis: Horoscopes is the lowest loading item on the C-factor but it is still in the "right" direction.) (b) Perhaps more important, it means that items relating to similar content areas will fall in the same area on the graph regardless of whether they are positively or negatively keyed. Thus Coloured immigration and Apartheid appear together in the two-dimensional space of Fig. 1 rather than in opposite quadrants, as they would do if they had been scored without any theoretical assumptions.

Since with this approach the items tend to fall into content clusters it is possible to suggest names for a number of sub-factors oblique to the two principal components. This has been done for an arbitrary number of item groups, and the array of vectors runs from morality (without necessary connection with religion), through religion itself, anti-sex attitudes, nationalism, conventionalism, punitiveness and finally racialism. These in turn can be seen to assist in the rather difficult task of finding a suitable label for principal component factor II. Clearly it is very reminiscent of Eysenck's T-factor, and indeed Toughmindedness-Tendermindedness may be regarded as a fairly appropriate title. Alternatively, it may be regarded as a factor concerned with Idealism versus Realism. Morality, religion, sexual abstinence and nationalism may all be regarded as different kinds of ideals, or are likely to be justified within an ideological framework, whereas behaving in a conventional manner, being punitive and practising racial discrimination are apparently expedient, and therefore realistic, courses, at least from the point of view of the individuals concerned.

Note that the suggestion made earlier (Chapter 1) that religion and racialism may be virtually independent yet both good measures of conservatism appears to be upheld, at least in so far as it is possible to tell from this two-dimensional picture. It may be necessary to stress, however, that this is not the whole picture of the organization of social atitudes by any means. The third and fourth principal components are by definition orthogonal to both of these and they each account for nearly as much variance as Factor

II. These will now be considered briefly. (The question of the special relationship between religion and racialism will be dealt with in Chapter 7).

Factor III, which was identified as being concerned with opposition to *sexual freedom* with the British sample, shows a very similar pattern of loadings in the Netherlands and New Zealand. Thus the following items all load negatively in a reasonably consistent manner: Divorce (−0·46, −0·46, −0·52), Legalized abortion (−0·37, −0·34, −0·50), Birth control (−0·30, −0·16, −0·55), Striptease (−0·49, −0·26, −0·20), Nudist camps (−0·42, −0·40, −0·07), Women judges (−0·43, −0·24, −0·27) and Working mothers (−0·28, −0·21, −0·22). Since these items are not all overtly sexual it is interesting to consider the intuitive relationships amongst them. They appear to fall into three groups: Firstly, the highest loading items (Divorce, Abortion, and Birth control) all concern responsibility in marriage and childbirth, and in particular the role of the woman as a wife and mother. The second area is that of sex viewed as a source of voyeuristic pleasure (Striptease, Nudist camps), and finally there are two "women's liberation" items (Women judges, Working mothers). These items are therefore more logically related than they might at first seem, since the factor is as much concerned with the role of women in society as it is with sexual freedom in general. Opposed to these items concerned with sex, marriage, and the role of women are a few items that are generally in the area of *militarism-punitiveness*: Military drill (0·41, 0·30, 0·36), Birching (0·39, 0·22, 0·37), etc.

Factor IV was identified as a *religious* factor with the British sample, and again, this interpretation appears to be well sustained in the other two cultures. The items which have consistent loadings in all three cultures have a distinctly religious flavour about them: Church authority (−0·53, −0·25, −0·27), Bible truth (−0·40, −0·29, −0·27), Birth control (−0·53, −0·30, −0·27), Sabbath observance (−0·32, −0·22, −0·34), Divine law (−0·22, −0·20, −0·24). Interestingly, the one item in the scale which is clearly concerned with superstitious belief also loads in the same direction (Horoscopes: −0·27, −0·24, −0·24). Considering the content of these items, the factor is not so much religion in general, as the rather more fundamental and dogmatic religion which is associated with the Roman Catholic Church and the more puritan of Protestant denominations and sects. Such an interpretation is perhaps further supported by an examination of the positive loading items which oppose those concerned with religion and superstition. Most of these relate to a flippant or frivolous philosophy of life, e.g. Casual living (0·39, 0·35, 0·17), Pyjama parties (0·34, 0·25, 0·32), Student pranks (0·22, 0·20, 0·34).

These results, then, indicate a remarkable degree of cross-cultural stability in the principal component factor structure of the C-Scale, and therefore the organization of social attitudes in general. Some indication of the extent of this stability can be gained from Table II which shows product-moment correlations amongst the three cultures on each of these first four principal components. Note that correlations do not provide an ideal measure of factor similarity because they are dependent upon common variance; the intercorrelations on the C-factor are thus spuriously low in one sense because it is a general factor comprised of positive loadings only. Nevertheless, it is clear that there is a great deal of consistency in the factors from one culture to another, and this has occurred despite certain demographic and educational differences across the three samples concerned and despite differences in levels of response as indicated by item means (Bagley, 1972).

TABLE II

Correlations of factor loadings among three cultures of the Conservatism Scale
(From Wilson and Patterson, 1970)*

	Factor I	Factor II	Factor III	Factor IV
r of English factor with corresponding Dutch factor	0·483	0·682	0·536	0·548
r of English factor with corresponding New Zealand factor	0·585	0·771	0·736	0·513
r of Dutch factor with corresponding New Zealand factor	0·586	0·713	0·615	0·696

*With 48 d.f., $p < 0.001$ for all correlations.

It would have been possible to examine these loadings in greater detail, showing further consistencies and discussing some of the reasons why certain apparent discrepancies have occurred, e.g. because of the ways in which they might have been interpreted in the different cultures. Unfortunately, space does not permit this.

III. Oblique Rotations

A. ORTHOGONAL VERSUS OBLIQUE SOLUTIONS

The principal components method has two major features which characterize it as a factor analytic technique: (a) It places the first factor in such a position that maximum variance is absorbed from the correlation matrix. (b) Each subsequent factor is required to be orthogonal to all the previously extracted factors, i.e. completely independent of them. The former characteristic makes it particularly well suited to the task of testing for a general factor underlying the field, which is how it was used by Wilson (1970). The restriction of orthogonality has the advantage that items or subjects can be economically described by locating them within a familiar and readily understood Euclidean space model. When only two principal component factors are employed, in particular, the items or subjects can be laid out very conveniently on a two-dimensional graph which is exceptionally easy for the reader to interpret (e.g. Fig. 1).

Many would argue, on the other hand, that there are advantages in using a factor analytic technique which allows oblique factors to emerge. While it is often said that such factors tend to "make more psychological sense", this is not really true; what they actually do is correspond more with commonsense or intuitive expectation in that the factors so obtained identify items of similar content (Nias and Wilson, 1972). Thus, in the case of the C-Scale, oblique rotation might be expected to yield factors corresponding to the different attitude areas represented in the questionnaire (religion, race, sex, punitiveness, etc.). The structure of social attitudes derived in this way may actually be *less* interesting psychologically because it can at best only serve to quantify and clarify what would probably be obvious from a content analysis of items anyway. (In fact, if this did not turn out to be the case, the factor analyst would no doubt try an alternative solution, e.g. by rotating a different number of principal components, and continue this process until the statistical result is congruent with his *a priori* expectation, or until he feels able to claim that factor analysis supports his hypothesis.)

Nevertheless, as suggested in the introduction, there is a certain amount to be gained from an examination of oblique factor solutions. They provide a summarized content analysis of the material covered in the scale, and a means of assessing the degree to which the different content areas are intercorrelated without recourse to the correlations between pairs of individual items. Also, it is possible to conduct a further factor analysis on the matrix of intercorrelations among the primary factors which reduces them to a smaller number of psychologically more interesting "higher-order" factors.

B. First-Order Promax Factors

Probably the best-known and most widely used technique that does not impose the restriction of orthogonality is called "promax" (Hendrickson and White, 1964) which rotates varimax factors towards a criterion of oblique simple structure. A promax rotation of C-Scale factors is reported by Bagley (1970), who used the same sample of 200 English males employed in Wilson's (1970) study. Whereas Wilson was concerned only with the unrotated principal components, Bagley put the data through the complete Hendrickson-White procedure in order to investigate the primary factor structure of the C-Scale.

Table III gives loadings on the first five, and most readily interpretable first-order promax factors obtained by rotating the first ten principal components, and gives possible titles for them. Note: in this table the signs are arranged so that a negative loading means that an unfavourable response to the item would be scored positively on the factor. It was felt that in this case such a scoring method would be less confusing than the standard procedure of scoring all items in the hypothetically conservative direction (as in Table I).

Factor I has high loadings on items concerned with the maintenance of military strength, harsh punishment and political conservatism. While it might be well summarized by the term "authoritarianism", and probably corresponds more literally to this description than does the Adorno *et al.*

TABLE III

Highest loading items on five promax factors in the C-Scale.
(Modified from Bagley, 1970)

Factor	Interpretation	Highest loading items			
I	Militarism-punitiveness	Birching	0·72	Disarmament	−0·76*
		Patriotism	0·67	Socialism	−0·60
		Military drill	0·60	Co-education	−0·43
		Death penalty	0·53	White lies	−0·38
		Conventional clothes	0·51	Coloured immigration	−0·36
		Royalty	0·48		
		Empire-building	0·39		
II	Anti-hedonism	Horoscopes	0·45	Striptease	−0·72
		Licensing laws	0·44	Pyjama parties	−0·70
		Chastity	0·35	Casual living	−0·49
				Computer music	−0·36
				Mixed marriage	−0·36
III	Racialism	White superiority	0·82	Mixed marriage	−0·57
		Apartheid	0·70	Working mothers	−0·52
		Empire-building	0·43	Coloured immigration	−0·47
		Horoscopes	0·39	Women judges	−0·47
				Learning Latin	−0·47
				Beatniks	−0·31
IV	Religious fundamentalism	Church authority	0·44	Legal abortion	−0·76
		Bible truth	0·34	Birth control	−0·76
				Divorce	−0·66
V	Anti-art	Censorship	0·34	Jazz	−0·71
				Modern Art	−0·43

*Negative loading means that disagreement is scored on the factor.

concept, in order to avoid confusion we will refer to it as *Militarism-punitiveness*.

Factor II has its highest loadings on items which concern sexual freedom, but it also deals with pleasure-seeking as a general philosophy of life, and is therefore most appropriately labelled *Anti-hedonism*. Inspection of the item loadings suggest that this factor might differentiate men from women to some extent, though a sex difference could not have been responsible for the emergence of the factor in this analysis because the sample was all male.

Factor III is dominated by racial items and has therefore been termed *Racialism*. It is interesting to note that the two items in the scale which are concerned with the status of women (Women judges and Working mothers) also have high loadings. An even more generalized intolerance of outgroups and minorities is suggested by the negative attitudes towards Latin (a foreign language) and Beatniks (a deviant minority) which also go with this factor.

Factor IV has been labelled *Religious fundamentalism*, but this should be clarified by noting that the loadings on items concerned with the role of women as agents of reproduction (Birth control, Abortion, Divorce) are even higher than those which refer directly to religious beliefs and values. These items seem intuitively to fall somewhere between the areas of religion and opposition to sex freedom, so it is interesting to find that in this analysis they cluster unambiguously with the overtly religious items. It seems likely that Roman Catholics would tend to score high on this factor since it appears to embody a number of values which are recognized as characteristic of that Church in particular. Regarding this factor also, it should be remembered that the sample was all male; females may well show a different attitude and belief structure in these areas.

Factor V loads on relatively few items but each of these suggests opposition to progressive or expressive ("decadent"?) art forms, which was one of the hypothesized components of the conservative personality (Chapter 1).

TABLE IV

Intercorrelations amongst five promax factors in the C-Scale.
(From data of Bagley, 1970)

		I Militarism- punitiveness	II Anti- hedonism	III Racialism	IV Religious fundamentalism
II	Anti-hedonism	0·36			
III	Racialism	0·46	0·28		
IV	Religious fundamentalism	0·18	0·20	0·29	
V	Anti-art	0·04	0·15	−0·03	0·03

The intercorrelations amongst these first five promax factors are shown in Table IV. The highest correlation is that between racialism and the militarism-punitiveness factor (0·46) which supports one of the major suppositions of Adorno *et al.* that racialism is related to, and perhaps a manifestation of, authoritarianism. Anti-hedonism is also correlated with militarism-punitiveness (0·36), but most of the other correlations are fairly low (although in a direction consistent with the finding of a general factor of conservatism. The anti-art factor, in particular, appears to be independent of the others except for one barely significant correlation with anti-hedonism, which might have been expected to emerge more clearly considering that both imply opposition to various kinds of "free expression".

Bagley also attempted to interpret five more promax factors in this analysis. Although they were becoming progressively limited and obscure, he labelled them as follows: VI *Youthful-reactionary* (Evolution theory —0·66, Teenage drivers 0·64), VII *Naturalistic* (Fluoridation —0·68, Suicide —0·47), VIII *Protestant* (Divine law 0·68, Inborn conscience 0·63, Moral training 0·59, in combination with low loadings on Birth control, Abortion, and Divorce); IX *Propriety* (Cousin marriage —0·86, Chaperones 0·42, Strict rules 0·42); *Anti-youth* (Student pranks —0·75, Censorship 0·38, Beatniks —0·31). From the point of view of developing a sub-factor scoring system for the C-Scale these latter promax factors are less important because they are specific to only two or three items each.

C. HIGHER-ORDER PROMAX FACTORS

Bagley then proceeded to reduce these ten promax factors down to two "higher-order factors" which correlated 0·60 together (again confirming the general factor finding). The first of these two factors he called *Conservative-religious*, and the second he termed *Anti-intellectual-racialist*. Bagley interpreted these results as suggesting that there are two kinds of conservatives: "The first we might term the 'Heath–Macmillan type' who is in favour of traditional values, favours scholarships, and is not particularly addicted to racialist items. The second type of conservative we might term the 'Alf Garnett type', who favours censorship and control, who dislikes the values of scholarship, and is clearly racialist."

This distinction strongly suggests a social class difference, and fortunately, Bagley was able to provide an occupational breakdown of mean factor scores in order to investigate this question (Table V). Clerks were found to have the highest mean score on the first factor and technical apprentices on the second; students were the most liberal on both. The differences were shown to be highly significant. While both factors show some negative relationship with social class, this is much more striking with respect to the Anti-intellectual-racialist factor, suggesting that it might be characterized as "working class conservatism".

TABLE V

Means and S.D.s. of scores on the two higher-order promax factors in the C-Scale
for four occupational groups.
(Modified from Bagley, 1970)

Occupational group	Factors	
	I Conservative-religious	II Anti-intellectual-racialist
Technical apprentices (N = 50)	8·60 (4·71)*	10·38 (5·14)
Clerks (N = 50)	10·12 (6·47)	6·68 (4·89)
Businessmen and Professionals (N = 50)	7·64 (6·16)	5·54 (3·98)
Students (N = 50)	5·88 (5·17)	3·34 (3·73)

*Means based on the ten highest loading items on the factor.
S.D.s given in parenthesis.

IV. Comparison with Previous Findings

How does the organization of social attitudes as revealed by factor analysis of the C-Scale compare with that discovered in previous studies using more conventional attitude scales? Adorno *et al.* and Rokeach showed a remarkable lack of interest in factor analysis as a method for testing hypotheses concerning the structure of attitudes, preferring to rely on their own intuition on this matter at all stages of their research.

It was Eysenck (1947, 1954) who produced the classic work on the organization of social attitudes as measured by conventional questionnaires. Testing alternative hypotheses regarding the interrelationships amongst different political groups (Labour, Conservative, Liberal, Fascist, and Communist), he found that they were best described by reference to two major orthogonal factors which he labelled *conservatism-radicalism* (R), and *toughmindedness-tendermindedness* (T).

Ferguson (1941) also found two major orthogonal factors in social attitudes which he called *humanitarianism* and *religionism*, and Eysenck pointed out that these were mathematically equivalent to his R and T factors in the sense that one solution could be converted into the other by simple orthogonal rotation (Fig. 2). There is no absolute answer to the question of where best to locate the axes in a two-dimensional Euclidean space. Eysenck's solution has the disadvantage that there are very few items which fall squarely along the T-axis, but on the other hand, there is probably some justification to his argument that it makes more psychological sense, e.g. the R-factor corresponds fairly closely to the well-known "left–right" political variable, and the T-factor is supposed to relate to the personality dimension of extraversion–introversion.

As noted previously, the first two principal components in the C-Scale do bear a fairly close relationship to Eysenck's R- and T-factors (and there-

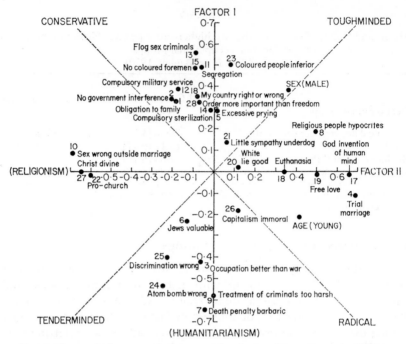

FIG. 2. Two main factors underlying social attitudes. (From Eysenck, 1971).

fore, through rotation, to Ferguson's two factors also). Nevertheless, two differences between the present findings and those of Eysenck do appear. The first difference concerns the relative importance of the two orthogonal factors; Whereas Eysenck found his R and T factors to be approximately equal in importance in terms of the amount of variance that they accounted for, factor analyses of the C-Scale have fairly consistently produced a general factor of almost overwhelming importance compared to the second and subsequent factors. Since there are only minor differences in the attitude content areas sampled by the two questionnaires (perhaps a tendency for Eysenck's Social Attitudes Inventory to contain more items concerned with the politico-economic sphere) it is probable that the failure for the second factor to appear so prominently in the C-Scale is attributable to the new item format that has been adopted. Eysenck postulates that the T-factor is the projection of extraversion–introversion onto the attitude field, while the *content* of the attitudes of these different personality types is determined by their position on the radicalism-conservatism axis. "It would follow from this hypothesis that there should be very few, if any, *pure* T items; tendermindedness and toughmindedness should always appear in conjunction with either right-wing or left-wing tendencies" (Eysenck, 1956, p. 431). In other words, what is implied is that R is a function of attitude *content* while T is a function of item *context*. Since context effects were deliberately eliminated in the new item format of the C-Scale, it was to be expected that the second principal component would be considerably reduced in importance relative to the first.

The second difference between Eysenck's findings and those relating to the C-Scale concerns the exact location of the two orthogonal axes within the space shown in Fig. 2. Detailed examination of the content of items loading on the first two principal components in the two questionnaires suggests that whereas Eysenck's R factor corresponds closely to the political *left-right* continuum, the general factor found by Wilson is more of a personality characteristic, "conservatism *with a small c*". This is assumed to vary amongst supporters of all the major political parties, and is somewhat closer to the Adorno *et al.* concept of *authoritarianism*. It follows that Wilson's second factor, which may be distinguished by the label *idealism-realism*, is also rotated a little bit around from the Eysenck T-factor. This means, in effect, that the Wilson solution is about midway between the Ferguson and Eysenck solutions, and mathematically equivalent to both of these.

V. Some Procedures for Scoring Sub-Factors in the C-Scale

It was noted earlier that factor analytic studies of the scale might help to provide a basis for the development of a system of keying other dimensions besides the general conservatism factor. This will now be attempted, where possible in accordance with empirical results, but remembering the limitations of the factor analytic technique for purposes such as these, the items selected for scoring on the factors will be chosen according to intuitive and theoretical criteria as well. This means that the scoring procedures suggested here should be regarded as working hypotheses which are subject to modification in the light of future evidence.

Consideration of the studies reported in this chapter suggests the usefulness of scoring the C-Scale for two principal components and four promax factors. The principal components may be described as "psychological" factors because they cut across a variety of different attitude areas, while the promax factors correspond to specific attitude content and may therefore be referred to as "content" factors (Nias and Wilson, 1972).

The items which are scored on the two principal components are shown in Table VI. Factor I is, of course, *conservatism-liberalism* as scored by the original procedure given in the Manual. Factor II, called *realism-idealism*, may be regarded as equivalent to a slightly rotated version of Eysenck's T-factor. Individuals scoring towards the "realistic" end of this dimension would tend to be racialistic, punitive, hedonistic and conforming, and to be generally predisposed to express attitudes and act in a "selfish", expedient manner. Individuals scoring towards the "idealistic" end of the dimension would tend to derive their attitudes from systematic ideologies, be they moral, religious, or political. From Table VI it will be seen that this second principal component is scored on thirty-six items, eighteen of them positively keyed (i.e. Yes = 2, ? = 1, and No = 0) and eighteen negatively keyed (Yes = 0, ? = 1, No = 2). Since the principal components upon which these two factors are based are by definition orthogonal, scores derived from this equal-weight scoring system should be fairly independent also, although this will require empirical verification.

TABLE VI

A suggested keying for two orthogonal "psychological" factors in the C-Scale.
(All items scored on 0, 1, 2 system)

	Factor	Positively keyed items	Negatively keyed items
I	Conservatism (versus liberalism)	All odd-numbered items	All even-numbered items
		(As for original scoring procedure given in Manual)	
II	Realism (versus idealism)	1. Death penalty	2. Evolution theory
		4. Striptease shows	5. Sabbath observance
		11. Horoscopes	9. Self-denial
		17. White superiority	14. Co-education
		18. Cousin marriage	15. Divine law
		20. Suicide	16. Socialism
		21. Chaperones	19. Moral training
		23. Empire-building	27. Chastity
		26. Computer music	28. Fluoridation
		31. Conventional clothes	29. Royalty
		33. Apartheid	30. Women judges
		34. Nudist camps	35. Church authority
		38. White lies	36. Disarmament
		39. Birching	37. Censorship
		43. Straitjackets	45. Learning Latin
		44. Casual living	47. Inborn conscience
		46. Divorce	48. Coloured immigration
		50. Pyjama parties	49. Bible truth

The keying system for the four oblique "content" factors is given in Table VII. The labels attached to them are fairly self-explanatory, but the degree to which these four specific factors are intercorrelated must also be established empirically, since they are by no means identical to the promax factors isolated by Bagley (1970). One extra criterion that was used in deciding which items should be scored on the four factors was the restriction that no item should appear in more than one factor. This condition was imposed in order to avert a source of very artificial overlap amongst the content factors, i.e. scoring the same item on several of them. Each factor contains twelve items, but (except in the case of *Religion-puritanism*) this time it was not possible to arrange for a balance in the direction of keying. Since the new item format of the C-Scale is less prone to acquiescence effects than the traditional format (Chapter 4) this lack of balance might be expected to be less important than it otherwise would have been. A computer program that may be used for scoring all six attitude factors is given in Chapter 6 Appendix 1.

TABLE VII

A suggested method of keying for four oblique "content" factors in the C-Scale.
(All items scored on a 0, 1, 2 system)

Factor name	Positively keyed items	Negatively keyed items
I Militarism-punitiveness	Military drill Birching Death penalty Patriotism Royalty Straitjackets Strict rules School uniforms	Disarmament Socialism Co-education White lies
II Anti-hedonism	Chastity Chaperones Licensing laws Self-denial Moral training Censorship	Striptease shows Pyjama parties Casual living Nudist camps Suicide Computer music
III Ethnocentrism and out-group hostility	White superiority Apartheid Empire-building	Coloured immigration Mixed marriage Working mothers Women judges Learning Latin Beatniks Teenage drivers Student pranks Jazz
IV Religion-puritanism	Bible truth Sabbath observance Divine law Church authority Inborn conscience Horoscopes	Legalized abortion Birth control Divorce Evolution theory Cousin marriage Fluoridation

These two scoring systems (based on psychological and content factors respectively) may be regarded either as alternative or complementary approaches. Their utility would depend upon the particular problem at hand. In both cases an equal-weight method has been recommended because factor scoring has been found to result in little gain. In any case, it is probably unjustified since precise factor loadings would not be expected to remain absolutely stable from one study to another. For some purposes, it may be more convenient or meaningful to treat each individual item separately. This enables the researcher to discover for himself the way in which the items cluster in particular circumstances (e.g. Wilson and Lillie, 1972); this may often be a profitable approach in the present state of knowledge.

VI. Some Preliminary Norms for C-Scale Subfactors

Table VIII shows means and S.D.s for four diverse groups of subjects. Two of these groups (the John Birchers and Dutch Reformed Church-goers) are generally very conservative and tend to be high also on Realism, Militarism-punitiveness, Anti-hedonism, Ethnocentrism, and Religion-puritanism, while the two student groups are low on C and all the sub-factors.

TABLE VIII

Means and (S.D.s.) on Six Attitude Factors for Four Diverse Samples

	Cons.	Real.	Mil-Pun	Anti-hed.	Ethno.	Relig.
John Birch Society (U.S.A.)* (N = 25)	72·8 (6·8)	54·2 (4.6)	18·1 (1·9)	17·4 (2.5)	14·1 (3·5)	18·6 (2·4)
Dutch Reformed Church Congregation (S. Africa) (N = 40)	68·3 (6·2)	51·7 (4·6)	15·3 (2·7)	17·6 (2·1)	16·2 (3·0)	17·6 (2·9)
Teachers' College Students (U.K.) (N = 358)	35·6 (11·7)	29·4 (7·9)	9·3 (4·1)	11·0 (4·8)	6·6 (3·5)	8·2 (4·1)
University Students (U.S.A.) (N = 91)	34·9 (13·8)	30·2 (7·1)	9·2 (4·3)	9·8 (4·7)	6·5 (3·4)	8·2 (4·2)

* Special thanks are due to Dr. J. J. Wright, California Institute of Technology, for testing this group at their San Marino headquarters.

Figure 3 shows means for several groups of white South Africans (40 members of a Dutch Reformed Church congregation, 26 Afrikaans-speaking office workers, 21 English-speaking office workers, 14 housewives, 11 medical practitioners, and 4 students), and Table IX shows the inter-correlations between general conservatism and the four content factors for the whole group of 116 South Africans. It appears that for this group at least, the four main content factors contribute about evenly to the total C-Score, again demonstrating the importance of the general factor in social attitudes.

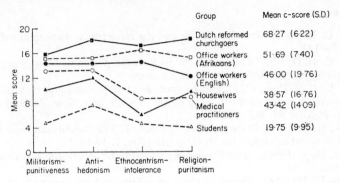

FIG. 3. Mean scores on conservatism and the four content sub-factors of the C-Scale for several groups of white South Africans. (From data of Wilson and Shutte, 1973.)

TABLE IX

Intercorrelations among attitude scales (N = 116).
(From data of Wilson and Shutte, 1973)

	Conservatism	Milpun.	Anti-hed.	Ethnoc.
Militarism-punitiveness	0·75			
Anti-hedonism	0·81	0·45		
Ethnocentrism-intolerance	0·72	0·47	0·46	
Religion-puritanism	0·72	0·38	0·49	0·40

VII. Summary

Despite the established predominance of a general factor in attitudes it is still possible to interpret several other orthogonal and oblique factors in the C-Scale. On the basis of a review of factor analytic studies of the C-Scale to date, a system of scoring for two principal components and four oblique (promax-like) factors has been developed. The first principal component is general *Conservatism* (versus Liberalism) which is scored as before; the second principal component has been called *Realism* (versus Idealism), although its similarity to Eysenck's tough-tendermindedness is noted. The four oblique factors represent the major attitude content areas in the C-Scale, and have been labelled: (i) Militarism-punitiveness (*Mil-pun.*), (ii) Anti-hedonism and opposition to sexual freedom (*Anti-hed.*), (iii) Ethnocentrism and outgroup hostility (*Ethno.*), and (iv) Religion-puritanism (*Relig.*). Some preliminary standardization data are provided (means, S.D.s and intercorrelations among attitude scales for some diverse groups of Ss).

92 G. D. WILSON

References

Bagley, C. R. (1970). Racial prejudice and the conservative personality. *Pol. Stud.* **18**, 134–141.

Bagley, C. R. (1972). "The Dutch Plural Society: A Comparative Study of Race Relations." Oxford University Press, London.

Bagley, C. R., Wilson, G. D. and Boshier, R. (1970). The Conservatism Scale: A factor-structure comparison of English, Dutch and New Zealand samples. *J. soc. Psychol.* **81**, 267–268.

Eysenck, H. J. (1947). Primary social attitudes: 1, The Organization and measurement of social attitudes. *Int. J. Opin. Att. Res.* **1**, 49–84.

Eysenck, H. J. (1954). "The Psychology of Politics." Routledge and Kegan Paul, London.

Eysenck, H. J. (1956). The psychology of politics and the personality similarities between Fascists and Communists. *Psychol. Bull.* **53**, 431–438.

Eysenck, H. J. (1971). Social attitudes and social class. *Brit. J. soc. clin. Psychol.* **10**, 201–212.

Ferguson, L. W. (1941). The stability of the primary social attitudes, 1. Religionism and humanitarianism. *J. Psychol.* **12**, 283–288.

Hendrickson, A. E. and White, P. O. (1964). "Promax": A quick method of rotation to oblique simple structure. *Brit. J. math. statist. Psychol.* **17**, 65–70.

Nias, D. K. B. and Wilson, G. D. (1972). Interpretation of the factor structure of the C-Scale: A reply to Boshier. *Brit. J. soc. clin. Psychol.* **11**, 324–325.

Wilson, G. D. (1970). Is there a general factor in social attitudes? Evidence from a factor-analysis of the Conservatism Scale. *Brit. J. soc. clin. Psychol.* **9**, 101–107.

Wilson, G. D. and Lillie, F. J. (1972). Social attitudes of humanists and salvationists. *Brit. J. soc. clin. Psychol.* **11**, 220–224.

Wilson, G. D. and Patterson, J. M. (1970). "Manual for the Conservatism Scale." N.F.E.R., Windsor, England.

Wilson, G. D. and Shutte, P. (1973). The structure of social attitudes in South Africa. *J. soc. Psychol.* in press.

Measurement and Structure of Children's Attitudes*

6

DAVID K. B. NIAS

Institute of Psychiatry, University of London

I. An Attitude Scale for Children

Because of the promising results from the adults' C-Scale, Insel and Wilson (1971) decided to construct a children's version. This was an obvious step since the C-Scale approach would appear to have even greater advantages in the case of children; less concentration and verbal sophistication being required for meaningful responses to the short items. Moreover, there is clearly a need for a satisfactory measure of social attitudes in children. A number of reliable tests are available for the assessment of intelligence and personality, but no real attempt has been made to tackle the problem of assessing children's attitudes. The neglect of this area of study seems surprising in view of the importance attached to the stages of

*This chapter is based in part upon data presented elsewhere (Nias, 1972).

childhood and adolescence in the development of attitudes. In this connection, Wilson and Patterson (1970) suggested that "conservatism" reflects the internalization of "parental" prohibitions. A children's attitude measure would thus seem useful as a technique for studying attitude formation, the relationship of attitudes to personality traits at different stages of development, and the effects of exposure to various family and social influences.

Insel and Wilson (1971) attempted to construct an equivalent form of the adults' scale by "translating" the items into a form that would be more suitable for school-children. This was generally achieved by making the items more concrete or specific, but without changing their sense, e.g. "Sabbath observance" was changed to "Sunday school". Four items did not need to be changed, and a few that seemed applicable only to adults had to be replaced altogether, e.g. it was difficult to find children's items concerned with politics and science. The exact wording of the items finally selected was arrived at following interviews with children aged 8 to 13 years. This procedure was intended to help ensure that the items would be understood by this age-group, but data have yet to be provided on the proportions of children who can actually read and define the different items. Therefore, the lower age limit of 8 years should not be taken too literally, especially since the sample came from schools in a "middle-class area". The same lay-out was used as in the adults' scale, including the alternation of hypothesized "conservative" and "liberal" items. The scale is reproduced in Table I.

The present chapter has five main aims. First, to critically evaluate the success of the children's version in terms of its equivalence to the adults' scale. Second, to examine the factor structure of children's attitudes and to compare this with the structure in adults. Third, to examine the implications of the factor analytic results for scoring the children's scale. Fourth, to examine sex differences in factor structure and item means. Fifth, to examine the relationship of children's attitudes to personality.

II. Comparison with the Adults' Scale

In order to investigate the equivalence of the children's version to the adults' scale, Insel and Wilson (1971) administered both measures to 185 girls, aged 12 to 16 years, from two schools. The correlation between the two scales was 0·86, and so they may be viewed as approximately equivalent for pupils around the borderline age-group as regards the suitability of the two scales. This evidence of high concurrent validity may not seem all that surprising when the close similarity of the items in the two scales is considered, but it does help demonstrate that the children were able to complete the two scales in a consistent fashion.

TABLE I

The Children's Scale of Social Attitudes.
(From Insel and Wilson, 1971)

Which of the following do you favour or believe in?
(Circle "Yes" or "No". If absolutely uncertain, circle " ?". There are no right or
wrong answers; do not discuss; just give your first reaction.)

1. Hanging thieves	Yes	?	No	26. Computers	Yes	?	No
2. Space travel	Yes	?	No	27. Saying prayers	Yes	?	No
3. School uniforms	Yes	?	No	28. Going barefoot	Yes	?	No
4. Bikinis	Yes	?	No	29. The Queen	Yes	?	No
5. Sunday school	Yes	?	No	30. Women doctors	Yes	?	No
6. Bearded men	Yes	?	No	31. Hard work	Yes	?	No
7. Saluting the flag	Yes	?	No	32. Drinking beer	Yes	?	No
8. Modern art	Yes	?	No	33. Atomic bombs	Yes	?	No
9. Obedience	Yes	?	No	34. Nude swimming	Yes	?	No
10. Comics	Yes	?	No	35. Church	Yes	?	No
11. Miracles	Yes	?	No	36. Chinese food	Yes	?	No
12. Dancing	Yes	?	No	37. Politeness	Yes	?	No
13. Army drill	Yes	?	No	38. Telling fibs	Yes	?	No
14. Mixed schools	Yes	?	No	39. Whipping criminals	Yes	?	No
15. The Ten Command-				40. The Germans	Yes	?	No
ments	Yes	?	No	41. Strict rules	Yes	?	No
16. The Russians	Yes	?	No	42. The Beatles	Yes	?	No
17. Whites only	Yes	?	No	43. Killing enemies	Yes	?	No
18. Kissing	Yes	?	No	44. Laughing in class	Yes	?	No
19. Strapping bad boys	Yes	?	No	45. Fox hunting	Yes	?	No
20. Swearing	Yes	?	No	46. Divorce	Yes	?	No
21. Servants	Yes	?	No	47. Confessing sins	Yes	?	No
22. Miniskirts	Yes	?	No	48. Coloured people	Yes	?	No
23. Saving money	Yes	?	No	49. Bible reading	Yes	?	No
24. Playing pranks	Yes	?	No	50. Playing doctors	Yes	?	No
25. Policemen	Yes	?	No				

The internal consistency of the two measures was assessed by correlating the score for "conservatism" obtained on the first twenty-five items
with that obtained on the second twenty-five, and applying the Spearman-
Brown correction for test length. The split-half consistency coefficients
thus obtained were 0·89 for the children's and 0·84 for the adults' measure.
These figures represent a satisfactory degree of internal consistency for
measures that cover a broad range of areas. The slightly higher figure for
the children's scale is consistent with the hypothesis that the easier items
should give rise to more systematic responding, thus supporting the logic
of the children's "translation". With younger children it might be predicted that the difference in internal consistency between the two scales
should be larger.

The discriminative validity of the two scales was checked by comparing the mean scores obtained from the two schools. One was a Catholic convent school and the other was a State secondary school, situated in the same area. Results consistent with the hypothesis that the Catholic pupils should obtain higher scores for "conservatism" were found with both measures (Fig. I). Even though these results were very highly significant, not too much can be claimed for this demonstration of validity since the attitude differences between the two schools could be due to any of a number of factors, quite apart from religion. It may be noted from Fig. 1 that the adults' scale appears to have slightly better discriminative ability. This may be due to the adults' scale having more strongly worded items, thus helping to maximize the attitude differences between the two schools.

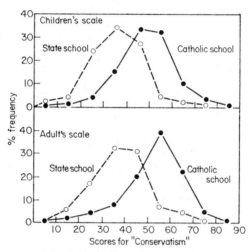

FIG. 1. Distribution of scores for "conservatism" from two schools. (From Insel and Wilson, 1971.)

This study by Insel and Wilson tells us that the two measures were answered in a similar fashion by a group of school-children, and that their answers were reasonably consistent and meaningful. We must now ask to what extent the responses of children differ from those of adults, and in particular the extent to which the attitudes of children are organized in a different way to adults. This latter question has implications for the scoring of the children's version, and hence for any comparison of children's and adults' scores. Insel and Wilson assumed that the children's version could be scored for "conservatism" in the same way as the adults' scale, but this procedure may not be justified if the structuring of the items making up the total score for "conservatism" is appreciably different for children and adults.

III. Factor Structure

A. PROCEDURE

Research with the adults' scale has strongly supported the assumption that an important general factor underlies all, or very nearly all, social attitudes. This picture, however, may not be the case with children. In order to check on this a factor analysis was carried out for a sample of school-children. It was decided to test 11 and 12 year olds, since the wording of the scale would seem most appropriate at about this age.

The scale was administered to 217 boys and 224 girls at an English comprehensive school. These children, who had recently transferred from several different primary schools in the area, represented a wide cross-section in terms of intelligence and social background. The scale was completed anonymously and was administered with the standard instructions, which were read aloud to the pupils. Most of the children were able to complete the scale within about ten minutes; any difficulties were seen as arising from poor reading ability rather than from lack of understanding of the items. Boys and girls were kept separate for the analysis. There were no immigrant children in the sample; such a group would have required separate analysis since some of the items (in particular those on racial issues) would take on a different meaning.

B. PRINCIPAL COMPONENTS

Means and standard deviations were computed for each item in the scale, together with the intercorrelations among the items. A principal components analysis was then carried out. This method is particularly appropriate for testing the hypothesis that the items in a scale intercorrelate to form a general factor.

For both boys and girls, there were twenty eigenvectors with latent roots greater than unity, but only the first four of these components involved more than a few items with high loadings, which could at the same time be readily interpreted. The nature of the first component will be discussed in detail below. The second component consisted mainly of ethnocentric and anti-sex items for boys, and of ethnocentric items for girls. The third consisted of punitive items for both sexes. The fourth consisted of sex and anti-punitive items for boys and of sex and religious items for girls.

The latent roots for the first component were 6·14 and 7·33 for boys and girls respectively. For the fifty-item test, these latent roots thus account for 12·3 and 14·7 per cent of the total variance, and convert to co-efficient alphas (i.e. the average of all possible split-halves) of 0·85 and

E

0·88. These coefficients being similar to the 0·89 obtained by Insel and Wilson, again compare very favourably with those from other personality or attitude scales that cover a broad range of areas. The second component was only half the size of the first, accounting for 6·3 and 7·2 per cent of the total variance for boys and girls respectively.

The item loadings for the first principal component are listed in Table II. For both boys and girls, this component seems to be mainly concerned with religion and respect for authority. For example, the three highest loadings are as follows (loadings for girls are given in brackets): Saying prayers 0·67 (0·71), Bible reading 0·65 (0·72), and Church 0·66 (0·70). The next group of items with high loadings are concerned with "good" behaviour, e.g. Obedience 0·58 (0·64), Politeness 0·56 (0·58), and Swearing −0·51 (−0·61). A third group of high loading items are concerned with established authorities, e.g. Policemen 0·58 (0·62), Saluting the flag 0·49 (0·54), and The Queen 0·52 (0·48).

C. COMPARISON WITH ADULTS

The first principal component appears rather narrow in scope compared with the general factor of conservatism found in adults. The variances are slightly smaller than those reported for adults (Wilson and Patterson, 1970). Moreover, the highest loading items can all be labelled in terms of the three areas identified above. Table III lists the fifteen highest loading items to illustrate this point. On the basis of the adults' research, a number of other areas might have been expected among these high loading items. This difference between adults and children cannot be dismissed as due to lack of equivalence between the two sets of items, since there is Insel and Wilson's evidence of a 0·86 correlation between them. From Table II it can be seen that there are a number of items with low loadings, and that these cover several different areas, e.g. Comics −0.02 (−0·03), Mixed schools 0·10 (0·01), Bikinis −0·06 (−0·06), and Strapping bad boys 0·09 (−0·03).

Using the scoring procedure of Insel and Wilson, as many as nineteen items load in the "wrong" direction, for both boys and girls. That is, there are nineteen items that load in the opposite direction to that predicted from the research with adults. The highest loading items in this category are concerned with ethnocentrism and punitiveness. The ethnocentric items include Coloured people 0·35 (0·39), The Germans 0·21 (0·37), and Whites only −0·14 (−0·24). The punitive items include Killing enemies −0·37 (−0·09), Fox hunting −0·24 (−0·04), and Whipping criminals −0·19 (−0·06). As can be seen from these figures the relevant items for girls are concerned more with ethnocentrism; punitive items for girls while generally loading in the "wrong" direction tend to have low loadings. Since this first component is concerned mainly with religion, this sex

TABLE II

Means, Standard Deviations and Item Loadings*

Item	Mean	S.D.	1st P.C.	4 Promax Factors			
				Relig.	Ethno.	Punit.	Sex
1. Hanging thieves	1·8 (1·6)	0·97 (0·86)	−24 (01)	−05 (00)	11 (−00)	55 (56)	−02 (−29)
2. Space travel	2·7 (2·2)	0·75 (0·96)	12 (18)	00 (−01)	−31 (−28)	11 (01)	08 (17)
3. School uniforms	1·6 (2·0)	0·89 (0·99)	34 (38)	15 (12)	−09 (−13)	13 (−04)	−38 (−21)
4. Bikinis	2·7 (2·9)	0·66 (0·33)	−06 (−06)	09 (17)	−12 (03)	21 (02)	33 (61)
5. Sunday school	1·4 (1·8)	0·77 (0·93)	53 (58)	61 (74)	17 (10)	−02 (−02)	−10 (22)
6. Bearded men	2·1 (2·0)	0·95 (0·94)	18 (08)	−09 (−25)	−51 (−31)	07 (11)	−01 (−01)
7. Saluting the flag	2·2 (2·0)	0·95 (0·93)	49 (54)	63 (61)	08 (01)	10 (24)	03 (04)
8. Modern art	2·2 (2·7)	0·96 (0·72)	13 (−07)	−08 (−15)	−41 (12)	12 (−00)	−02 (13)
9. Obedience	2·1 (2·5)	0·96 (0·84)	58 (64)	35 (42)	−19 (−05)	01 (00)	−33 (−10)
10. Comics	2·9 (2·9)	0·45 (0·41)	−02 (−03)	17 (08)	03 (−08)	24 (−01)	22 (13)
11. Miracles	2·0 (2·0)	0·96 (0·95)	24 (38)	44 (39)	14 (−22)	−01 (−06)	22 (−07)
12. Dancing	1·9 (2·8)	0·98 (0·61)	20 (07)	27 (−01)	−22 (10)	04 (−09)	32 (20)
13. Army drill	2·2 (1·8)	0·96 (0·91)	21 (47)	19 (49)	−13 (06)	18 (22)	−04 (19)
14. Mixed schools	2·6 (2·8)	0·78 (0·60)	10 (01)	05 (−08)	−31 (−40)	−12 (00)	29 (18)
15. The Ten Commandments	2·0 (2·1)	0·95 (0·94)	54 (65)	64 (85)	17 (01)	−07 (12)	−03 (27)
16. The Russians	1·9 (1·9)	0·93 (0·91)	17 (32)	−10 (−06)	−36 (−62)	−33 (06)	04 (−07)
17. Whites only	1·9 (1·9)	0·96 (0·95)	−14 (−24)	20 (04)	55 (73)	23 (08)	−08 (05)
18. Kissing	2·7 (2·8)	0·72 (0·52)	−09 (−15)	19 (18)	−05 (12)	−05 (−05)	62 (74)
19. Strapping bad boys	1·5 (1·6)	0·82 (0·88)	09 (−03)	04 (21)	−20 (24)	51 (59)	−18 (−10)
20. Swearing	1·8 (1·6)	0·92 (0·84)	−51 (−61)	−21 (−47)	33 (−03)	−03 (12)	29 (29)
21. Servants	1·8 (1·6)	0·93 (0·85)	−16 (−23)	−23 (−08)	−19 (−04)	51 (40)	−16 (−24)
22. Mini skirts	2·8 (3·0)	0·64 (0·24)	−15 (−14)	03 (07)	−18 (−10)	03 (28)	57 (16)
23. Saving money	2·7 (2·8)	0·64 (0·54)	36 (31)	28 (13)	−05 (−07)	06 (00)	−18 (−09)
24. Playing pranks	2·1 (1·9)	0·94 (0·95)	−42 (−50)	−25 (−29)	03 (01)	26 (13)	20 (40)
25. Policemen	2·5 (2·7)	0·87 (0·66)	58 (62)	37 (35)	−33 (−19)	−19 (−11)	−02 (−15)
26. Computers	2·6 (2·3)	0·76 (0·89)	08 (21)	05 (14)	−07 (−49)	19 (22)	−08 (−05)

Item	Mean	S.D.	1st P.C.	4 Promax Factors			
				Relig.	Ethno.	Punit.	Sex
27. Saying prayers	1·8 (2·1)	0·94 (0·94)	67 (71)	69 (80)	04 (−03)	−13 (−03)	−04 (02)
28. Going barefoot	1·9 (2·3)	0·97 (0·92)	−17 (−20)	−24 (−17)	−36 (−16)	12 (−03)	22 (43)
29. The Queen	2·3 (2·7)	0·91 (0·70)	52 (48)	64 (65)	08 (13)	−00 (11)	06 (−06)
30. Women doctors	2·2 (2·9)	0·93 (0·50)	25 (24)	32 (10)	−16 (−18)	−02 (02)	37 (−03)
31. Hard work	2·0 (2·2)	0·98 (0·93)	50 (44)	37 (23)	−21 (−15)	03 (13)	−12 (−00)
32. Drinking beer	2·5 (2·1)	0·84 (0·92)	−43 (−37)	−25 (−39)	03 (−07)	12 (37)	30 (01)
33. Atomic bombs	1·7 (1·2)	0·94 (0·45)	−18 (−01)	−09 (01)	02 (−12)	40 (26)	−04 (−01)
34. Nude swimming	2·2 (1·6)	0·91 (0·84)	−32 (−37)	−09 (−18)	−07 (06)	−10 (32)	62 (21)
35. Church	1·8 (2·2)	0·94 (0·93)	66 (70)	78 (83)	09 (−04)	−06 (−09)	08 (13)
36. Chinese food	2·0 (2·1)	0·98 (0·94)	17 (03)	15 (−14)	−38 (−15)	15 (−13)	27 (13)
37. Politeness	2·3 (2·5)	0·91 (0·81)	56 (58)	41 (35)	−38 (−36)	02 (−10)	04 (−07)
38. Telling fibs	1·8 (1·4)	0·92 (0·79)	−43 (−59)	−19 (−53)	07 (−02)	15 (14)	36 (15)
39. Whipping criminals	1·9 (1·7)	0·97 (0·92)	−19 (−06)	04 (05)	12 (−03)	54 (67)	04 (01)
40. The Germans	1·8 (1·9)	0·94 (0·91)	21 (37)	−22 (06)	−59 (−62)	−35 (08)	−03 (−01)
41. Strict rules	1·6 (1·6)	0·88 (0·88)	35 (42)	17 (31)	−17 (−01)	17 (18)	−34 (−10)
42. The Beatles	2·0 (2·2)	0·97 (0·94)	−17 (11)	−06 (11)	−18 (−31)	09 (35)	40 (05)
43. Killing enemies	1·9 (1·5)	0·95 (0·80)	−37 (−09)	−07 (−06)	23 (27)	45 (46)	12 (−05)
44. Laughing in class	2·6 (2·5)	0·77 (0·86)	−31 (−30)	−09 (−20)	06 (−32)	−19 (28)	50 (38)
45. Fox hunting	1·5 (1·2)	0·83 (0·53)	−24 (−04)	−04 (−19)	04 (−09)	51 (26)	11 (−55)
46. Divorce	1·7 (1·5)	0·93 (0·81)	−18 (−08)	−18 (−01)	−29 (−13)	06 (33)	31 (14)
47. Confessing sins	1·9 (2·0)	0·92 (0·92)	37 (45)	44 (49)	10 (−04)	−07 (−05)	04 (27)
48. Coloured people	1·9 (2·2)	0·94 (0·92)	35 (39)	−01 (10)	−68 (−76)	−20 (−04)	11 (−08)
49. Bible reading	1·8 (2·0)	0·93 (0·94)	65 (72)	71 (78)	01 (−12)	−01 (03)	−00 (06)
50. Playing doctors	1·4 (1·7)	0·74 (0·86)	09 (30)	08 (28)	−23 (09)	12 (23)	15 (−20)

* Results for girls are given in brackets (N = 217 boys and 224 girls). Decimal points omitted for factor loadings.

TABLE III

Principal component loadings above 0·40*

Rank	Item	Loading for Boys (Girls)		Category
1.	Saying prayers	0·67	(0·71)	Religion
2.	Bible reading	0·65	(0·72)	Religion
3.	Church	0·66	(0·70)	Religion
4.	Obedience	0·58	(0·64)	Good behaviour
5.	Policemen	0·58	(0·62)	Authority
6.	The Ten Commandments	0·54	(0·65)	Religion
7.	Politeness	0·56	(0·58)	Good behaviour
8.	Swearing	−0·51	(−0·61)	Good behaviour
9.	Sunday school	0·53	(0·58)	Religion
10.	Saluting the flag	0·49	(0·54)	Authority
11.	Telling fibs	−0·43	(−0·59)	Good behaviour
12.	The Queen	0·52	(0·48)	Authority
13.	Hard work	0·50	(0·44)	Good behaviour
14.	Playing pranks	−0·42	(−0·50)	Good behaviour
15.	Confessing sins	0·37	(0·45)	Religion

*Boys and girls loadings averaged for rank order

difference may be interpreted to mean that "religious" boys are more opposed to punitive measures than "religious" girls.

Thus the first principal component for these children consists mainly of attitudes in favour of religion, good behaviour, and established authorities, and to a lesser extent of attitudes *against* ethnocentrism and punitiveness. This finding of a negative relationship between these two sets of attitudes provides a rather striking contrast to the usual positive relationship between them in the general factor for adults. Possible reasons for this difference will be taken up in the last section of this chapter.

D. VARIMAX

To provide a complementary solution to that given by the principal components, the first five were rotated towards orthogonal simple structure using the Varimax method (Kaiser, 1958). This procedure differs from the unrotated principal components method by distributing the variance more evenly among the factors.

The areas identified by the first four principal components emerged this time as separate factors, which were more homogeneous in content. The first four factors could be readily identified as relating to religion, ethnocentrism, punitiveness, and sex. The fifth factor consisted of relatively low loadings, and could not be meaningfully interpreted. The variances accounted for by the first four factors were 10·2 (13·0), 6·0 (6·8), 5·2 (5·2), and 6·2 (4·8) per cent respectively.

E. Promax

Rotation towards oblique simple structure was also investigated, using the Promax method (Hendrickson and White, 1964). This procedure is designed to provide "cleaner" factors since, unlike the above two methods, it does not impose the restriction of orthogonality, but instead attempts to approximate an "ideal" graphical solution. In addition, it provides the potentially useful information of the correlations between these "natural" factors.

The same four factors emerged as with the Varimax analysis, but they were very slightly more sharply defined. The fifth factor again could not be interpreted. Table II lists the item loadings for the first four factors. Examination of the loadings may be seen to provide justification for the labels given to the factors. Examples of items with high loadings from each factor are as follows:

"Religion": Church 0·78 (0·83), Saying prayers 0·69 (0·80), and Bible reading 0·71 (0·78). "Ethnocentrism": Coloured people −0·68 (−0·76), Whites only 0·55 (0·73), and The Germans −0·59 (−0·62). "Punitiveness": Whipping criminals 0·54 (0·67), Hanging thieves 0·55 (0·56), and Strapping bad boys 0·51 (0·59). "Sex" or "Hedonism": Kissing 0·62 (0·74), Bikinis 0·33 (0·61), and Nude swimming 0·62 (0·21).

The product-moment correlations between these four factors are given in Table IV. It may be noted that the relationship between the factors is consistent with that implied by the results from the first principal component. In particular, religion and ethnocentrism correlate negatively for both boys (−0·36) and girls (−0·19).

TABLE IV

Correlations between the four promax factors*

	Rel.	Eth.	Pun.	Sex
Religion		−0·19	−0·13	−0·37
Ethnocentrism	−0·36		0·10	−0·08
Punitiveness	−0·08	0·01		0·14
Sex	−0·26	0·12	0·10	

*Results for girls are above the diagonal

F. Sex Differences

The pattern of the factor analytic results is remarkably similar for boys and girls. This agreement may be taken as strong confirmatory evidence for the reliability of the results, in so far as the two sets may be viewed as replications of each other. In spite of this similarity, however, it may be instructive to look at instances where differences did occur.

A slight difference between the sexes on the first principal component has already been mentioned; punitive items tend to have higher negative loadings for boys than for girls. On the four Promax factors, there are a number of items that show slight differences between the sexes. Although differences for individual items may be largely attributable to chance effects, there are two *sets* of items that appear to form meaningful groups. First, for the "Religion" factor, items concerned with "good" (or bad) behaviour tend to have higher loadings for girls, e.g. Telling fibs -0.19 (-0.53), Swearing -0.21 (-0.47), and Laughing in class -0.09 (-0.20). This suggests that "bad" behaviour is considered more "irreligious" by girls. Second, the nature of the "Sex" factor appears, as might be expected, slightly different for boys and girls. Items such as Miniskirts 0.57 (0.16), Nude swimming 0.62 (0.21), and Women doctors 0.37 (-0.03) have higher loadings for boys, while Bikinis 0.33 (0.61), Going barefoot 0.22 (0.43), and Kissing 0.62 (0.74) have higher loadings for girls. Items with "sexual" significance appear to be of a more subtle nature in the case of girls.

These results may be viewed as serving the two overlapping functions of providing evidence for the general validity of the scale, and of providing findings that are interesting in their own right. With regard to the latter, it does seem particularly important to investigate sex differences in attitudes at ages when these are being developed.

IV. Scoring the Children's Scale

The factor analytic results have an immediate application for scoring the children's scale. Two main ways are suggested. First, the scale could be scored for the first principal component obtained in this study. This could be done by the method of factor scoring in which each item is given a weight according to the size of its loading, or by simply assigning an equal weight to each of the high loading items and treating the remainder as "passenger" items. Further studies would, of course, be necessary to delineate this component more accurately. On the basis of the present evidence it seems to combine a broad factor of religion with social respectability and acceptance of authority.

Second, the scale could be scored for the four content areas obtained by the Promax or the Varimax method. Because these factors consist essentially of logical clusterings of items, and because they have been found in adults, it would seem that they could be replicated more closely than the first principal component, especially if different age groups were to be considered. Moreover, because these factors are easily interpreted (i.e.

TABLE V

Suggested items for scoring the four attitude scales*

Religion	Ethnocentrism	Punitiveness	Sex
Sunday school 0·61 (0·74)	Bearded men −0·51 (−0·31)	Hanging thieves 0·55 (0·56)	Bikinis 0·33 (0·61)
Miracles 0·44 (0·39)	The Russians −0·36 (−0·62)	Army drill 0·18 (0·22)	Dancing 0·32 (0·20)
The Ten Commandments 0·64 (0·85)	Whites only 0·55 (0·73)	Strapping bad boys 0·51 (0·59)	Kissing 0·62 (0·74)
Saying prayers 0·69 (0·80)	Women doctors −0·26 (−0·18)	Servants 0·51 (0·40)	Miniskirts 0·57 (0·16)
The Queen 0·64 (0·65)	Chinese food −0·38 (−0·15)	Atomic bombs 0·40 (0·26)	Going barefoot 0·22 (0·43)
Church 0·78 (0·83)	Politeness −0·38 (−0·36)	Whipping criminals 0·54 (0·67)	Nude swimming 0·62 (0·21)
Confessing sins 0·44 (0·49)	The Germans −0·59 (−0·62)	Killing enemies 0·45 (0·46)	Laughing in class 0·50 (0·38)
Bible reading 0·71 (0·78)	Coloured people −0·68 (−0·76)	Fox hunting 0·51 (0·26)	Divorce 0·31 (0·14)

* Loadings for girls are given in brackets.

they immediately make sense), any study involving their use would allow a relatively clear evaluation.

Suggested items for such a scoring procedure are presented in Table V. The selection of eight items for each scale is based on a compromise between the Promax results, various practical considerations such as having each item represented on only one factor, and face validity—subjective grounds seem necessary because of the danger of including items that have given high loadings only by accident. Future work will, of course, provide the test for the present selection of items. Exact Promax loadings have been given only for the sake of interest. There is little justification for using these as a basis for assigning differential weights to the items within a given scale, since they are unlikely to remain stable from one factor analysis to another. In any case, it has been reported for the adults' scale that there is surprisingly little loss in using an equal-weight scoring procedure (Bagley, 1970). The computer program presented in Appendix 1 can be employed to score the four scales in this way.

Means and standard deviations for the four scales are listed in Table VI. It may be interesting to note that girls score higher on religion and sex (remember this is a group of 11 and 12 year olds), and boys on ethnocentrism and punitiveness. The correlations between the scales are given in Table VII. The similarity of these coefficients with those from the factor scores in Table IV indicates that appropriate items have been selected.

TABLE VI

Means and standard deviations for the attitude and personality Scales*
(N = 210 boys and 220 girls)

Scale	Means	S.D.
Religion	7·1 (8·7)	4·7 (4·9)
Ethnocentrism	7·8 (6·5)	4·0 (4·0)
Punitiveness	6·3 (4·1)	3·7 (3·1)
Sex	10·5 (11·5)	3·3 (2·6)
Psychoticism	6·4 (4·5)	3·2 (2·6)
Extraversion	16·9 (16·8)	2·9 (2·6)
Neuroticism	11·9 (13·2)	4·5 (4·6)
Lie	8·4 (10·9)	4·1 (4·6)

*Results for girls are given in brackets

It is not, of course, essential for a scoring system to be based on factor analysis. The method has the obvious limitation that it can only indicate how variables are structured for a specified group of people. For certain problems, such as investigating the development of "extreme" types, an empirically based scoring key may be more appropriate. Thus it is

D. K. B. NIAS

TABLE VII

Intercorrelations for the attitude and personality scales*

Scale	Rel.	Eth.	Pun.	Sex	P.	E.	N.	L.
Religion		−0·23	0·08	−0·25	−0·31	−0·09	−0·11	0·52
Ethnocentrism	−0·23		0·11	−0·10	0·17	−0·10	0·11	−0·03
Punitiveness	−0·16	0·18		−0·08	0·15	0·05	0·13	0·04
Sex	−0·19	−0·20	0·02		0·19	0·25	0·03	−0·50
Psychoticism	−0·29	0·21	0·24	0·17		0·04	0·35	−0·42
Extraversion	0·16	−0·13	0·05	0·19	0·02		−0·21	−0·11
Neuroticism	−0·04	0·00	−0·01	0·03	0·16	−0·04		−0·24
Lie	0·37	−0·05	0·10	−0·37	−0·35	−0·02	−0·17	

* Results for girls are above the diagonal coefficients of 0·14 and are significant at the 0·05 level (two-tail test).

possible that Insel and Wilson's scoring system, or something similar, may prove to be a useful predictor of adult "conservatism". This could arise if "extreme conservatism" is manifested in much the same form at different ages. Insel (1971) has provided some evidence along these lines by demonstrating high correlations between children's scores for "conservatism" and those of their parents (Table VIII).

Another approach would be to treat each item separately. This procedure, which becomes feasible with computer facilities, would enable very detailed and refined analyses to be carried out. This would seem to be the safest non-factor analytic approach to adopt at present. It also has the advantage that all the items can be made use of; it may be noted that the Promax scoring method described above uses only thirty-two of the fifty items for the four scales. Finally, it may be pointed out that each of the methods suggested here may have their uses in certain studies; there is no reason to rigidly adopt only one scoring procedure.

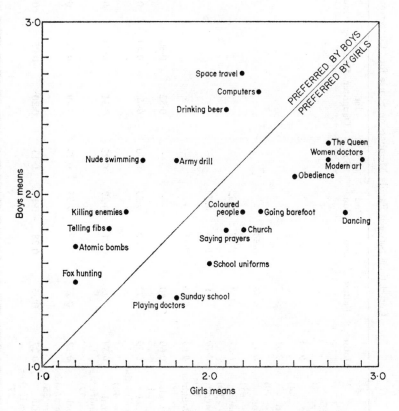

FIG. 2. Items with largest mean differences between the sexes.

TABLE VIII

Correlations between Family Members on Scores for "Conservatism" (From Insel, 1971)*

	Mother	Father	1st Son	2nd Son	3rd Son	1st Daughter	2nd Daughter	3rd Daughter	Maternal GM	Maternal GF	Paternal GM	Paternal GF
Mother (N = 97)												
Father (N = 94)	0·66											
1st Son (N = 70)	0·61	0·62										
2nd Son (N = 41)	0·55	0·56	0·50									
3rd Son (N = 10)	0·57	0·40	0·57	0·52								
1st Daughter (N = 83)	0·70	0·41	0·44	0·39	—							
2nd Daughter (N = 39)	0·63	0·44	0·41	—	—	—						
3rd Daughter (N = 8)	0·60	0·40	—	—	—	0·52	0·50					
Maternal Grandmother (N = 48)	0·59	0·32	0·39	0·33	0·30	0·40	0·40	0·50				
Maternal Grandfather (N = 37)	0·34	0·28	0·21	0·29	0·22	0·31	0·38	0·40	0·66			
Paternal Grandmother (N = 35)	0·22	0·52	0·39	0·35	0·28	0·30	0·32	0·38	0·36	0·28		
Paternal Grandfather (N = 27)	0·27	0·35	0·28	−0·17	0·13	0·20	0·05	0·20	0·27	0·38	0·59	

*Children under 14 years were tested with the children's scale.   Coefficients in italics are rsignificant at the 0·05 level.

V. Sex Differences in Item Means

In contrast to the similar picture given by the factor analytic results, the item means illustrate a number of fairly large differences between the sexes. Means and standard deviations are listed in Table II. "Yes" responses were scored three, "?" responses two, and "No" responses one. Therefore, the means are within the range one to three, with high scores indicating a predominance of "Yes" responses. Since the standard deviations are all below 1·0, it may be calculated that all differences of 0·2 or over between item means are statistically significant.

Figure 2 illustrates the extent to which selected items have been answered "Yes" (i.e. high means), and the extent to which sex differences have occurred. For example, boys are relatively more in favour of Nude swimming 2·2 (1·6), Space travel 2·7 (2·2), and Atomic bombs 1·7 (1·2), while girls are more in favour of Dancing 1·9 (2·8), Women doctors 2·2 (2·9), and Modern art 2·2 (2·7). In looking for groups of items that differentiate the sexes it may be noted that girls tend to endorse religious items, such as Church 1·8 (2·2) and Sunday school 1·4 (1·8), while boys tend to endorse punitive items such as Killing enemies 1·9 (1·5) and Fox hunting 1·5 (1·2). These differences are consistent with those from the Promax scales (Table VI).

As with the sex differences in the factor analytic results noted earlier, the present results again serve the overlapping functions of demonstrating validity and potentially interesting findings. The differences, illustrated in Fig. 2, do seem to make good sense in that they are generally in the direction that might have been predicted from what is known about sex differences in the related fields of personality and interests.

VI. Relationship of Attitudes to Personality

The school-children employed in the factor structure study were also given a revised version of the Junior Eysenck Personality Inventory (Eysenck, 1965). Their scores on this test were correlated with the four content area scores obtained from the attitude scale, using the items listed in Table V. The means and standard deviations are given in Table VI, and the correlations in Table VII. Seven boys and four girls, who had not satisfactorily completed both tests, were dropped from this part of the analysis.

The means and intercorrelations for this particular version of the personality inventory are comparable with those obtained with other groups of children; this indicates that we are, at least, not dealing with an atypical sample. Table VII shows that a number of the correlations between attitudes and personality are significant for both sexes. Thus, Psychoticism is fairly closely related to Religion (negatively), Punitiveness, and Ethnocentrism; these correlations are consistent with the emerging picture of the high P scorer as insensitive, anti-social, hostile, and even psychopathic. Psychoticism is also correlated with Sex, which is consistent with the sensation-seeking component of P. Similarly, among students there is a tendency for high P scorers to be high on 'libido' or sex drive as assessed by a self-report inventory (Eysenck, 1970). Extraversion is correlated with Sex, which is also consistent with results from students. Neuroticism is not related to any of the attitude scores.

Before leaving the interpretation of these correlations it is relevant to note those involving the Lie scale. L is correlated with Religion and with Sex (negatively), thus indicating some degree of overlap in content. The relationship of L to attitudes on Religion and Sex suggests that children's views in this area may be determined to a large extent simply by what they consider to be right or wrong, whether in the religious sense or more generally in terms of what they have "internalized" from their parents and teachers. As children get older it may be predicted that their attitudes will become more complexly determined, especially when motivational factors begin to exert an influence. This point will be discussed further in the next section.

VII. Theoretical Considerations

The main finding to emerge from the studies described in this chapter seems to be the difference between children and adults in the way that attitudes are structured. In seeking explanations for this difference it would seem most relevant to examine the very different influences that probably operate on attitude development in children compared with adults.

The "conservative" syndrome as it appears in adults is generally believed to develop as a result of a complex interaction of personality, motivation, and various learning experiences (Eysenck, 1954). One popular theory suggests that there is a generalized tendency in some people to feel threatened in the face of a changing environment. For example, it has been argued that racial attitudes are likely to develop in people who feel threatened in their position at work by the arrival of immigrants. In a similar way, a strict sexual morality may develop as a reaction to feelings of conflict and jealousy in people who feel ill-at-ease or at a disadvantage in a "permissive" society. These theories, although difficult to substantiate, may, at least, serve to illustrate the kind of processes that are more likely to apply to adults than to children.

The attitudes of children would seem to be determined more by simpler social or cognitive processes, and in particular by the direct influence of their parents and teachers. Because items referring to religion feature strongly in the children's first principal component, it seems possible that religious education may have played a large role in the formation of their attitudes generally. In other words, religious beliefs may be generalized to other areas of behaviour to a much greater extent in children than in adults. For example, children might be strongly influenced by religious tenets, such as "love thy neighbour", when deciding where they stand on racial issues. Religious beliefs certainly appear to be more widespread among children than adults; scores for religious items in the present sample were around the mid-point, which is appreciably higher than those obtained for adults (Wilson and Patterson, 1970). Moreover, the contribution of social desirability in determining children's attitudes is indicated by the fairly high correlation of 0·37 (0·52 for girls) between Religion and the L scale of the personality inventory.

Thus it is being suggested that a complex or broad "psychological" dimension such as "conservatism" would be expected to emerge when attitudes are determined by an interaction of personality, motivation, and other influences, as seems to be the case with adults. In contrast, when these complex determinants are not present, then factor analysis seems likely to group items that are clearly of similar content, such as all being directly concerned with religion (Nias and Wilson, 1972). Because the attitudes of children appear to be determined by simpler social processes, and to the extent that these attitudes reflect the teaching of their parents, school and church, it seems reasonable that the structuring is clear-cut and consistent with social desirability and the Christian ethic.

VIII. Summary

Results obtained with the children's scale of social attitudes appear to be very reliable and meaningful, for both boys and girls. Interestingly, the structuring of these attitudes appears to be *qualitatively* different from that found in adults. With adults, religion is aligned with ethnocentrism and punitiveness as part of a general factor of "conservatism". With children, the only general factor to emerge is a broad religion and "good" behaviour dimension, in which ethnocentric and punitive items load *negatively*. While it appears that the factor structure in adults needs to be explained in terms of a complex interaction of various influences including personality dispositions and motivation, the structure in children can be explained more simply in terms of what they consider to be right and wrong. Because of this different factor structure, it does not seem appropriate to score the children's scale for "conservatism". The scale can, however, readily be scored for the clearly defined content areas of religion, ethnocentrism, punitiveness, and sex. These factors have been correlated with the personality dimensions of psychoticism, extraversion, and neuroticism. The relationships are consistent with those found in adults although there appears to be more overlap with the personality trait of social desirability in the case of children. Social desirability is associated with responses to the personality dimensions of psychoticism and neuroticism, and especially to the attitude areas of religion and sex; this overlap is not surprising bearing in mind the hypothesized absence of other more "psychological" determinants.

References

Bagley, C. (1970). Racial prejudice and the "conservative" personality: a British sample. *Pol. Stud.* **18**, 134–141.

Eysenck, H. J. (1954). "The Psychology of Politics." Routledge and Kegan Paul, London.

Eysenck, H. J. (1970). Personality and attitudes to sex: a factorial study. *Personality* **1**, 355–376.

Eysenck, S. B. G. (1965). "Manual of the Junior Eysenck Personality Inventory." University of London Press, London.

Hendrickson, A. E. and White, P. O. (1964). Promax: a quick method for rotation to oblique simple structure. *Br. J. statist. Psychol.* **17**, 65–70.

Insel, P. M. (1971). Family similarities in personality, intelligence and social attitudes. Ph.D. thesis, University of London, 1971.

Insel, P. M. and Wilson, G. D. (1971). Measuring social attitudes in children. *Br. J. soc. clin. Psychol.* **10**, 84–86.

Kaiser, H. F. (1958). The varimax criterion for analytic rotation in factor analysis. *Psychometrika,* **23**, 187–200.

Nias, D. K. B. (1972). The structuring of social attitudes in children. *Child Dev.* **43**, 211–219.

Nias, D. K. B. and Wilson, G. D. (1972). Interpretation of the factor structure of the C-Scale: a reply to Boshier. *Br. J. soc. clin. Psychol,* **11**, 324–325.

Wilson, G. D. and Patterson, J. R. (1970). "Manual for the Conservatism Scale." N.F.E.R., Windsor, England.

APPENDIX 1

A flexible scoring programme developed at the Institute of Psychiatry by
P. O. White and J. D. Parrish, which may be used for scoring the six
attitude factors in the C-Scale.

```
            PROGRAM SCORE(INPUT,OUTPUT,PUNCH,TAPE5=INPUT,TAPE6=OUTPUT,TAPE7=PU
           XNCH)
         C QUESTIONNAIRE SCORING PROGRAM FOR2 OR 3 RESPONSE CATEGORIES
         C YES/NO ITEMS PUNCHED 0-1, OR 1-2, ETC. MAY BE SCORED 0-1, 0-2, OR 0-3, ETC.
         C YES/QUERY/NO ITEMS - 0-1-2, OR 1-2-3, ETC. MAY BE SCORED 0-1/2-1, 0-1-2, ETC
         C LOGICAL TAPE UNITS USED - TAPE5=INPUT, TAPE6=OUTPUT, TAPE7=PUNCH (OPTIONAL).
000003         DIMENSION W(10,100),D(100),S(10),TITLE(20),VF(80)
         C READ TITLE CARD (80 COLS)
000003         READ (5,50) TITLE
000011         READ(5,100)NS,NV,IVF,NSCORE,XMULT,XADD
         C READ PROBLEM CARD (6 INTEGERS IN 5 DIGIT FIELDS STARTING IN COL. 1)
         C PARAMETERS ARE 1)NS=NO. OF SCALES 2)NV=NO. OF ITEMS 3)IVF=NO. OF  VARIABLE
         C FORMAT CARDS 4)NSCORE=NO. OF RESPONSE CATEGORIES(2 OR 3) 5)XMULT=CONSTANT TO
         C MULTIPLY STANDARD SCORES 0-1 (0-1/2-1) TO OBTAIN DESIRED SCORES 6)CONSTANT TO
         C ADD TO ACTUAL RESPONSE SET TO GIVE STANDARD RESPONSE SET 1-2 (1-2-3).
000031         WRITE(6,200)TITLE,NS,NV,IVF,NSCORE,XMULT,XADD
000053         IVF=IVF*20
000055         READ(5,50)(VF(I),I=1,IVF)
         C READ VARIABLE FORMAT CARD(S) (80 COLS PER CARD). BEST TO BEGIN (A4, - - - - -
000070         WRITE(6,250)(VF(I),I=1,IVF)
000103         DO 10 J=1,NS
000105         READ(5,400)  (W(J,K),K=1,NV)
         C READ NS VECTORS OF ITEM WEIGHTS, 2 COLS FOR EACH WEIGHT, 40 PER CARD
         C +1 FOR POSITIVELY KEYED, -1 FOR NEGATIVELY KEYED ITEMS, OTHERS LEFT BLANK.
000120      10 WRITE(6,500)  (W(J,K),K=1,NV)
000137      30 READ(5,VF)IOBS,(D(K),K=1,NV)
         C READ DATA ACCORDING TO V. FORMAT. DATA TERMINATED BY STOP (COLS 1-4).
000154         IF(IOBS.EQ.10HSTOP        )STOP
000160         DO 40 K=1,NV
000162         D(K)=D(K)+XADD
000165         IF(NSCORE.EQ.2.AND.D(K).EQ.2.)D(K)=3.
000200         IF(D(K).LT.1..OR.D(K).GT.3.)GO TO 6000
000212      40 CONTINUE
000214         DO 3000 J=1,NS
000216         S(J)=0.
000217         DO 3000 K=1,NV
000221         IF(W(J,K).EQ.0.)GO TO 3000
000224         IGO=D(K)+W(J,K)+1.
000231         GO TO (3000,1000,2000,1000,3000),IGO
000242    1000 S(J)=S(J)+.5*XMULT
000246         GO TO 3000
000247    2000 S(J)=S(J)+1.*XMULT
000253    3000 CONTINUE
000260         WRITE(6,4000)IOBS,(S(K),K=1,NS)
000275         WRITE(7,5000)IOBS,(S(K),K=1,NS)
         C REMOVE COMMENT LABEL FROM PREVIOUS CARD TO PUNCH RESULTS.
000312         GO TO 30
000313    6000 WRITE (6,7000) IOBS
000321         GO TO 30
000322      50 FORMAT(20A4)
000322     100 FORMAT(4I5,2F5.0)
000322     200 FORMAT(1H1,20A4/1H0,4I5,2F5.0)
000322     250 FORMAT(1H0,20A4)
000322     400 FORMAT(40F2.0)
000322     500 FORMAT(1H0//(1X,40F3.0))
000322    4000 FORMAT(1H0,(1X,A10,10F6.1))
000322    5000 FORMAT(A10,10F6.1)
000322    7000 FORMAT(1X,17HBAD DATA SUBJECT ,A10)
000322         END
```

Part III

RESEARCH AND THEORY

Religion, Racialism and Conservatism

7

GLENN D. WILSON
Institute of Psychiatry, University of London
and
CHRISTOPHER BAGLEY
*Centre for Social Research, Sussex University**

I. Introduction

There may appear to be a paradox implicit in the general factor theory of social attitudes outlined in previous chapters. The finding that both ethnic intolerance and expressed commitment to fundamentalist-type religion load positively on the general conservatism factor might be interpreted as meaning that these two areas are themselves positively correlated. This would seem paradoxical considering that the Christian ethic supposedly emphasizes charity and brotherly love. As noted in Chapter 1, however, it is quite possible for religion and racialism to be totally independent or even negatively correlated to a slight extent, yet both be measures of conservatism in that they load the same way on the general factor.

This chapter may be regarded as an elaboration on Chapter 5, in that it is concerned with the precise relationship between two of the subfactors of conservatism within the general structure of social attitudes. In particular, it deals with some studies relevant to the question of the relationship between religious beliefs and practices on the one hand and racial prejudice on the other.

II. Promax Rotation of the C-Scale

A recent study by Bagley *et al.* (1973) compared promax factors in the C-Scale for large samples of English, Dutch, and New Zealand subjects.

*Now at University of Surrey, Guildford.

In spite of considerable demographic differences among the three samples (Table I) the promax procedure in each case yielded two independent factors which Bagley *et al.* identified as referring to *religious* and *racialist* values respectively. The exact correlations between these factors were

TABLE I

Demographic composition and C-Scale scores of the samples in the study by Bagley *et al.* (1973).

	English subjects	Dutch subjects	New Zealand subjects
Sample size	212	279	350
Per cent male	100	48	34
Mean age (with S.D.)	20·28 (2·10)	35·99 (14·67)	35·10 (9·49)
Mean C-score (S.D.)	35·92 (9·72)	41·59 (13·79)	43·21 (11·28)

TABLE II

Highest loading items on the first two promax factors in the c-Scale for three European cultures*
(From Bagley *et al.*, 1973)

Factor	England	Netherlands	New Zealand
I "Religion"	*Bible truth*	*Divine law*	*Church authority*
	Divine law	*Bible truth*	*Bible truth*
	Church authority	*Sabbath observance*	*Divine law*
	Sabbath observance	*Church authority*	*Sabbath observance*
	Divorce	Self-denial	
	Legalized abortion		
II "Race"	*Apartheid*	Military drill	Death penalty
	White superiority	*Mixed marriage*	Disarmament
	Coloured immigration	*Coloured immigration*	Military drill
	Mixed marriage	Disarmament	Socialism
		Death penalty	Birching
		White superiority	*Apartheid*
		Conventional clothes	*Coloured immigration*
		Apartheid	*Mixed marriage*

*The top eight items are listed where their loading is greater than 0·1 disregarding the sign. Items in italics are represented in all three cultures.

−0·01, −0·00 and 0·00, which is quite remarkable considering that the promax method does not impose orthogonality. (Many other promax factors were obtained at the first level, but Bagley *et al.* were concerned only with the relationship between these two, together with a consideration of certain demographic variables and measures of religious behaviour.)

Table II shows the eight highest loading items for each culture on these two major promax factors. Clearly, the first factor is dominated by religious items in each case. The second factor is slightly more complex, being exclusively racial with the English sample, but mixed with militaristic and punitive items in the Dutch and New Zealand samples.

Bagley *et al.* went on further to conduct a higher order rotation of the first-order promax factors in their English sample. This produced two more generalized factors which correlated 0·34 one with another. One factor was concerned with religious and puritanical views and had a C-Scale loading of 0·68. This higher-order factor structure was rather different from that described in a previous study (Bagley, 1970a), which probably reflects demographic differences between the samples used.

In general, the results of this promax analysis indicate that religious attitudes and beliefs do not predict expressed prejudice in heterogeneous samples. They differ from many previous findings discussed in Chapter 5 which have shown positive correlations between religion and prejudice. Most of these previous studies had used samples that were more homogeneous in some respects than Bagley's, but it is not clear why this variable should influence the factor structure of the C-Scale. All that can be said at present is that religious and racial attitudes tend to be opposed on a second attitude factor orthogonal to conservatism and that in some samples they will be totally independent of each other.

III. Religious Behaviour, Conservatism, and Prejudice

For the Dutch and New Zealand subjects in the Bagley *et al.* study information was available on a large number of demographic variables including religious affiliation and behaviour. In another paper by Bagley and Boshier (1972) the extent to which these variables, taken independently of each other, would predict conservatism and prejudice was examined by the method of multiple regression analysis. This technique examines, in turn, the correlation of each demographic variable with the dependent variable, partialling out the correlation of that variable with each of the other predictors.

The Dutch sample comprised 200 adult residents of The Hague aged 21 to 60 (100 males and 100 females), stratified so as to be representative of the age and occupational structure within this age group, and seventy-nine young professionals (aged 18 to 30) attending courses of professional education in Amsterdam. Ss were approached by Dutch interviewers using a Dutch translation of the C-Scale (see Bagley, 1973). In addition to the C-Scale, they completed a six-item scale measuring prejudice towards Surinamers (Black immigrants from the former Dutch colony of Surinam in South America). This scale was a translation of one used in a British study of prejudice (Bagley, 1970b, c).

Variables studied in the Dutch sample were: scores on the C-Scale and the prejudice scale; occupational categories, age and sex, religious affiliation; and religious behaviour, including the degree to which the subject contributed to church funds, held some office or performed some role in his church, and frequency of attendance.

The New Zealand subjects were 329 adults attending University extramural courses in Wellington. The age-distribution was similar to that of the Dutch Ss, but compared to the Dutch Ss the N.Z. sample tended to be biased towards females and middle class Ss. Variables in the N.Z. sample were C-scores; age, sex, and occupation; years of education; level of qualification; religious affiliation; and "social integration", measured by S's feeling that Wellington was his true home.

TABLE III

Multiple regression predicting conservatism in 279 Dutch subjects
(From Bagley and Boshier, 1972)

Variable	Original correlation with conservatism	Correlation with conservatism after multiple regression	t value of correlation
Church giving	0·22	0·55	10·87
Church attendance	0·09	0·50	9·48
Age	0·59	0·49	9·28
Young professional workers	−0·53	−0·39	6·91
Sex (female)	0·29	0·31	5·35
Re-Reformed church member	0·17	0·30	5·16
Roman Catholic	0·24	0·20	3·46
No religion	−0·11	−0·19	3·20
Clerical worker	0·17	0·16	2·75
Church function	0·02	0·14	2·35
Unskilled worker	0·26	0·12	1·98
Dutch Reformed church member	−0·09	0·12	1·97
Church affiliation, but not a regular attender	0·23	0·11	1·80
Professional worker	0·11	−0·10	1·70
Skilled worker	0·01	−0·09	1·52
Variables not in the regression set			
Score on six-item prejudice scale*	0·38	0·28	4·87
Multiple correlation	—	0·81	—

*This variable, although significant, was not included in the regression set because it is an aspect of conservative values.

Table III shows the results of the multiple regression analysis on the Dutch Ss with conservatism as the dependent variable. The highest correlation with C after controlling on all other variables was the extent of contribution to church funds, followed by frequency of church attendance (i.e. religious activity). Both of these correlations had increased markedly after the other variables had been partialled out, indicating that there are some paradoxical features among the original correlations. This may be accounted for by the fact that the seventy-nine young professionals were recruited through sectarian educational institutions and therefore tended to be involved with their church even though their C-scores were fairly low. For the main sample, however, religious behaviour was related to high C,

TABLE IV

Multiple regression predicting conservatism in 329 New Zealand subjects
(From Bagley and Boshier, 1972)

Variable	Original correlation with conservatism	Correlation with conservatism after multiple regression	t value of correlation
Church attendance	0·41	0·35	6·74
No religion	−0·49	−0·24	4·36
Years of University education	−0·30	−0·23	4·20
Roman Catholic	0·34	0·21	3·83
Student	−0·15	−0·16	2·86
Age	0·19	0·15	2·78
Church of England	0·12	0·13	2·41
Other Protestant	0·09	0·11	2·00
Clerical	0·07	0·05	1·01
Presbyterian	0·03	0·05	1·00
Variables not in the regression set			
Retired	0·04	0·04	0·71
Methodist	0·02	−0·04	0·69
Years of secondary education	−0·16	−0·03	0·57
Jewish	−0·01	−0·03	0·50
Skilled worker	−0·04	−0·03	0·49
Level of qualifications	−0·28	−0·02	0·40
Social integration	−0·01	−0·02	0·38
Sex (female)	0·12	0·02	0·27
Holds some formal office	−0·04	−0·01	0·24
Years of primary education	0·01	−0·01	0·20
Housewife	−0·16	0·01	0·20
Professional worker	0·15	0·01	0·10
Baptist	0·03	0·00	0·01
Multiple correlation	—	0·66	—

and combining the two samples (the quota sample and the young professionals) tended to obscure the original correlation of religious behaviour with conservatism. It is a strength of the multiple regression technique that such peculiarities in the data can be sorted out.

Age, female sex, the status of young professional (negative), and membership of the Re-Reformed (extreme Calvinist) Church were the other main predictors of conservatism, and the multiple correlation of all fifteen variables in the regression set with C was 0·81. Scores on the prejudice scale showed a significant correlation with C even after controlling for all other variables, but prejudice was not included in the regression set because it is an aspect of conservatism rather than a demographic predictor.

For the New Zealand Ss, the best predictor of C after controlling for other variables was frequency of church attendance (Table IV). Having no religion was a significant inverse predictor of C independently of other

TABLE V

Multiple regression predicting prejudice in 279 Dutch subjects
(From Bagley and Boshier, 1972)

Variable	Original correlation with prejudice	Correlation with prejudice after multiple regression	t value of correlation
Church affiliation, but not a regular attender	0·42	0·36	6·36
Unskilled worker	0·21	0·16	2·64
Sex (female)	0·09	0·13	2·24
Age	0·25	0·13	2·22
Professional worker	0·09	0·09	1·45
No religion	−0·12	−0·08	1·39
Roman Catholic	0·20	0·07	1·20
Variables not in the regression set			
Conservatism score	0·38	0·20	3·86
Young professional worker	−0·25	−0·04	0·64
Re-Reformed church member	0·08	0·02	0·39
Church giving	−0·11	−0·02	0·39
Dutch Reformed church member	−0·13	−0·01	0·23
Clerical worker	−0·03	−0·01	0·22
Skilled worker	0·01	0·01	0·17
Church attendance	−0·15	0·00	0·06
Church function	−0·11	−0·00	0·03
Multiple correlation	—	0·51	—

variables, as was extent of university education. Roman Catholic affiliation also predicted C independently of other variables, and the multiple correlation based on ten variables was 0·66.

The most notable difference between the results for the Dutch and N.Z. samples was the relative failure of age to predict C in the latter culture (0·15 as against 0·49). Similarly, sex predicted C in the Netherlands but not in N.Z.

Finally, regression analysis was carried out on the Dutch data using scores on the prejudice scale as the dependent variable (Table V). In this case, the only variable that predicted prejudice with any power was nominal church affiliation (i.e. claiming church membership but not attending regularly). The C-score also predicted prejudice towards Surinamers but was not included in the regression set because prejudice is a recognized component of conservatism. Roman Catholicism was related to prejudice before controlling for other variables, but the regression analysis revealed that most of this correlation could be attributed to the effects of other demographic variables. The Catholics more than other groups tended to show nominal rather than active church participation and they were overrepresented among the unskilled working class.

This finding that nominal rather than active church involvement is related to prejudice was strongly supported by an examination of the position of the demographic "marker" variables in relation to the two orthogonal promax factors of religion and racialism identified by Bagley et al. (1973). Predictably, total C-score correlated with both the religious and racial factors about evenly, meaning that general conservatism embodies both of these attitude areas. Regularity of church attendance and extent of contribution to church funds fell in the region of the religious factor, but declared (i.e. nominal) religious affiliation fell *between* the religious and racial axes (like C-scores). Furthermore, data available for the Dutch sample only showed that "church defaulters" (persons who declared a religious affiliation but who "rarely or never" attended church) were definitely in the area of the racialist factor rather than the religious.

On the basis of these results Bagley et al. concluded that individuals who have a superficial attachment to the established church but are not actively involved in church life are significantly more prejudiced than active church members (and those who do not claim any religious affiliation). They went on to suggest that the reason why some studies have found a significant positive association between racialist and religious attitudes may be traced to the large proportion of the population who pay "lip service" to religion by endorsing conservative opinions in the realm of religion and morality as well as coming out in favour of militaristic and racialist viewpoints.

IV. Attitudes of Salvationists and Humanists

Another study relevant to the question of the relationship between religious and racial attitudes is that of Wilson and Lillie (1972) who compared the attitudes of "Salvationists" with those of "Humanists". A comparison of these two groups was thought to be of particular interest because they might both be described as "tenderminded" in the Eysenck terminology, and differing primarily in the areas of religious beliefs and attitudes.

The C-Scale was administered separately to a group of 43 Salvation Army officer cadets (17 males and 26 females) and a group of 31 members of the Young Humanist Association (16 males and 15 females). The Salvationists ranged in age from 19 to 36 with a mean of 25; the Humanists were aged 18 to 33, also with a mean of 25. Both groups were told that the results would be used only for group research and that they would be individually anonymous.

Since there were no significant differences between males and females in either group the data were collapsed across sex. The two groups were clearly separated on the general conservatism dimension (Figure 4, Chapter 4), but Wilson and Lillie went on to examine the extent to which this separation could be accounted for by the explicitly religious items in the scale. This was done by the very simple technique of plotting mean item scores for the Salvationists against those of the Humanists (Fig. 1) so that the discriminative power of each individual item was indicated by its distance from the diagonal. Loci above the diagonal represent higher conservatism on those items by the Salvationists; loci below the diagonal indicate higher conservatism for the Humanists.

The items which separate the two groups most powerfully do tend to be overtly religious (Bible truth, Sabbath observance, Divine law, Church authority). These are all located on or above the arbitrary level six, at which Salvationist means are six times as high as those of Humanists. Also aligned in the region of level six are a number of social issues upon which Christians have been traditionally more conservative than non-Christians (Birth control, Divorce, Abortion, Evolution). In the region of level three (Salvationist means about three times those of Humanists) are items which refer to sexual freedom and hedonism as a life philosophy (Censorship, Nudist camps, Striptease, Pyjama parties, Chastity, Chaperones, Self-denial, Casual living, White lies), and also punitive-militaristic items (Death penalty, Birching, Straitjackets, Strict rules, Empire-building, Disarmament, Military drill). Around level two are items concerned with political conservatism (Socialism, Patriotism, Royalty) and conventional-conforming attitudes and behaviour (School uniforms, Licensing laws, Women judges, Working mothers, Mixed marriage, Beatniks).

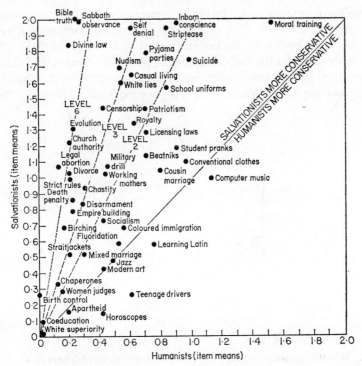

FIG. 1. Mean item scores of Salvationists plotted against mean item scores of Humanists. The degree to which each item discriminates the two groups is indicated by its distance from the diagonal. (From Wilson and Lillie, 1972.)

Thus, although the explicitly religious items are primary discriminators of the two groups, the Salvationists are also more conservative than the Humanists on a wide variety of other issues—consistent with the general factor hypothesis. They are more strongly opposed to sexual freedom, more punitive, militaristic, politically conservative, and conventional in their attitudes and beliefs.

There is, however, at least one area in which the attitudes of the two groups do not differ, and this is racial prejudice (White superiority, Apartheid, Coloured immigration). In fact, both the Salvationists and Humanists show very low levels of ethnocentrism compared to the population at large. So although the Salvationists are relatively conservative in most respects, they are apparently "true Christians" in the sense that they are tolerant of racial minorities.

The importance of this study to the question of the structure of attitudes in general, and the relationship between religious and racial attitudes in particular, is based upon the fact that it offers an approach to the investigation of attitude clustering different from that of factor analysis. The patterning of items revealed in Fig. 1 is interesting because it is consistent to a large extent with that obtained by principal components analysis (Chapter 5). In both cases the results suggest that four of the major attitude areas represented in the C-Scale (religion, sex, punitiveness, and racialism) are arranged in that same order, such that adjacent pairs are closely associated and separated pairs relatively uncorrelated. According to this

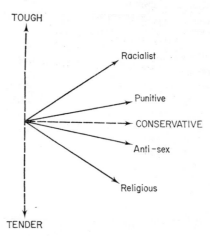

FIG. 2. Hypothesized relationships between the four main subfactors in the C-Scale general conservatism, and Eysenck's T factor (From Wilson and Lillie, 1972).

hypothesis (Fig. 2), religion and sexual attitudes would be fairly highly correlated, likewise sex-punitiveness and punitiveness-racialism, but religion and racialism would be relatively (perhaps even totally) independent. This hypothesis has found some support from the findings concerning the principal component and promax factor structures of the C-Scale. The Wilson and Lillie study shows that this ordering of attitudinal sub-factors is quite well sustained with respect to the magnitude of the item-mean differences between Salvationists and Humanists. Comparisons of other pairs of criterion groups would of course be necessary before firm conclusions based on this method of analysis could be reached.

V. Conclusions

The results of the studies outlined above, taken together with previous results, suggest the following conclusions:

1. Although religious attitudes and beliefs tend, in general, to be positively related to ethnocentrism and prejudice (Chapter 5), these two subfactors of conservatism tend to be less strongly associated than other pairs

of attitude clusters and with some subject samples may emerge as completely independent one from another. They may therefore be thought of as marking polar positions on a second major factor in social attitudes orthogonal to conservatism–liberalism. This second factor may be described as realism versus idealism or toughmindedness versus tendermindedness.

2. The extent to which the religious and racial attitude factors approach independence apparently depends upon the extent to which the people in the sample who express religious attitudes and beliefs have actually absorbed Christian ethics through involvement with their church. Evidence for this hypothesis comes from the finding that nominal church affiliation without actual participation in church affairs predicts racial prejudice better than religious behaviours that indicate close church involvement. Such a view is also supported by the finding that people very committed to a religious way of life (e.g. Salvationists) exhibit very low levels of prejudice compared to the general population, while those who show a peripheral attachment to religious values (e.g. John Birchers) tend to show a high degree of prejudice. In the next chapter, Webster and Stewart demonstrate that in a sample composed entirely of committed Christians (Baptist clergy) religious fundamentalism is quite strongly related to ethnocentrism ($r = 0.58$). Thus it would appear that prejudice is most strongly expressed by two groups: those who have a nominal or superficial interest in religion, and those who are dogmatic and fundamentalist in their religious beliefs. People who are liberal in their religious beliefs and active in their church tend to be relatively free of prejudice, as do people who claim no religious beliefs (e.g. Humanists).

In seeking an explanation for these findings it would seem necessary to consider the possible influences of personality dynamics. If we are to accept that prejudice against minority groups may serve an ego-protective function (e.g. enhancing one's self-esteem by putting down others) then the correlation with nominal religiosity may arise because claiming to be devout and Godly is also ego-enhancing. Similarly, if prejudice arises out of fear of people who are different, then the expression of religious attitudes may reflect a fear of God or death. However, individuals who are fully assimilated into a religious environment can hardly avoid becoming committed to the ethical code of their religion, usually including an emphasis on "love of fellow men", and this is presumably why they express less prejudice. Finally, an excessively dogmatic and inflexible adherence to a set of religious beliefs may also be viewed as ego-defensive, thus again being associated with expressions of prejudice.

References

Bagley, C. R. (1970a). Racial prejudice and the conservative personality. *Pol. Stud.* **18**, 1340–41.

Bagley, C. R. (1970b). "Social Structure and Prejudice in Five English Boroughs." Institute of Race Relations, London.

Bagley, C. R. (1970c). On the construction and reliability of a prejudice scale. *Race.* **11**, 372–374.

Bagley, C. R. (1973). "The Dutch Plural Society: A Comparative Study of Race Relations." Oxford University Press, London.

Bagley, C. R. and Boshier, R. Demographic predictors of conservation and racial prejudice. Submitted for publication 1972.

Bagley, C. R., Boshier, R. and Nias, D. K. B. (1973). The orthogonality of religious and racial-punitive attitudes in three societies. *J. soc. Psychol.* in press.

Wilson, G. D. and Lillie, F. J. (1972). Social attitudes of humanists and salvationists. *Brit. J. soc. clin. Psychol.* **11**, 220–224.

Theological Conservatism

8

ALAN C. WEBSTER and
ROBERT A. C. STEWART

Massey University, New Zealand

I. Introduction

An important area contributing to conservatism as a general factor in social attitudes is religious or theological conservatism. There has been growing interest over the last decade or so in the relationship of religious beliefs and behaviour with variables such as dogmatism, authoritarianism, ethnocentrism, conservatism and prejudice (Dittes, 1969). Instruments commonly used in these studies have included the Rokeach Dogmatism Scale (Rokeach, 1960), the F-Scale and E-Scale (Adorno *et al.*, 1950). Although the Wilson-Patterson C-Scale has some different bases from these scales, it has been shown to correlate significantly with each of them (e.g. Crano, 1968). The present authors (Webster and Stewart, 1969) found a relationship of 0·59 between C- and D-Scales, and 0·65 between the C-Scale and the New Zealand Ethnocentrism Scale (adapted for the present study from the Australian Ethnocentrism Scale of Beswick and Hills, 1969). Because of their overlap with the C-Scale, some of the relevant work using these instruments is discussed.

F

Typical of the studies using the Rokeach Dogmatism Scale, Kilpatrick *et al.* (1970) found in a sample of 245 male and 250 female undergraduates that churchgoers were more dogmatic than non-churchgoers. Using their Australian Ethnocentrism Scale, Beswick and Hills (1969) found that rate of church attendance was uncorrelated with ethnocentrism, but the 12 per cent of their sample of 273 who described themselves as "agnostic" or "atheist" were significantly less ethnocentric than the others.

One of the major principles of the Christian faith is a belief in the importance of love and goodwill towards one's fellow man. It might be expected, then, that the more devout the individual, the less prejudiced he would be. In one study at least (O'Reilly and O'Reilly, 1954) this does not appear to be the case at all. These authors devised a test of "religious devoutness" based on the extent to which subjects agreed with the Catholic Church on certain social, moral and religious questions. Anti-Semitism and prejudice against Black people were also measured in the subjects (92 men and 120 women who were seminary and university students). The more devout showed themselves to be relatively anti-Jew and anti-Negro, at a statistically significant level.

Allport and Ross (1967) reviewed the literature from 1946 and concluded that "on the average, religious people show more intolerance in general". (p. 432). These authors, however, constructed a test which separated "extrinsic" and "intrinsic" orientations to the church and religion, and showed that higher prejudice scores related to the "extrinsic" orientation, rather than the "intrinsic". A third *indiscriminately pro-religious* type was the most prejudiced of all. (Allport considers that religion is internalized in the case of the "intrinsic" believer, whereas the "extrinsic" believer merely *uses* religion for his own ends.)

Is there a difference in dogmatism and prejudice between people who are equally "intrinsic" in their belief, but at opposite ends of a theological conservatism—liberalism dimension? Recent re-examination of leading studies has suggested that a major weakness in many studies of religiousness and its psychological correlates has been the failure to differentiate styles or modes of intrinsic religion. For example, Brown (1962, 1966) developed a unifactor theory of the structure of religious belief which was questioned by Allen and Spilka (1967) on the ground that, like Allport's extrinsic-intrinsic model, it does more to differentiate religiousness from non-religiousness than to analyse *within* religious belief or *among* committed believers. Dittes (1967) has argued similarly.

What is needed, therefore, is control not only of *content* but also of *commitment* of belief. To control for content means to identify, measure and hold constant by research design and statistical analysis the different conditions of belief content which are thought to relate to dependent variables. To control for commitment means, if Allen and Spilka (1967) be accepted, to recognize that the meaning of religiousness should be studied among the religiously committed.

Cryns (1970) studying dogmatism in Catholic clergy, found that those in the active ministry were significantly more dogmatic than either ex-priests or ex-seminarians. Control for commitment and for content of belief are both in doubt here. Stanley in Australia (1963b, 1964) controlled for commitment but used only a one-item question to distinguish fundamentalists from non-fundamentalists. (For a comparison of single item and multiple item scales for measuring religious values see Gorsuch and McFarland, 1972). Similarly Ranck (1955) in a large study of American theological seminaries, did not analyse the content of belief, and Webster (1966) studying American, Australian and New Zealand groups, while showing that lower dogmatism and greater inner orientation characterized students at theological schools reputed to be more liberal, did not obtain a measure of theological belief.

The present study represents an advance on most previous work in that attention is paid to both the content of belief and to the distinctive religious factor of demonstrated commitment. In particular it is argued that general conservatism as a correlate of religiousness can be better understood when it is recognized that religious belief itself falls on a conservative—liberal continuum.

II. Concepts and Measures in the Present Study

A. HYPOTHESES

The earlier studies appear to indicate that a general personality tendency to prefer stability and control in belief and behaviour, and to protect beliefs, customs, and status from threat or change, might be expected to be associated with theological conservatism. It also seems likely that older individuals, representing earlier beliefs and attitudes, will be more conservative. Since reputedly more liberal theological schools have yielded higher scores on measures of "psychological health", it seems reasonable to expect that use of a measure of theological belief would confirm this tentative observation. In view of the fact that to hold liberal beliefs is by definition to deviate from the norm, it could be expected that individuals of liberal belief will hold deviant beliefs also about functions and roles within the church. From the theoretical basis of the self-actualization concept, which posits a positive, optimistic attitude to human development as a necessity for personality health, it would follow that if an individual holds such views of his own nature, he will be less likely to have felt the need for a radical change such as in religious conversion. Therefore there would be a contrast on open, liberal, self-actualizing attitudes between those who see themselves as "converted" and those who cannot remember ever having not been religious.

On these grounds, four general hypotheses were formulated:

(1) There will be a positive relationship between general conservatism, theological conservatism, dogmatism and ethnocentrism.

(2) All these traits will increase with age.

(3) There will be a positive relation between theological liberalism, role conflict and psychological health.

(4) Perception of oneself as having grown uninterruptedly into Christian faith will be more strongly associated with open, liberal and self-actualizing attitudes than perception of oneself as having been "converted".

B. Theological Conservatism-Liberalism

Whereas some studies (e.g. Stanley, 1963) used only one belief item and its logical opposite as a criterion of fundamentalism, the present researchers attempted to develop a more comprehensive inventory. (It has been shown by Gorsuch and McFarland, 1972, that while single-item scales are good measures of an intrinsic pro-religious position, multiple-item scales are better measures of traditional Christian orthodoxy). On *a priori* grounds a set of fifteen orthodox statements of major conservative theological beliefs was generated, and a further fifteen items devised representing liberal versions of the same set of major beliefs. An item-analysis based on the research data showed twelve conservative items (Th C) and twelve liberal items (Th L) to consistently differentiate between high and low scorers. These twenty-four items were adopted as the Theological Inventory (Table I).

Table I

Loadings of belief items on principal factor of "Theological Conservatism"

Loadings	Positively loaded belief items
0·831	Christ changed real water into real wine.
0·699	There is a hell involving everlasting suffering after death for unbelievers.
0·689	A person of responsible years is either saved or unsaved.
0·687	God interrupts natural laws sometimes.
0·642	Christ will return to earth in physical form.
0·617	The dead body of Jesus came alive again.
0·578	Mary conceived Jesus without being known by a man.
0·539	The Holy Spirit gives people wisdom that is beyond their natural ability.
0·533	Philosophies and religions which do not come from the Bible are a threat.
0·473	Christian truth is found exclusively in the words of the Bible.
0·378	Human effort is of no avail for pleasing God.

Loadings	Positively loaded belief items
0·332	God visited Palestine in human form for a brief period about 2,000 years ago.
0·320	God has a separate existence from all other reality.

Negatively loaded belief items

−0·779	It is not necessary to hold that Jesus had no human father, since the idea of the virgin birth was to express his uniqueness which is now seen to be better supported by his life than by his conceptions.
−0·731	The miracle stories of the New Testament must be taken as the attempts of a pre-scientific age to express the ecstacy of heightened human experience.
−0·714	The idea of hell in an after-life is misleading as a basis for Christian living; it is hell here in the present that is the real concern of the Christian.
−0·698	The idea of a physical resurrection of Jesus is not as important as, and even serves to obscure the spiritual message of, the continuing Christ-spirit that the resurrection idea dramatizes.
−0·514	"Holy Spirit" refers to the Christian's experience and realization of the depth and power of shared love, commitment and meaning, thus "spirit" is a depth dimension of our existence.
−0·482	It is unlikely that any church in its official doctrine expresses the Christian faith validly for today.
−0·466	The concept "Christ" refers to a universal dimension of being that showed uninterruptedly through the man Jesus, and appears or "comes again" wherever the way of Jesus is genuinely followed.
0·459	Rather than giving supernatural gifts to people, the Holy Spirit symbolizes the fulfilment and realization of human capacities for meaning, energy and ecstacy.
−0·447	Salvation is best thought of as the process of self-discovery, integration and commitment.
−0·438	There are many sources of knowledge of God outside the Bible, including art, history, science and psychology.
−0·397	The idea of God is man's attempt to symbolize his reverence for that which is other than himself and thus to express his sense of the profound meaning of existence.
−0·387	God does his work through natural processes and therefore prayer must be basically a way of disposing the church to fulfil his purposes by natural, human, social and scientific means.
−0·356	Human effort and fulfilment, far from displeasing God, is his chief concern.

A *Theological Orientation Index* was calculated for each respondent, by obtaining the ratio of conservative (Th C) to liberal (Th L) responses.

C. General Conservatism-Liberalism

This has been fully discussed in Chapter 1. It was measured for the present study by the C-Scale developed originally in New Zealand by Wilson and Patterson (1968; see Chapter 4).

D. Open and Closed Mindedness (Dogmatism)

Rokeach (1960) assumes that in any given situation a person will act appropriately to the extent that he is able to receive and evaluate the relevant information in his situation. Any influence generated in his own personality which lessens the individual's ability to receive information and to process it objectively may be considered irrelevant and a threat to efficiency in information-processing. Irrelevant internal pressures such as the need for safety, or an anxious linkage of reward or punishment to the behaviour, will tend to make the response to the situation irrational or inappropriate. The more open the belief system, the more the individual will be able to evaluate and act on information on its own merits. He will be more governed by his own self-actualizing forces than will one whose internal forces interfere with his ability to receive information. He will also be more able to resist externally imposed reinforcements and less influenced by these in the way he evaluates and acts upon information.

The *Dogmatism (D) Scale* developed by Rokeach to measure open-closed mindedness, has been found to discriminate reliably and validly between "known" groups. It has also been shown (Kaplan and Singer, 1963) that people who score highly on the D-Scale demonstrate, as a group, significantly lower acuity in hearing, taste, smell and touch—apparently supporting the theory that dogmatism is a general closing off from life. Lower dogmatism scorers have also been found by Rokeach to be better problem solvers, more inventive, more ingenious and flexible.

E. Psychological Health

Known also as the concept of self-actualization, this is a theory of man's "optimum behaviour", an attempt to explain the fact that when his basic needs are dependably met, man "seeks to exercise and fulfil his potentialities". (Maslow, 1954, 1962; Rogers, 1961; Allport, 1961; Erikson, 1963; Jourard, 1964; Fromm, 1964). These authors and others of the "Third Force" school in psychology have argued that a complete view of man as a social being must take account of his best rather than his worst, i.e. healthy rather than sick people. Observation of people living at what these workers consider to be a superior level has produced certain generalizations about the characteristics of psychologically healthy or self-actualizing people.

The *Personal Orientation Inventory* (P.O.I.) was developed by Shostrom (1963) to measure people's level of self-actualization. The instrument was standardized for New Zealand by Webster (1968). A test of differences between the present sample and the standardization sample (853 young adults) showed that ministers as a whole were more able to "live in the present" (Time Competency Scale, $p < 0.0001$), more self accepting (Self Acceptance Scale, $p < 0.01$), more integrated (Synergy Scale, $p < 0.0001$) and better at interpersonal relations (Contact Scale, $p < 0.01$), but were poorer in awareness of their own feelings (Feeling Reactivity Scale, $p < 0.01$). The P.O.I. provides two major scales (TC and I) and ten sub-scales.

F. OTHER MEASURES

1. *Job dissatisfaction* (JD). A score was derived from three questions dealing with enjoyment of the job, acceptance of its definition, and desire to stay in the job.
2. *Role conflict* (RC). Each respondent ranked seven current pastoral tasks, first in order of actual time spent on them, secondly in order of preference and thirdly in order of "ideal importance". The total discrepancy in ranking berween preferred order and the actual and ideal was utilized as an indication of relative role conflict in the individual.
3. *Ethnocentrism* (E). This was measured by an adaptation of the Australian Ethnocentrism Scale (Beswick and Hills, 1969), to include reference to "Maori", "New Zealand", etc., where "Aborigine", "Australia" and other local reference occurred. The validity of the scale for New Zealand is intuitive and though the present study yielded the expected trends and relationships, further study of our adaptation will be required.
4. *Psychological Needs* were measured by use of the Edwards Personal Preference Schedule (E.P.P.S.; Edwards 1953), a widely used inventory yielding scores on fifteen major personality needs.
5. Information was also asked on age, education, and mode of becoming Christian ("conversion" versus steady growth).

III. Sample and Method

The population chosen for study consisted of all the accredited ministers (not including missionaries) on the official national list of a New Zealand Protestant denomination. Questionnaires were sent to 176 accredited individuals, including four women. Of the ninety-three responses only four were from other than the 150 or so active ministers. Two responses were from women. Thus the results are best taken as those of almost 60 per cent of the active ministers. Average age of respondents was 40·8 years. (S.D. = 11·0). Response rate was better from younger individuals and for those with university degrees. No group, however, was conspicuously lacking in response. Six returns came too late to be used and three were invalid, while a further seven omitted to complete one or more scales. The final sample consisted of eighty-four for general data, seventy-seven for those computations which required complete sets of data. Initial analyses of the hand-scored data were carried out by use of the computer unit at Massey University, while an additional factor analysis was carried out at Victoria University.*

The possibility of systematic bias exists, since it is not known whether the reasons for non-response were such as would have influenced the results in a complete sample. But the response was good as postal surveys go, and may with reasonable confidence be regarded as representative of one denomination's ministry. For purposes of the present discussion it is more important that the sample contained considerable variability on a theological conservatism—liberalism dimension than that it conform to random sampling demands.

IV. Intercorrelations Among the Personality, Attitude and Belief Variables

Results relevant to the prediction that there would be a positive relationship between theological conservatism, general conservatism, dogmatism and ethnocentrism are shown in Tables II, III and IV. Table II shows that the generally conservative minister is highly likely to be theologically conservative, ethnocentric, dogmatic and dependent on others (Outer Support), while unlikely to be theologically liberal, independent (Inner Support), flexible in values (Existentiality), sensitive to feelings (Feeling Reactivity) or constructive in his view of human nature (Nature of Man). Other results in Table II show him to be less job dissatisfied, to have less role conflict, greater need for deference, order and endurance, and less need for autonomy and for heterosexuality. Tables III and IV show that the theologically conservative minister, the dogmatic and the ethnocentric are almost identical in attitudes and orientation to the generally conservative. Examination of the correlation coefficients shows, however, that the strongest relationships are those between theological belief and general conservatism, while general conservatism is also the highest correlate of both ethnocentrism and dogmatism. Likewise it may be noted that the strongest correlates of the self-actualizing "support scales" (Inner and Outer) are theological belief and general conservatism.

The strong confirmation of this first prediction is seen also in Figs. 1 and 2. The upper 25 per cent and lower 25 per cent, i.e. the top and bottom nineteen, were selected, first on their Dogmatism scores, secondly on their T.O.I. scores. The average P.O.I. scores were computed and a t-test applied to ascertain whether the differences were significant.

*By kind co-operation of Professor C. J. Adcock, who gave valuable advice on the analysis. The present authors take full responsibility, however, for the interpretation given in this report.

TABLE II

Correlates of General Conservatism (C)

Conservatism Scale	
Job dissatisfaction	−0·31†
Role conflict	−0·24*
Theological conservatism	0·75‡
Theological liberalism	−0·72‡
Ethnocentrism	0·65‡
T.O.I.	−0·73‡
Dogmatism	0·58‡
Edwards Personal Preference Schedule	
N. Deference	0·26*
N. Order	0·24*
N. Autonomy	−0·30†
N. Endurance	0·28*
N. Heterosexuality	−0·33†
Personal Orientation Inventory	
Outer support	0·51‡
Inner support	−0·50‡
Self-actualizing value	−0·32†
Existentiality	−0·51‡
Feeling reactivity	−0·47‡
Spontaneity	−0·32†
Nature of man, constructive	−0·39‡
Synergy	−0·30†
Acceptance of aggression	−0·25*
Capacity for intimate contact	−0·29*

*$p \leq 0.05$; †$p \leq 0.01$; ‡$p \leq 0.001$

TABLE III

Correlates of Theological Conservatism (ThC), Theological Liberalism (ThL), and Theological Orientation Index (T.O.I.)

Theological Conservatism	
Job dissatisfaction	−0·39‡
Role conflict	−0·31†
Theological liberalism	−0·78‡
Conservatism	0·75‡
Ethnocentrism	0·58‡
T.O.I.	−0·89‡
Dogmatism	0·62‡
N. Order (E.P.P.S.)	0·30†
N. Autonomy (E.P.P.S.)	−0·27*
N. Intraception (E.P.P.S.)	−0·25*
Outer support (P.O.I.)	0·56‡
Inner support (P.O.I.)	−0·54‡
Self-actualizing Values (P.O.I.)	−0·30†
Existentiality (P.O.I.)	−0·56‡
Feeling reactivity (P.O.I.)	−0·41‡

Theological Conservatism	
Spontaneity (P.O.I.)	−0·26*
Self-acceptance (P.O.I.)	−0·28*
Nature of man, constructive (P.O.I.)	−0·42‡
Synergy (P.O.I.)	−0·29*
Acceptance of aggression (P.O.I.)	−0·30†
Capacity for intimate contact (P.O.I)	−0·38‡
Theological Liberalism	
Job dissatisfaction	0·37‡
Theological conservatism	−0·78‡
Conservatism	−0·72‡
Ethnocentrism	−0·55‡
T.O.I.	0·88‡
Dogmatism	−0·40‡
N. Order (E.P.P.S.)	−0·28*
N. Autonomy (E.P.P.S.)	0·33†
N. Heterosexuality (E.P.P.S.)	0·25*
Outer support (P.O.I.)	−0·50‡
Inner support (P.O.I.)	0·49‡
Self Actualizing Values (P.O.I.)	0·39‡
Existentiality (P.O.I.)	0·44‡
Feeling reactivity (P.O.I.)	0·41‡
Spontaneity (P.O.I.)	0·27*
Nature of man, constructive (P.O.I.)	0·46‡
Synergy (P.O.I.)	0·27*
Acceptance of aggression (P.O.I.)	0·24*
Capacity for Intimate Contact (P.O.I.)	0·24*
Theological Orientation Index	
Job dissatisfaction	0·41‡
Role conflict	0·26*
Theological conservatism	−0·89‡
Theological liberalism	0·88‡
Conservatism	−0·73‡
Ethnocentrism	−0·54‡
Dogmatism	−0·47‡
N. Order (E.P.P.S.)	−0·27*
N. Autonomy (E.P.P.S.)	0·37†
Outer support (P.O.I.)	−0·58‡
Inner support (P.O.I.)	0·56‡
Self actualizing values (P.O.I.)	0·39‡
Existentiality (P.O.I.)	0·57‡
Feeling reactivity (P.O.I.)	0·44‡
Spontaneity (P.O.I.)	0·32†
Self acceptance (P.O.I.)	0·25*
Nature of man, constructive (P.O.I.)	0·41‡
Synergy (P.O.I.)	0·28*
Acceptance of aggression (P.O.I.)	0·33†
Capacity for intimate contact (P.O.I.)	0·38‡

*p ≤ 0·05; †p ≤ 0·01; ‡p ≤ 0·001

TABLE IV

Correlates of Ethnocentrism (E), and Dogmatism (D).

Ethnocentrism Scale	
Theological conservatism	0·58‡
Theological liberalism	−0·55‡
Conservatism	0·65‡
T.O.I.	−0·54‡
Dogmatism	0·40‡
Edwards Personal Preference Schedule	
N. Deference	0·24*
N. Heterosexuality	0·23*
Personal Orientation Inventory	
Outer orientation	0·34†
Inner orientation	−0·31†
Existentiality	−0·31†
Feeling reactivity	−0·28*
Nature of Man	−0·25*
Acceptance of aggression	−0·24*
Dogmatism Scale	
Theological conservatism	0·62‡
Theological liberalism	−0·40‡
Conservatism	0·58‡
Ethnocentrism	0·40‡
T.O.I.	−0·47‡
Edwards Personal Preference Schedule	
N. Autonomy	−0·30†
N. Intraception	−0·31†
Personal Orientation Inventory	
Time incompetence	0·24*
Time competence	−0·26*
Outer orientation	0·48‡
Inner orientation	−0·50‡
Existentiality	−0·46‡
Feeling reactivity	−0·29*
Spontaneity	−0·30†
Self acceptance	−0·34†
Nature of man	−0·31†
Synergy	−0·30†
Capacity for intimate contact	−0·39‡

*p ≤ 0·05; †p ≤ 0·01; ‡p ≤ 0·001

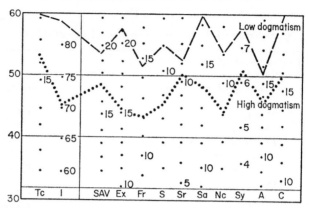

FIG. 1. Self actualization scores for high and low dogmatics (N.Z. young adults norms).

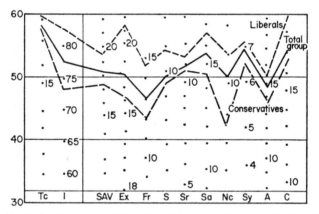

FIG. 2. Self actualization scores of Baptist ministers: total group, theological liberals and theological conservatives (N.Z. young adults norms).

Figure 1 shows the P.O.I. profiles for the high and low dogmatics using the N.Z. Young Adult norms (presented as T-scores with a mean of fifty). Low dogmatics were significantly more self-actualizing on all scales except Self-regard. They also showed significantly lower theological and general conservatism (both differences significant at $p < 0.0001$), lower ethnocentrism ($p < 0.001$) and a higher need for autonomy ($p < 0.05$). The mean C-score of the low dogmatics (42·3) is close to that of N.Z. professionals (43·78), while that of the high dogmatics (59·8) is close to that of housewives (60·98). According to the Wilson and Patterson (1968) standardization data, housewives were the most conservative of the major occupational groups in N.Z.

Differences in self-actualization between liberal and conservative scorers on theological orientation (Fig. 2) were similar to those of high versus low dogmatism, although the contrast was slightly less on the average. Since there is such a strong association of theological and general conservatism, it is safe to say that the profiles of theological liberals and conservatives given in Fig. 2, would typify the low and high scorers in general conservatism also. Reference to Tables II and III confirms that the correlations of general conservatism and theological conservatism with P.O.I. scales are of similar magnitude.

It seems clear that the open-minded, the theologically liberal and the generally liberal are as a group more self-actualizing than the young adult standardization sample, while the dogmatic, and theologically and generally conservative are less self-actualizing than the young adults. Note that the differences between ministers grouped on the basis of theological position are greater than those between ministers and others.

The second prediction, that dogmatism, general conservatism and ethnocentrism would increase with age, was tested in a comparison between the older and younger halves of the sample. It was found that although age might explain variation on job dissatisfaction, need for heterosexuality, need for exhibition (the older group scored lower on these three) and needs for deference and endurance (the older scored higher), no differences appeared on any of the other attitudes as a function of age.

In view of the failure to find an age difference on the main belief and attitude variables it was decided to check for an association of these critical indices with education. A chi-square analysis of the number of high and low scorers on P.O.I. and on dogmatism among the university graduates and non-graduates failed to reveal any association with educational level either. This result was taken as an indicator that other major variables would also not be associated with education.

The third prediction was that there would be a positive relation between theological liberalism, role conflict and psychological health. Thus it was expected that ministers who were theologically liberal, open-minded and psychologically healthy would be free both to perceive and to express more role conflict.

Tables V and VI give data showing that the expected differences in terms of role conflict and the related construct, job dissatisfaction, were confirmed. Table V shows that those with lesser role conflict tend to be more theologically conservative, more generally conservative, more dogmatic and more dependent. Greater job dissatisfaction, more liberal theological orientation and more self-actualizing orientation are also revealed in ministers who question the existing order. Table VI while showing the job-dissatisfied to be less theologically conservative, shows them also to have less need for abasement, greater need for heterosexuality, and greater ability to handle aggression.

TABLE V

Attitude differences between ministers with greater and lesser role conflict

Attitude	Mean scores		p
	Low conflict (below median) N = 38	High conflict (above median) N = 38	
Role conflict	3·4	8·9	0·0001
Theological conservatism	62·5	51·3	0·01
General conservatism	54·8	48·8	0·05
Dogmatism	163·0	151·1	0·05
Outer support	50·0	45·6	0·05
Job dissatisfaction	6·4	8·5	0·01
Theological orientation	75·0	114·0	0·05
Inner support	75·4	79·8	0·05
Existentiality	17·0	19·0	0·05
Feeling reactivity	12·6	13·8	0·05
Self-acceptance	14·7	16·5	0·05
Acceptance of aggression	14·1	15·5	0·05

TABLE VI

Attitude differences between ministers with
greater and lesser job dissatisfaction

Attitude	Mean scores		p
	Low dissat. (below median) N = 38	High dissat. (above median) N = 38	
Job dissatisfaction	5·1	9·8	0·001
Theological conservatism	60·7	53·2	0·05
Need for abasement	15·9	13·3	0·01
Need for heterosexuality	7·3	11·1	0·01
Acceptance of aggression	14·0	15·5	0·01

The fourth prediction was that ministers professing "steady growth" into Christian faith would be more likely than the "converted" to display open, liberal and self-actualizing attitudes.

Table VII presents the data relevant to this prediction. Of the seventy-seven in the total group, the fifty who professed conversion were much more likely to be theologically conservative, generally conservative, ethnocentric and dependent. The nearly one third who professed "steady growth" into Christian faith were more liberally oriented in theology, had a greater need for heterosexuality and were more flexible in application of

TABLE VII

Attitude differences between ministers professing conversion
and those professing steady growth into faith

Attitude	Mean scores		p
	Converted N = 50	Steady growth N = 27	
Theological conservatism	62·2	47·7	0·01
General conservatism	55·4	45·5	0·01
Ethnocentrism	74·2	67·0	0·01
Theological orientation	70·0	138·0	0·0001
Need for heterosexuality	7·9	11·3	0·01
Outer support	49·8	44·5	0·05
Existentiality	17·1	19·5	0·05

values. This finding is similar to that of Stanley (1963) who found dogmatism, authoritarianism and conversion to be linked. It is contrary to Kildahl (1958), however, who in a study of theological seminary students found nothing to support his hypotheses that "sudden converts" were more likely than persons with a gradual religious development to perceive authority figures as more threatening, to be more authoritarian, to be more depressed, to be less humanitarian and to be more religiously conservative. The difference in findings may perhaps be seen to arise from the different social meaning of conversion and steady growth in different contexts. In the present sample, "conversion" would be seen by the conservative as a more approved *rite de passage*, while in Kildahl's sample of Lutheran students this social pressure would be less likely; i.e. conversion would not be socially valued over gradual development.

V. Factor Analysis of Theological and General Attitude Scales

As already indicated (Table I), factor analysis of the Theological Inventory, using Thurstone's centroid method (Olson, 1964) yielded a single-factor solution. Successive Tucker's phi values for the five factors extracted were 0·29, 0·81, 0·89, 0·88, 0·87. The levelling off of phi after the first factor indicates that it is really only necessary to extract one (Fruchter, 1954; Olson, 1964).

According to Cooley and Lohnes (1971, p. 150), "It is usually desirable to retain enough factors for rotation to demonstrate that all major factors have been accounted for and that some nearly unique factors (significant loadings on only one test) have been reached". Would the theological conservatism scale remain intact if a criterion allowing the extraction of more factors was used and if more variables were incorporated in the matrix?

TABLE VIII

Loadings of theological, personal, social and ethnic orientations and selected life variables, on the first six principal component factors*

Scale	Loading on factor						h^2 (for 13 factors)
	I	II	III	IV	V	VI	
Theological conservatism (ThC)	0·93	0·19	0·07	−0·21	0·04	0·06	0·99
General conservatism (C)	0·79	0·15	−0·13	−0·11	0·07	−0·12	0·77
Inner orientation (I)	−0·76	0·63	0·02	−0·00	0·00	0·07	0·99
Dogmatism (D)	0·60	−0·03	0·04	−0·31	0·13	−0·16	0·70
Ethnocentrism (E)	0·55	0·14	−0·22	−0·16	0·12	−0·09	0·51
Job dissatisfaction (JD)	−0·45	−0·06	0·02	−0·12	0·23	0·25	0·67
Conversion	0·40	−0·27	−0·20	0·31	−0·00	0·03	0·63
Role conflict	−0·22	−0·14	0·03	0·30	−0·03	0·30	0·68
Percent of total variance in factor	34·3%	9·5%	5·9%	5·3%	4·5%	4·3%	
Cumulative percentage of variance in factors	34·3%	43·9%	49·7%	55·1%	59·5%	63·8%	
Communalities estimate for 13 factors (estimated by interative sums of squares)							81·6%

*The analysis is based on a matrix which included all the items of the theological scale. The ThC scale loaded more highly than any single belief item on Factor I, supporting the internal consistency of the scale. Highest loading items on Factor I were concerned with the miracle of changing water to wine (0·83), the virgin birth (−0·76 and 0·71), hell (−0·68 and 0·68), miracles as pre-scientific explanations (−0·67), individual salvation (0·64) and the physical return of Christ (0·62). Items concerning the physical resurrection of Jesus, Bible authority, church doctrine, and Holy Spirit versus natural wisdom also loaded above 0·50. All items in the scale loaded in the same direction on Factor I.

To answer this question a further factor analysis including forty-seven variables was carried out. This time the limit on the number of factors to be extracted was taken as the number of eigenvalues greater than unity. By this procedure thirteen factors were extracted, accounting for 81·57 per cent of variance. The first six factors contained 63·8 per cent of total variance. Factor I remained clearly the major factor, containing 34·3 per cent of the variance. Inspection of the communalities for the variables reported in Table VIII shows that a satisfactory amount of variance on discrete scales has been extracted by the factors. This further analysis suggests a unifactor basis of conservatism for religious, social, personal and cognitive-affective traits. Theological and general conservatism are the most salient components and are opposed to the ego-independence of the I-scale. A protective function for conservatism is further indicated by its associations with the self-insulation of dogmatism, the out-group prejudices of ethnocentrism, and the institutional identification suggested by the higher job satisfaction and lower role conflict within the factor.

Both orthogonal and oblique rotations to thirteen factors were also inspected, but neither obtained more independence of variables than the principal components analysis, and the resulting factors were less meaningful. The principal component solution was therefore accepted as evidence for a general factor of conservatism with several minor factors cutting across it, namely: (II) Inner support (−); (III) Ethnocentrism (−); (IV) Open-mindedness, growth into belief, and role conflict; (V) Age (a specific factor); and (VI) Role conflict (−). The almost complete absence of belief items in the "self-actualizing" or inner support factor (II) suggests that although conservative belief runs counter to self-actualizing tendencies, self-actualizing tendencies do not necessarily predict liberal beliefs. Most of the variance on the I-scale is in Factor I, however, and is thus dependent upon conservatism. Although not included in the factor analysis, ThL and T.O.I. may be assumed to belong within Factor I (see correlations of general C with the three theological scales in Table II).

VI. Conclusions

On his own report, the religiously conservative minister typically falls far short of personality freedom. This clear finding may be seen as contrasting with the claims made by fundamentalists such as Billy Graham for the advantages of a conservative religious commitment. It appears that the "abundant life" or, in psychological terms, greater self-extension, is more likely to be found in the theological liberal than in the theological conservative within a committed religious sample. (It should be recognized, however, that the *content* of conservative belief may be less important than the fact that these beliefs represent conformity. Thus in another sample, conformity to a liberal party line may well be found to correlate with prejudice and general conformity).

As suggested earlier, it is reasonable to suppose that the group of subjects in the present study would have an "intrinsic" rather than "extrinsic" orientation to religion (Allport, 1966; Allport and Ross, 1967). With reasonable control over this factor, it has been shown that conservatism, dogmatism, ethnocentrism and non-self-actualization fall on a common dimension with theological conservatism, supporting Wilson's (1970) identification of a "general factor of conservatism".

This study, of course, has been conducted within the framework of one Protestant denomination only. (An additional study is at present being conducted using a carefully selected sample of Catholic clergy and ministers of the four Protestant denominations in New Zealand which are negotiating for union—Webster and Mullan, in preparation). Nevertheless, the pervasiveness of the conservatism factor throughout personality, beliefs and attitudes as shown in this study suggests a mjaor variable in life-style which goes far beyond the limited and unrepresentative sample from which responses were obtained.

References

Adorno, T. W., Frenkel-Brunswick, E., Levinson, D. J. and Sanford, R. N. (1950). "The Authoritarian Personality." Harper, New York.

Allen, R. O. and Spilka, B. (1967). Committed and consensual religion: a specification of religion-prejudice relationships. *J. sci. Stud. Religion*, 6, 191–206.

Allport, G. (1961). "Pattern and Growth in Personality." Wiley, New York.

Allport, G. (1966). The religious context of prejudice. *J. sci. Stud. Religion*, 5 448–451.

Allport, G. and Ross, J. M. (1967). Personal religious orientation and prejudice. *J. Personality soc. Psychol.* 5, 432–443.

Beswick, D. G. and Hills, M. D. (1969). An Australian Ethnocentrism Scale. *Aust. J. Psychol.* 21, 211–225.

Brown, L. B. (1962). A study of religious beliefs. *Br. J. Psychol.* 53, 259–272.

Brown, L. B. (1966). The structure of religious belief. *J. sci. Stud. Religion*, 5, 257–272.

Cooley, W. W. and Lohnes, P. R. (1971). "Multivariate Data Analysis." Wiley, New York.

Crano, W. R. (1970). Personal communication to G. D. Wilson 1968, reported in Wilson and Patterson. (1970).

Cryns, A. G. (1970). Dogmatism of Catholic clergy and ex-clergy: a study of ministerial role perseverance and open-mindedness. *J. sci. Stud. Religion.* 9, 239–243.

Dittes, J. E. (1967). Comment. *J. sci. Stud. Religion.* 6, 235.

Dittes, J. E. (1969). Psychology of religion. In "Handbook of Social Psychology". (Lindsay, G. and Aronson, E. , eds.). 2nd edtn., vol 5: 602–659. Addison-Wesley, Reading, Mass.

Edwards, A. (1954). "Edwards Personal Preference Schedule Manual." The Psychological Corporation, New York.

Erikson, E. (1963). "Human Strength and the Cycle of Generations." Unpublished paper, Syracuse University.

Fromm, E. (1964). "The Heart of Man: Its Genius for Good and Evil." Harper and Row, New York.

Fruchter, B. J. (1954). "Introduction to Factor Analysis." Van Nostrand, New York.

Gorsuch, R. L. and McFarland, S. G. (1972). Single *vs.* multiple-item scales for measuring religious values. *J. sci. Stud. Religion.* 11, 53–64.

Jourard, S. (1964). "The Transparent Self." Van Nostrand, Princeton, N.J.

Kaplan, M. and Singer, E. (1963). Dogmatism and sensory alienation: an empirical investigation. *J. consult. Psychol.* **25**, 6, 486–491.

Kildahl, J. P. (1958). Personality correlates of sudden religious converts contrasted with persons of gradual religious development. *Diss. Abstr.* **18**, 2210–2211.

Kilpatrick, D. G., Sutker, L. W. and Sutker, Patricia B. (1970). Dogmatism, religion and religiosity, a review and re-evaluation. *Psychol. Rep.* **26**, 15–22.

Maslow, A. H. (1954). "Motivation and Personality." Harper, New York.

Maslow, A. H. (1962). "Toward a Psychology of Being." Van Nostrand, Princeton, N.J.

Olson, P. K. (1964). Correlation matrix with optional factor analysis and rotation of factors. New York: IBM 1620 Users Group Program.

O'Reilly, C. T. and O'Reilly, E. J. (1954). Religious beliefs of Catholic college students and their attitudes toward minorities. *J. abnorm. soc. Psychol.* **49**, 378–380.

Ranck, J. (1955). Religious conservatism-liberalism and mental health. In "The Minister's Own Mental Health." (Oates, W. E., ed.). Channel Press, New York.

Rogers, C. (1961). "On Becoming a Person." Boston. Houghton Mifflin Co.

Rokeach, M. (1960). "The Open and Closed Mind." Basic Books, New York.

Shostrom, E. (1963). "A Manual for the Personal Orientation Inventory." San Diego: Educational and Industrial Testing Service.

Stanley, G. (1963a). Personality and attitude characteristics of fundamentalist theological students. *Aust. J. Psychol.* **15**, 121–123.

Stanley, G. (1963b). Personality and attitude characteristics of fundamentalist university students. *Aust. J. Psychol.* **15**, 199–200.

Stanley, G. (1964). Personality and attitude correlates of religious conversion. *J. sci. Stud. Religion*, **4**, 60–63.

Stewart, R. A. C. and Webster, A. C. (1970). Scale for theological conservatism, and its personality correlates. *Percept. Mot. Skills.* **30**, 867–870.

Webster, A. C. (1966). "Patterns and Relations of Dogmatism, Mental Health and Psychological Health in Selected Religious Groups." Unpublished doctoral dissertation. Syracuse University.

Webster, A. C. (1968). "The Standardization of a Measure of Self-Actualization." Unpublished report, Massey University, N.Z.

Webster, A. C. and Mullan, D. S. "The New Zealand Ministry Study." Sponsored by the New Zealand National Council of Churches. In peparation.

Webster, A. C. and Stewart, R. A. C. (1969). Psychological attitudes and beliefs of ministers. *Anvil: A Baptist Quarterly*, **1**, 11–17.

Wilson, G. D. and Patterson, J. R. (1968). A new measure of conservatism. *Br. J. soc. clin. Psychol.* **7**, 264–269.

Wilson, G. D. and Patterson, J. R. (1960). "Manual for the Conservatism Scale." N.F.E.R. Publishing Co., Windsor, England.

Wilson, G. D. (1970). Is there a general factor in social attitudes? Evidence from a factor analysis of the conservatism scale. *Br. J. soc. clin. Psychol.* **9**, 101–107.

Conservatism and Superstitious Behaviour*

9

ROGER BOSHIER

University of Auckland, New Zealand

I. Introduction

Superstition, a "somewhat odd and esoteric topic" (Jahoda, 1969), has not been taken seriously by attitude researchers. However, despite the fact most people appear shamefaced and deny behaving in a superstitious manner when asked by an interviewer, one person in six is reputed to believe in ghosts, one in four are uncertain as to whether ghosts exist and one in fourteen say they have actually seen or heard a ghost. Citing results from the few available surveys on superstition, Jahoda notes that one English person in three has been to a fortune-teller, one person in ten believes they have a lucky number, and whilst "astrology" is not widely understood, about two-thirds of the adult population read their horoscope at least occasionally.

In New Zealand, urbanization has eroded traditional Maori beliefs in supernatural forces although both casual observation and empirical research (Clark *et al.,* 1971) suggests there has been a resurgence of interest

*Thanks are due to David Harre of N.Z.B.C. Northern Television, and the following interviewers—Christine Flinn, Jenny Boshier, Robyn Wilson, Elizabeth Thom, Robert Hancock, John Groom, Patricia Keiller, Vivian Theobald, Cheryl Brown, Douglas Pratt, Henry Heald.

in the occult, particularly among (primarily drug-taking) university students.

The antiquity of superstitious observances and beliefs concerning the "tohunga" in early New Zealand society, and witches and sorcerers else-where, coupled with the observance of superstitions in "civilized" societies, suggests superstition is a fruitful field for psychological study.

Examination of the scant literature on the subject impels one to the view that superstitious behaviours serve some psychological function. Jahoda goes so far as to suggest that superstition "far from being odd and abnormal . . . is in fact intimately bound up with our fundamental modes of thinking, feeling and generally responding to our environment". (1969, p. 146). It is therefore likely that people can be ordered in terms of how much superstitious behaviour they exhibit. It is also likely that superstition does not appear in vacuo but is related to other personality variables.

According to the "Authoritarian Personality" researchers (Adorno *et al.*, 1950) superstition was a central component of the highly conservative fascistic type person. This notion undoubtedly stemmed from Freud's somewhat circular explanation for superstitious behaviour whereby a cruel thought or death wish against oneself or another person arouses guilt which leads to an expectation of punishment manifesting itself as a super-stitious notion of misfortune. According to Adorno *et al.* superstitiousness "indicates a tendency to shift responsibility from the individual onto outside forces beyond his control; it indicates that the ego might already have 'given up', that is to say, renounced the idea that it might determine the individual's fate by overcoming external forces" (p. 236).

However, close examination of the "Authoritarian Personality" reveals an absence of empirical evidence supporting the above proposition. Adorno and his colleagues discuss what they considered are the antecedents of superstitious behaviour, and its relationship to anti-scientific thinking, illustrating with excerpts from case history interviews. However, item or factor scores derived from "superstition" items are not related to whole F-Scale or sub-scale scores. Nor was any alternative statistical analysis attempted.

The aim of the present sudy was to investigate the hypothesized rela-tionship between conservatism and superstition utilizing an unobtrusive behavioural measure of superstition.

II. Measurement

The constructors of the Conservatism Scale included items such as "horoscopes" and "inborn conscience" to tap superstition. Factor analysis of the C-Scale with oblique rotation (Boshier, 1972) revealed a second-order "superstition" and a third-order "superstitious retribution" factor. Bagley *et al.* (1970) have shown that in its unrotated form the C-Scale measures a "general conservation factor" with positive loadings on most items which account for a percentage of variance in excess of that account-ed for by other factors. However, the superstition items identified by Boshier's (1972) rotation made only a minor contribution to the unrotated "general" conservatism factor (e.g. "horoscopes" loaded only 0·10 in Wilson's London sample, 0·02 in Bagley's Dutch sample, and 0·03 in Boshier's New Zealand sample) so the question of whether superstition is a central component of conservatism is as yet unresolved. The C-Scale used in this study was modified so as to eliminate the items which directly tapped superstitious beliefs.

In developing a measure of superstition an effort was made to avoid simply correlating pencil-and-paper measures (because of the possibility that some people might express disbelief in superstitious ideas but *behave*, perhaps unconsciously, in a superstitious manner) by setting up a situation where actual superstitious behaviour could be measured.

Prior to the actual study of a checklist of behaviours commonly asso-ciated with the onset of bad luck or misfortune was assembled. This check-list contained such things as "breaking a mirror", "spilling salt" (without subsequently throwing some over one's shoulder), a black cat crossing one's path, wearing green, and walking under a ladder. A brief investiga-tion with thirty-eight pedestrians drawn at random in Auckland City, revealed that the behaviour associated with "bad luck" and known (but not necessarily believed) by nearly all interviewees, was walking under a ladder.

According to Radford (1947), this superstition has its origins in Holland where walking under a ladder was associated with being hanged. A ladder against a wall also forms a triangle which represents the Trinity and to defy it is to play into the hands of evil. In some countries, bad luck evoked by walking under a ladder, can be averted if the hapless person crosses two fingers until he sees a dog! The ladder superstition is also reputed to be allied with the "head taboo" found in South East Asia. The Thais for instance, consider a spirit called Khuan to reside in the head; the Burmese regard it as an indignity to have anything over their heads, whilst Cam-bodians will not walk beneath suspended objects. Radford concludes that ladder superstitions in most countries are allied to religious belief, caution, and the necessity of keeping the head unfouled.

Most people having heard of the ladder superstition, it was decided to explore the relationship between conservatism and superstition by erecting a ladder in a city street and administering the modified C-Scale to a sample of persons walking around and a sample of persons walking under it.

III. Method

Prior to the experiment, the density of pedestrian traffic in several Auckland mid-city streets was observed. These observations, coupled with what was already known about the average time taken to complete a C-Scale, suggested that the interviewers available for the experiment could be expected to interview every fifth person walking under and every fifth person walking round a ladder placed against a wall in High Street, Auckland, between the hours of 1·15–2.30 p.m. on a Thursday. The assistance of Northern Television was obtained in order to film the behaviour of pedestrians when confronted by an unoccupied ladder in the street.

On the day of the experiment a sixteen foot wooden extension ladder was placed against a wall. For two hours a concealed assistant observed and recorded pedestrian behaviour, adjusting the position of the ladder from time to time, until 50 per cent of pedestrian traffic from one direction was going under, and 50 per cent was going round the ladder. During the actual experiment the foot of the ladder was eighteen inches from the gutter but four feet from the wall against which it rested. Pedestrians had a clear view of the ladder. Care was taken to remove extraneous ropes and other encumbrances from the immediate area so that approaching pedestrians would not feel physically endangered.

Interviewing took place between the times given above. Every fifth person walking under the ladder in a southerly direction and every fifth person walking round the ladder in a southerly direction was stopped and invited to take part in a "survey on social attitudes", in which respondents completed the C-Scale. The ladder was not mentioned (only one respondent asked whether the "survey" and the ladder were related). Television cameras recording pedestrian and interviewer behaviour were concealed on the opposite side of the road.

IV. Results

Mean C-scores, were calculated separately for different age and sex groups, for hypothesized high-S (round the ladder) and low-S (under the ladder) respondents. The approximate age and sex of the non-respondents was also noted as was the fact of their having walked under or round the ladder.

A. AGE AND SEX

C-scores showed their usual relationship to age and sex, except that men aged 30 years or more were more conservative than women of the same age (Table I). Whereas our male respondents were a fairly representative sample of Auckland men, a high proportion of the young women interviewed were office workers and therefore not representative. Since previous research has shown that clerical sales workers are more conservative than workers in other occupational categories (Boshier, 1972), this might have contributed to the finding that young women were more conservative than young men.

TABLE I

Mean Conservatism scores for different age and sex groups

	Men			Women			t	df
	N	M	S.D.	N	M	S.D.		
50–59	7	52·00	12·26	8	45·00	20·12	0·79	13
40–49	12	51·33	16·25	4	42·00	24·64	0·87	14
30–39	9	37·55	17·22	5	33·40	22·72	0·38	12
20–29	30	30·70	15·60	12	41·16	24·19	1·66	40
10–19	13	29·28	14·68	8	41·12	10·74	1·97*	19
Total	71	38·32	16·97	37	40·64	15·21		

$t > 1·72$, df $= 19$, $p < 0·05$

B. SUPERSTITION

Table II demonstrates that "young" people were more inclined to walk under the ladder than "old" people.

TABLE II

The relationship between age and superstitious behaviour (per cent by row in parenthesis).

Age	Total	High–S (around ladder)	Low–S (under ladder)
10–29 years	63	24 (40·00%)	39 (60·00%)
30–49 years	30	18 (60·00%)	12 (40·00%)
50–59 years	15	8 (53·33%)	7 (46·67%)
Total	108	50	58

$* x^2 = 11·50$; df $= 2$, $p < 0·0005$ (one-tailed test)

Of the 108 respondents interviewed fifty-eight walked under (low-S condition) and fifty walked around (high-S condition) the ladder. The fifty-eight low-S respondents had a mean C-score of 38·08 (S.D. 16·74), while the high-S group had a mean C-score of 37·58 (S.D. 16·87). This difference was non-significant so at first glance there seemed to be no relationship between the two variables under study. However, as previous research has demonstrated the powerful effect of age on C-scores, an overall population average cannot be regarded as meaningful and it was decided to analyse the "under" and "around" respondents by age. As expected this revealed a different picture (Fig. 1).

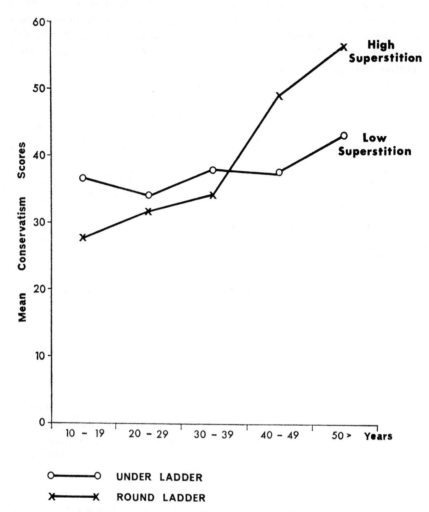

Fig. 1. Main C-scores at various age levels for SS walking round the ladder (high-S) and under (low-S).

In the younger age groups conservatism and superstition were not significantly related, but among persons over the age of 40 years the expected effect appears. The effect was most apparent in 50–59 year olds. The persons in this age group passing under the ladder had a mean C-score of 43·00 (S.D. 9·05) whilst the eight 50–59 year olds passing around the ladder had a mean C-score of 56·00 (S.D. 19·79). The difference (t = 1·59, df $= 13$, $0.05 < p < 0.1$) suggests that the conservatism superstition relationship is strongest in older people.

The unexpected result involving 10–29 year olds, that persons passing under the ladder had a higher mean C-score (M $= 36.53$, S.D. 12.06) than persons passing around the ladder (M $= 27.5$, S.D. 15.29) is puzzling, even though the difference is not statistically significant (t $= 1.39$, df $= 17$).

C. NON-RESPONSE

McClosky (1958) claims that "conservatism is not the doctrine of the intellectual élite or of the more intelligent segments of the population, but the reverse. By every measure available to us, conservative beliefs are found most frequently among the uninformed, the poorly educated, and ... the less intelligent" (p. 35). McClosky also claims that conservative postures are characteristic of social isolates, people who think poorly of themselves, "who are submissive, timid and wanting in confidence" (p. 37). McClosky's propositional statement type measure of conservatism is vulnerable to the same criticisms as those levelled at the F-scale, but his results are partly born out by Boshier's (1969) linking of conservatism with low self esteem (as measured by the Bills Index of Adjustment and Values) and Patterson and Wilson's (1969) finding that conservatives, more than liberals, prefer to remain anonymous when filling in the C-Scale. Bearing in mind the fact that non-respondents in survey research are known to come in disproportionate numbers from the poorly educated and depressed segments of society, it was decided to examine whether non-respondents in the present study (people who refused to complete the C-Scale) were more or less inclined than respondents to walk around the ladder (high-S condition).

Interviewers were accordingly instructed to note the sex and approximate age of non-respondents and whether or not they walked under or around the ladder. Of the thirty-five non-respondents 60 per cent walked around the ladder, compared to 45.81 per cent of respondents. The same tendency applied for both men and women.

Thus, non-respondents emerge as being more inclined to behave in a superstitious manner than respondents, although the relationships presented in Table III fail to reach the 0.05 level of significance. Survey researchers could now alert themselves to the possibility of non-respondents being more superstitious than respondents, as well as more conservative (Patterson and Wilson, 1969). Had the non-respondents actually completed the C-Scale it is likely that their scores would have significantly lifted the overall C-Scale mean for respondents walking around the ladder, giving further credence to Adorno's proposition concerning conservatism and superstition.

TABLE III

The relationship between superstitious behaviour and non-response (per cent by column in parenthesis)

| | Non respondents | | | Respondents | | |
	Total (%)	Men (%)	Women (%)	Total (%)	Men (%)	Women (%)
Round Ladder	21 (60·00)‡	12 (63·15)*	9 (56·25)†	50 (45·81)	37 (50·00)	13 (50·00)
Under Ladder	14 (40·00)	7 (36·85)	7 (43·75)	58 (54·13)	37 (50·00)	21 (60·00)
Total	35 (100·00)	19 (100·00)	16 (100·00)	108 (100·00)	74 (100·00)	34 (100·00)

*Men Non-Respondents compared with Men Respondents, $\chi^2 = 1.05$.
†Women Non-Respondents compared with Women Respondents, $\chi^2 = 1.43$.
‡Total Non-Respondents compared with total Respondents, $\chi^2 = 1.98$.

V. Conclusion

Considering the question of why conservatives aged over 40 years are more superstitious than liberals of the same age, it may be conjectured that avoiding a ladder is a realistic response based on past experience. In behaviouristic terms, avoiding ladders may start with accidental operant or secondary reinforcement (people and things fall off ladders, sometimes on to other people!). It is likely that ladder-avoidance starts as an empty gesture stemming from childhood superstition. Once a person starts avoiding ladders, if "bad luck" does not occur, ladder-avoidance behaviour is reinforced. If "bad luck" does occur it is easily seen as contingent upon other factors. (Avoidance behaviour would also be sustained by the widespread nature of the belief concerning ladders). If ladder-avoidance behaviour has been positively reinforced it is worth maintaining because it can do no harm! The same mechanism was seen during the Second World War when the protective superstitions employed by men in combat were often explained by the notion that there "might be something in it". Thus, articles of clothing or equipment associated with some previous experience of escape from danger were religiously carried into subsequent battles. Conservatives, almost by definition, should be more cautious than liberals when confronted by a ladder on a wall.

The fact that among younger respondents conservatism and superstition were not related presents two possibilities. The first is that among young people the hypothesized relationship between conservatism and superstition simply does not exist. The second is that superstition is as prevalent among the young as the old, and related to conservatism as hypothesized, but that ladder-avoidance is not a measure of superstition appropriate for young people. The research of Clark et al. (1971) into beliefs concerning occult and psychic phenomena suggests that superstition among young people takes new forms in which ladder-avoidance is irrelevant and old-fashioned. In this regard, the rejection of technology and intellectual endeavour by youthful "counter culture" groups may reflect the fact that superstitious behaviour is now a concomitant of liberalism rather than conservatism. Such a shift is implied in Kenniston's (1968) typology which distinguishes intellectual, entrepreneurial "activist" youth from drop-out drug-oriented and superstitious "alienated" youth.

Whilst no data concerning family background were collected, other C-scale studies have shown that old conservatives are more inclined towards fundamentalist religious belief than old liberals (Boshier and Pratt, 1972), that conservative parents tend to nurture conservative children (see Chapter 14) and use harsher and more punitive child-rearing methods than liberal parents (Boshier and Izard, 1972). It is thus probable that old conservative respondents came from more tyrannical home backgrounds than old liberals. Jahoda (1969) notes that a home background where discipline is relatively harsh and threatening, where parents exercise rigid control and are not to be questioned, is consistent with the development of a "belief that one's fate is in the hands of unknown external powers, governed by forces over which one has no control" (p. 139).

The above explanation is consistent with findings concerning "external" control of reinforcement: (Rotter, 1966; Lefcourt, 1966) and the ideas of life-cycle theorists. Neugarten (1963) for instance, notes that "in young adulthood, the thrust is towards the outer world, and towards mastery of the environment. In middle age, there comes a re-alignment and restructuring of ego processes and to the extent to which these processes become conscious a re-examination of the self. In old age there is a turning inward, a withdrawal of interest from the outer world and a new preoccupation with the inner world", accompanied by a resurgence of interest in religion, supernatural forces, presumably superstitious belief, and, as shown in Table II, superstitious behaviour.

Many of those passing around the ladder put themselves to considerable inconvenience in order to avoid going under the ladder. During the peak pedestrian traffic period, people were lining up on either side of the ladder to avoid passing under it. Our results were undoubtedly contaminated by chance effects e.g. a person whose "ladder-approach" behaviour indicated he would pass under was sometimes obstructed by a person passing under from the other direction and, as a consequence, he would walk around the ladder. The reverse effect seemed less frequent, a "conservative" intending to pass round the ladder, on being obstructed by a person passing round it from the other direction, was more inclined to wait until the way was clear and then walk around the ladder. In only a few instances did a person whose behaviour immediately prior to the ladder suggest that he would be a "superstitious" respondent and whose course was impeded, take the "risk" and pass under the ladder. To many, particularly young people, the ladder was of no consequence and they went under or around depending upon what was most convenient at the moment they reached it. On the other hand, some (generally older people) saw the ladder at a distance and adjusted their course so as to avoid passing beneath it. These observations are subjective (although the behaviour on which they were based is recorded on film) but they suggest that future research utilizing ladder-avoidance as a measure of superstition might attempt to distinguish between chance and deliberate avoidance behaviour. Selective sampling of persons whose behaviour suggests that they deliberately avoided the ladder, or manipulation of the difficulty required to be surmounted in order to avoid the "bad luck" condition, should sharpen relationships under study.

Whilst the present age-related findings only partly support the propositions of Adorno *et al.* concerning the conservatism/superstition relationship, they point to several possible research leads. Just as important is the demonstration that personality researchers can measure *behaviour*.

References

Adorno, R. W., Frenkel-Brunswik, E., Levinson, D. J. and Sanford, N. (1950). "The Authoritarian Personality." Harper and Row, New York.

Bagley, C., Wilson, G. D. and Boshier, R. W. (1970). The Conservatism scale; a factor structure comparison of English, Dutch, and New Zealand samples. *J. soc. Psychol.* **81**, 267–268.

Boshier, R. W. (1972). To rotate or not to rotate: the question of the Conservatism Scale. *Br. J. soc. clin. Psychol.* 1972, **11**, 313–323.

Boshier, R. W. (1969). The relationship between self concept and conservatism. *J. soc. Psychol.* **33**, 139–141.

Boshier, R. W. and Izard, A. (1972). Do conservative parents use harsh child-rearing practices? *Psychol. Repts.* **31**, 734.

Boshier, R. W. and Pratt, D. (1972). Conservatism and religious orthodoxy. Unpublished MS, University of Auckland.

Boshier, R. W. and Thom, E. (1973). Do conservative parents nurture conservative children? *Soc. Behaviour and Personality* (in press).

Clark, J. R., Bryan, G. and Greene, R. L. (1971). An occult phenomena scale with personality correlates of occult belief. Paper presented to the *N.Z. Psychol. Soc.* Christchurch.

Jahoda, G. (1969). "The Psychology of Superstition." Allen Lane, London.

Lefcourt, H. M. (1966). Internal versus external control: a review. *Psychol. Bull.* **65**, 206–220.

McClosky, H. (1958). Conservatism and personality. *Am. pol. Sci. Rev.* **52**, 27–45.

Neugarten, B. (1963). Personality changes during the adult years. In "Psychological Backgrounds of Adult Education". (Kuhlen, R. G., ed.). Centre for the Study of Liberal Education for Adults.

Patterson, J. R. and Wilson, G. D. (1969). Anonymity, occupation and conservatism, *J. soc. Psychol.* **78**, 263–266.

Radford, E. and M. A. (1947). "Encyclopedia of Superstitions." Rider and Co., London.

Rotter, J. B. (1966). Generalized expectancies for internal versus external control of reinforcement. *Psych. Monogr.* **80**, No. 1.

Wilson, G. D. and Patterson, J. R. (1970). "Manual for the Conservatism Scale." N.F.E.R. Publishing Co., Windsor, England.

10 Conservatism and Aesthetic Judgments

JOHN R. PATTERSON

University of Otago, New Zealand

I. Introduction

For a variety of reasons one is led to assert that the study of C-Scale status with respect to parameters of aesthetic judgments should be particularly enlightening.

As with most C-Scale studies reported in this volume, it affords one the opportunity to establish whether an appropriate assessment of that general attitudinal factor, customarily labelled "conservatism", will facilitate prediction of behaviour in contexts remote from that of the assessment. But in choosing actual art objects (here, reproduced paintings) as the array of stimulus instances to be judged, the experimenter should also enhance both the potential generality and interest of his findings.

That one should experimentally concern oneself with stimulus input that is representative of the "stuff" out of which most real-life judgments are formed has been persuasively argued by Brunswik (1947). Brunswik takes the reasonable position that results with "ecological validity" may be obtained only by the use of experimental materials drawn from, and hence representative of, the real situations to which one wishes to generalize. If the results obtained in the usual experiment are "significant" in the usual sense, one has some specifiable degree of confidence that they are generalizable to people other than those used as subjects; but the degree to which they are generalizable to new stimuli remains a matter of conjecture. Yet the latter kind of generalization is no less important than the former.

G

Experimental stimuli, traditionally kept as close as possible to the top of the S-R hierarchy of clearness, simplicity and univocality, bear little apparent relation to their real-life counterparts. So, for instance, the behaviour of experimental subjects responding to pairs of dots, as varied by Imai and Garner (1965) in distance, orientation and position, is likely to be qualitatively removed from their producing and utilizing judgmental categories that bear upon stimuli as complex as (say) Seurat's *An Afternoon at La Grande Jatte*. Admittedly, to satisfactorily generalize from any experimental stimuli, one requires sampling from a parent population characterized by certain determinate statistical parameters. Decidedly short of this, but serving as an interim measure, is the present more or less arbitrary choice of artefacts that are genuine in the sense that they are stimuli which are consensually conceived of as works of art in the context of presentation.

Substantive foci of the present studies are dictated by the contentions that aesthetic stimuli provide tractable and pertinent means of imposing conditions of input complexity, and that conservatism is a significant determinant of how individual judges will process such rich sources of multivariate stimulus information. This second contention shall be evaluated more fully in the sequel but in essence it is that variations in C-Scale status are associated with a differential tendency to simplify input.

Empirical appraisal of this presumed tendency clearly requires that some at least of the experimental stimuli can be temporally, if not concurrently, processed with regard to many different attributes. Not only does a medley of dimensions and values typify many paintings but there is also the advantageous fact that these static visual objects are given in their perceptual entirety. Indeed, their creation may be represented as a pre-eminent concern with perceptible unity or form (Fry, 1920). This procedurally healthy state of affairs may be contrasted with the common use of interstitial stimuli in cognitive research. It is true that there has been some emancipation from a pervasive psychophysical tradition of unidimensional stimulus manipulation, but to ask one's subjects to (say) participate in a military game situation (e.g. Schroder *et al.*, 1967; Streufert *et al.*, 1965 is not to provide them with a comparably construable set of distal events. Having subjects report their person "perceptions" (Beach and Wertheimer, 1962; Dornbusch *et al.*, 1965) is likely to maximize the extraneous influences of memory and inference.

Concept identification studies (Schneider and Giambra, 1971) offer another approach to the problem of providing multivariate sources of stimulus information but here, too, aspects of the stimuli usually only serve as "cues" i.e. as bases for "going beyond" by inference, whereas, in the aesthetic domain they are likely to assume much more than momentary signal status. Indeed, sustained examination of the intrinsic perceptual quality of aesthetic stimuli is their virtual *raison d'etre*.

In so far as researchers are disposed to define attitudes in terms of affect (Wilson and Patterson, 1968), then it would seem that with regard to stimuli of this kind the influence of conservatism should be heightened. After all, the starting point of most aesthetic inquiry has been the conviction that the stimulus constitution of an art object is the outcome of evocative intent (Fechner, 1876; Seurat, 1870; Kandinsky, 1912; Klee, 1924) and, the functional dependence of affective responses upon aesthetic stimulus variables has been experimentally demonstrated (Lundholm, 1921; Guildford, 1934 and the following: Mouton and Helson, 1956; Schaie, 1961).

The foregoing would seem to constitute a good *a priori* case for pursuing the study of conservatism in the light of experimental aesthetics. It may surprise, then, that there are few such studies and that these scratch little more than the surface. This state of affairs is understandable in so far as experimental analyses of aesthetic behaviour have proceeded in the virtual absence of a specifiable environment and a tractable taxonomy. Multi-dimensional scaling techniques would seem to promise means of redress, however.

It has been claimed that experimental aesthetics can provide an experimental environment the complexity of which will do justice to the conceptual capacity of the average respondent. A clear corollary is that interindividual differences with respect to information-processing will be maximized in so far as the available input comprises stimuli that may be perceived in many ways. One obvious basis of comparison is the extent to which an individual's behavioural complexity matches that of the provided environment. The second study under present consideration (Patterson *et al.*, 1972) bears upon such a consideration. Wilson *et al.* (1973) may be seen to have pursued another point of comparison: the extent to which an individual's disposition to handle input varies according to the level of stimulus complexity *per se*.

It is not unnatural that one should look at the variable of conservatism as a prime source of interindividual differences in both these respects. The import of much of the copious empirical literature pertaining to the highly conservative person justifies the frequent characterization of him as a cognitively simple being. It is noteworthy, too, that in their extensive look at the cognitive processes underlying social, problem-solving situations, Schroder *et al.* (1967) found a negative correlation between F and Dogmatism scale values and those on their measures of integrative complexity. The precise motivating logic behind the studies under consideration here is somewhat different, however.

II. Preferred Complexity

Wilson *et al.* (1973) start with the proposition that a generalized fear of uncertainty is the psychological variable which accounts for the organization of social attitudes along a general factor of liberalism-conservatism. They assume that with respect to any stimulus event uncertainty is commensurate with the conceptual degrees of freedom the given situation allows; and, they hypothesize that with respect to art objects the more complex they are in this sense the more aversive they seem to conservatives and the more attractive they seem to liberals.

Their experimental stimuli comprised twenty slide reproductions of paintings such the subsets of five represented four *a priori* categories: simple-representational (SR); simple-abstract (SA); complex-representational (CR); and complex-abstract (CA). "Complexity" was defined as the number and concentration of different elements contained within a painting as conceptualized by an art expert. Each subject was asked to rate the individually presented paintings according to his personal preference.

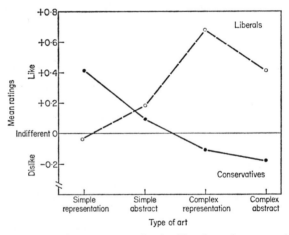

FIG. 1. Mean ratings on four art categories for liberals and conservatives. The four types of art are arranged in *a priori* order of stimulus uncertainty (From Wilson, *et al.*, 1973).

Mean like-dislike ratings for the four style-of-art quadrants are shown in Fig. 1. The groups labelled "liberal" and "conservative" were derived by splitting the thirty male and female Ss at the sample's median C-score (C-scores ranged from 11 to 57 with a median of 36·5). The group differences yielded significant t ratios ($p < 0.05$) for each category save SA. Correlational analysis revealed that the complexity dimension was the primary discriminator of the judgments of liberals and conservatives (r = −0·56, p < 0·01) rather than abstraction (r = −0·14, n.s.) The investigators concluded that these results "may be interpreted as providing support for the theory that conservatism represents a reaction against uncertainty, whether it be in terms of the alternatives in action that are available, or merely complexity and ambiguity in the environment to which the individual is exposed".

The Wilson *et al.* study is noteworthy in that it represents an attempt to test a proposition concerning the dynamics of conservatism in the context of *stimulus* uncertainty rather than at the *response* phase of behaviour. This is in keeping with Garner's (1970) plea that "if we want to understand how the organism processes information, we must be prepared to ask under what circumstances a particular form of processing is used. And one of the most important of these circumstances", says Garner, "has to do with the nature of the input itself. . . . For too long we have considered that a stimulus is a stimulus is a stimulus whose only function is to elicit behaviour. But all stimuli are not equivalent, and all information cannot be processed the same way."

The problem of the present study is that its circumstantial analysis is purely *a priori*. This is perfectly understandable in so far as the formidable complexity of most paintings would seem to render problematic the use of independent empirical operations to specify the properties ascribed to them. However, the lack of known commonality of dimension reference (between the art expert and Ss or across Ss) might be taken as an argument for the application of behaviourally derived, and analytically inferred, measures of subjective stimulus space. Be that as it may, the present study would seem to indicate the relevance of conservatism with respect to a respondent's preferred level of aesthetic complexity and, hence, the quality of his affective response.

III. Complexity of Process

Since Barron and Welsh (Barron, 1953) singled out the dimension of simplicity-complexity in relation to aesthetic preference, there has been a tendency (see reviewers Moyles *et al.*, 1969) to extend the variable to the intrapsychic domain. This is evident in the underlying rationale of the study just considered. Wilson *et al.* clearly do not view aesthetic preference as a consequence of stimulus properties alone but rather as a consequence of their being mediated by the "organismic" variable, conservatism. Patterson *et al.* (1972) have collected data in the expectation of finding such individual differences as might be determined by this presumed residuum of within person cognitive influence.

These investigators hypothesized that, in contradistinction to conservatives, liberals would (a) generate more dimensions in their conceptualization of complex stimuli (b) confer more equal information weight on such dimensions as are generated and (c) produce qualitatively different denotational reference in their dimensionality. In short they were asserting that the conservative person is cognitively "simple" in the sense of (say) the formulated type of information-processing system of Schroder *et al.* (1967). However, it was allowed that the notion of authoritarian liberals (Brown, 1968) constituted an argument for a curvilinear function. That is, an over-representation of cognitively simple persons among both the extremely high, and the extremely low, C-Scale population was considered possible.

Patterson *et al.* applied Coomb's nonmetric multidimensional unfolding procedures* to similarities judgments of reproduced paintings. Eighty-three New Zealand college students rated the overall similarity of paired combinations of seven such stimuli, and analyses of scale structure were separately computed for each individual subject.

C-Scale scores ranged from sixteen to sixty-seven with a median of 34·5 (the sample comprised fifty-two males and thirty-one females, aged between 16 and 19 years). To statistically appraise their experimental hypotheses, the investigators trichotomised this subject sample according to rank of respondents' C-scores. In addition, a separate, *ad hoc* measure of cognitive complexity was provided by responses to author White's "square-completion test". This test entails subjective estimation of the number of serially presented elemental bits (some uncued pseudo as well as those veridical) required to complete a previously presented square stimulus.

Contrary to expectation, Patterson *et al.* found no evidence to suggest that liberals and conservatives do not have at their disposal similarly extensive arrays of psychological dimensions for characterizing visual aesthetic stimuli, i.e. they found no significant difference in the number of dimensional units of information utilized by High and Low C-Scale scorers ($t = 0.44$; 53 df). Nor did these investigators find any differential tendency to unequally weight the available dimensional bases of response ($t = 0.45$; 53 df). Trend for the Medium scorers was comparable in both respects. Corroborating these findings was that of a modest correlation ratio value of 0·26 for estimated point of square completion as a function of respondent's C-Scale status.

The general conclusion would seem to be that, on the data of this study and in the present context, there are no grounds for contending that conservatives are intra-psychologically simpler respondents who, through want of cognitive capacity, conceive of their environment in terms of fewer, and less equably considered, bases of response than do more

---

*"Nonmetric multidimensional psychophysics is defined as the problem of constructing a stimulus space from order relations on interpoint distances, the solution being in the form of a set of simple orders," (Coombs, 1964).

complex counterparts. It may be noted in passing, that the average number of employed dimensions across all eighty-five judges was 1·92. This value is remarkable both for its constancy across Ss and for its modest size. No subject, liberal or conservative, employed more than three dimensions, and the standard deviation was only 0·35 of a dimensional unit. This is in accord with recent multidimensional scaling findings with respect to judgments in other stimulus domains. As Fenker and Brown (1969) have explicitly suggested, the consistency of these findings implies the operation of a geometrical analogue to Miller's magic number seven. However, the present assumption of an overall impoverishment of response space is subject to the provisos (1) that the logic of multidimensional scaling procedure is such that it cannot be taken as a necessarily exhaustive account of the task response space and (2) that experimental subjects may, in any case, have only utilized some specific subset of a presumably concept space. The possibility of the predicted liberal-conservative differences cannot be unconditionally excluded, therefore.

In so far as a liberal preference for complexity (Wilson *et al.*) does not seem to betoken a corresponding differential complexity of judgmental process, it would appear that the aesthetic judgments of liberals and conservatives entail differences in affective disposition *per se*. Wilson *et al.* imply this when they characterize conservative responses to complex art works as "aversive".

Consistent with this is the present study's evidence of a strong association between conservatism and the affectivity elicited by the stimuli. Patterson *et al.* found (see Table I) that all but two members of the experimental stimulus set elicited significant (at $p < 0.05$ level) t ratios with respect to the differences in like-dislike ratings accorded them by High and Low C-Scale scorers (expanding the binomial indicates that the chance probability of this occurrence is less than 0·0001). It is noteworthy that those

TABLE I

Mean like (7)—dislike (1) ratings accorded the stimuli by High, Medium and Low C-Scale scorers.

Stimuli*	A	B	C	D	E	F	G
High C Ss	1·20	2·14	3·70	2·10	4·14	4·25	3·65
Medium C Ss	1·32	3·06	3·82	2·28	3·82	3·00	3·72
Low C Ss	2·32	3·14	2·91	2·34	2·86	2·70	5·04
p < High/Low t's	0·05	0·05	n.s.	n.s.	0·05	0·01	0·01

*A—*Painting* (1957), Pierre Soulages; B—*Snob Party at the Princesse's* (1944), Joan Miro; C—*Young Woman*, Georges Rouault; D—*Pillars and Crosses* (1931), Paul Klee; E—*American Gothic* (1930), Grant Wood; F—*The Balcony* (1868), Edouard Manet; G—*Woman at a Mirror* (1932), Pablo Picasso.

paintings most preferred by the High C-Scale scorers (Manet's and Wood's) are both the most representational and among the least modern of the art works constituting the experimental set. Picasso's, the preferred painting of Low C-Scale scorers, contrasts in its relative abstraction and apparent recency of origin.

Perhaps more serendipitous is the investigators' further observation that High C-Scale scorers show an appreciably greater susceptibility to hedonic intrusion in their use of the similarity rating scale. Procedural constraints were meant to ensure that the latter should entail subjects cognizing only upon what they deemed to be the objective stimulus reference. However, for each subject, the experimenters rated the stimulus pairs in terms of a preference ordering inferentially derived from the given single stimulus like-dislike ratings, and correlations of these with the ostensive similarities ratings in hand were computed. Transformed into Fisher's z function, the resulting r's for High and Low C-Scale scorers were found to significantly ($p < 0.01$) differ (t = 3.90; 53 df). Findings of this kind are consistent with, if not confirmatory of, the present contention that liberals and conservatives differ not so much in the information-processing means they have at their disposal as in their emotively toned disposition to deal with some kinds of input rather than others.

Patterson *et al.* found some substantiation of their third hypothesis. Table II sets out differences in the nature of emergent dimensionality.

TABLE II

Percentage of each subject group employing the major analytically-derived dimensions.

Dimension label	Low C Ss	Medium C Ss	High C Ss
Extra-pictorial reference	39·3	64·3	70·4
Chromaticity	17·9	42·9	22·2
Age of painting	42·9	3·6	22·2
Hard-soft edge-ness	10·7	14·3	37·0
Realism–abstraction	21·4	3·6	18·5
Warm hues—Cold hues	14·3	25·0	7·4
Brightness—darkness	10·7	21·4	7·4

For instance, it can be seen that, relative to respondents of either extreme, Medium C-Scale scorers show an apparently greater tendency to view paintings in terms of dimensionalized aspects of colour treatment. Whereas a majority (70·4 per cent) of High C-Scale scorers based their similarity judgments to some extent on a dimension interpretable as meaningfulness (the degree of extra-pictorial reference evident in the stimuli in question), this was true of less than half as many Low C-Scale counterparts. On the other hand, only 22·2 per cent of High C-Scale respondents reacted to the relative contemporaneity of the stimulus set as against 42·9 per cent of the

Low C-Scale scorers. Again, while the relative "soft-hard edge-ness" ascribable to the stimulus paintings appeared to be a reactionary basis for 37 per cent of High C-Scale scorers, less than a third as many of the opposing group of respondents reacted to the same. The implication is that the "cognitive maps" utilized by liberals and conservatives tend to differ in their qualitative content if not in their discriminatory fineness or completeness.

IV. Some Propositions Concerning Dimension "Criteriality"

In the light of the studies just considered, there appears to be little doubt that preferred simplicity is a fundamental psychological accompaniment of tendencies towards conservatism. It would seem profitable to speculate upon the way in which such input preferences materialize themselves in the qualitatively opposed aesthetic—and perhaps most affective—judgments of liberals and conservatives. A pertinent context is provided by the problem of dimension "criteriality".

Everyday observation suggests that many people habitually compare and evaluate art objects on some bases more than upon others and that they may be characterized according to this recurring order of reference. One person may respond to paintings typically in terms of their verisimilitude and, in a decreasingly lesser extent, their subject, colour and composition; with another, order in this respect might be reversed; while in a third case, it might be ascribed to a quite different set of bases (say) spatial representation, chiaroscuro, calligraphy and texture. Patterson et al. s' experimental observations are consonant with these assertions. The problem is to explain such variation in the extent of dimensional contribution to total affective response.

A collation of otherwise diverse research studies convinced Patterson (1969) that a likely determinant of this observed preference for dimensional bases of response, whether these are stimulus-bound or conceptually-derived or both, is the relative ease of judgment associated with such bases. In fact, Patterson's experimental findings supported his contention that such criterial status is not simply a function of increasing ease of dimension judgment but rather the discrepancy of the same from a presumed prevailing norm or adaptation level (Helson, 1964) of judgmental ease. The present argument is that liberals and conservatives will be found to be characterized by a respectively positive and negative asymmetry of such functions.

It is already known that conservatives display a relatively strong preference for simple (cognitively undemanding) aesthetic stimuli, and that liberals display a contrariwise tendency (Wilson et al., 1973). One possible implication of this finding is that these similarly large, but qualitatively

opposed, discrepancies from the AL of judgmental-ease both entail reinforcement for whatever dimensional bases arouse such positive affect.
But it is further suggested that both a simple positive linear function for
the conservatives and its simple negative counterpart for the liberals are
belied by the respective probabilities that extreme positive discrepancies
from AL connote trivia and that extreme negative discrepancies entail
cognitive discomfort. However, evocation of some positive affect (and
commensurate reinforcement) also seems consistent with moderate discrepancies from AL: such positive departures from the usual may, in the
case of liberals, be subjectively regarded as "surprisingly easy" and their
negative counterpart, in the case of the conservatives, as just difficult
enough to be "challenging".

Figure 2, depicts the divergent discrepancy-from-level formulations
that are predicted according to this semi-intuitive argument. These may be
interpreted as systematic deviates of a general function advanced by
McClelland and Clark (in 1953; see Nelson, 1964, p. 382) to account for
the hedonic tone of sensory stimulation. The affective correlate of dimensional ease of judgment is similarly expected to entail internal response-
produced stimuli, and it is also assumed that criterial status derives from
the pairing of dimensional stimulation with the conditions producing such
affective arousal.

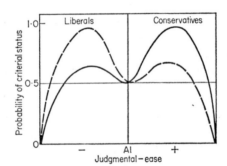

FIG. 2. Dimension "criteriality" as a theorized function of high and low conservatism.

This proposed functional differentiation would readily account for the
marked variation in affective tone that liberals and conservatives typically
display with respect to aesthetic stimulation. The fact that the nature and
weighting of their respective dimensionality is also different is a necessary
corollary of these formulations.

V. Conclusion

The foregoing encourages one to conclude that (a) the attitudinal factor
of conservatism is again demonstrably pertinent with respect to the pre-

diction of behaviours seemingly remote from that of its own assessment and (b) aesthetic stimuli are likely to constitute a lucrative domain for the teasing out of such theoretical conundrums as undoubtedly underlie this demonstrated pertinence.

References

Barron, F. (1953). Complexity-simplicity as a personality dimension. *J. abnorm· soc. Psychol.* **48**, 163–172.

Brown, R. (1968). "Social Psychology," Collier Macmillan.

Brunswik, E. (1947). "Systematic and Representative Design of Psychological Experiments." U.C.P., Berkeley.

Beach, L. and Wertheimer, M. (1962). A free response approach to the study of personal cognition. *J. abnorm. soc. Psychol.* **62**, 367–374.

Coombs, C. H. (1964). "A Theory of Data." Wiley.

Dornbusch, S. M., Hastorf, A. H., Richardson, S. A., Muzzy, R. E. and Vreeland, R. S. (1965). The perceiver and the perceived. *J. pers. soc. Psychol.* 434–440.

Fechner, G. T. (1876). "Vorschule der Aesthetic." Breitkopf and Härtel.

Fenker, R. M. and Brown, D. R. (1969). Pattern perception, conceptual spaces and dimensional limitations on information processing. *Mult. behav. Res.* **4**, 257–271.

Fry, R. (1920). An essay in aesthetics. In "Fry's Vision Design". Phoenix.

Garner, W. R. (1970). The stimulus in information-processing. *Am. Psychol.* **25**, 350–358.

Guilford, J. P. (1934). The affective value of colour as a function of hue, tone and chroma. *J. expl. Psychol.* **17**, 342–370.

Helson, H. (1964). "Adaptation-Level Theory." Harper and Row.

Imai, S. and Garner, W. R. (1965). Discriminability and preference for attributes in free and constrained classification. *J. expl. Psychol.* **69**, 596–608.

Kandinsky, W. (1912). "Uber das Geistige in der Kunst." Piper and Co.

Klee, P. (1924). "Uber die Moderne Kunst." Benteli.

Lundholm, H. (1921). The affective tone of lines: experimental research. *Psychol. Rev.* **28**, 43–60.

Mouton, J. S. and Helson, H. (1956). Total impression as a function of the dimensions of aesthetic objects. Unpublished study, cited by Helson (1964).

Moyles, E. W., Tuddenham, R. D. and Block, J. (1969). Simplicity/complexity or symmetry/asymmetry? A re-analysis of the Barron-Welsh Art Scales. In "Psychology and the Visual Arts". (Hogg, J., ed.). Penguin.

Patterson, J. R. (1969). Ease of judgment as a determinant of the degree to which stimulus dimensions serve as criteria for aesthetic responses, Unpublished M.A. Thesis, Univer. of Canterbury.

Patterson, J. R., White, K. G. and Patterson, Sue. (1972). Conservatism as a primary predictor of aesthetic judgments. Unpublished study.

Schaie, K. W. (1961). Scaling the association between colours and mood tones. *Am. J. Psychol.* **74**, 266–273.

Schneider, G. A. and Giambra, L. M. (1971). Performance in concept identification as a function of cognitive complexity. *J. pers. soc. Psychol.* **19**, 261–273.

Schroder, H. M., Driver, J. and Streufert, S. (1967). "Human Information Processing." Holt, Rinehart and Winston.

Seurat, G. (1926). Letter of Seurat to Beaubourg, 28 August, 1870, published by Rey, R. Apropos du cirque de Seurat. *Beaux Arts.*

Streuffert, S., Suedfeld, P. and Driver, J. (1965). Conceptual structure information search and information utilization. *J. personal soc. Psychol.* **2**, 735–741.

Wilson, G. D., Ausman, J. and Mathews, T. R. (1973). Conservatism and art preferences. *J. Pers. soc. Psychol.* in press.

Wilson, G. D. and Patterson, J. R. (1968). A new measure of conservatism. *Brit. J. soc. clin. Psychol.* **7**, 264–269.

Conservatism and Response to Humour

11

GLENN D. WILSON

Institute of Psychiatry, University of London

I. Introduction

The importance of humour as a psychological phenomenon has long been recognized, both by psychoanalytic and empirically oriented psychologists. Its main interest lies in the fact that it apparently offers an indirect approach to the investigation of the most salient needs, motives and conflicts of an individual or group, including some that might not be accessible by direct verbal report either because they are not consciously recognized or because they are socially unacceptable. Thus, to the psychoanalyst humour is a "window to the unconscious mind"; to the experimental psychologist it is a source of fascinating data involving many variables that may be controlled or manipulated.

What insights can be gained into the nature of conservatism by examining the differences between liberals and conservatives in their response to various kinds of humour? This chapter outlines a number of studies of conservatism in relation to humour and their findings are discussed in terms of the light that they throw on the dynamics of conservatism. The first of these studies is concerned with the relationship between the conservatism dimension and self-rated preferences among several different categories of cartoon. The second study replicates and extends some of the results from the first using other-person ratings of videotaped responses to cartoon humour. The remaining studies to be discussed are concerned with the connections between conservatism, sexual attractiveness, and the enjoyment of seaside postcards that may be broadly characterized as "risqué".

II. Cartoon Peferences

Wilson and Patterson (1969) tested the hypothesis that persons scoring high on the C-Scale, having "chronically mobilized inhibitions", would be less appreciative than liberals of humour involving the transparent expression of sex and aggression, but not of humour that is either purely formal or in which libidinal content is comparatively veiled.

Six categories of humour were selected for study (Table I). It was not claimed that this classification is comprehensive in any sense, just that it provides a sample of humour types that vary along a formal-libidinal dimension (called "tendentiousness" by Freud). A search was then made of magazines such as "Punch" and "Playboy" for a set of cartoons that appeared to correspond fairly unambiguously to each of the six chosen humour categories. The list of category definitions was given to four

TABLE I

Categories of humour employ
(By Wilson and Patterson, 1969)

Category	Definition	Example
Puns	Play on the sound and meaning of words	A carrier staggering under the weight of a grandfather clock is asked: "Have you got the time on you?"
Incongruity	Familiar elements appearing out of usual context	A butcher with an animal-plan erected on a music stand is applying his hacksaw to a side of meat in the manner of a double-bass player.
Antiradical	Ridicule of radical or Bohemian elements in society	As they pass by a hardware store, a beatnik is shielding his girl-friend's eyes from the sight of a bath and washbasin.
Antiauthority	Ridicule of conventionally respected persons and institutions	A truck-driver waiting at a stop-light is casually stubbing out his cigarette on the helmet of a motorcycle cop also waiting beneath him.
Sick	Delight in the morbid, gruesome, and sadistic	A little girl is swinging joyfully on the legs of a man who has just hanged himself.
Sexual	Participation in, or anticipation of, sexual pleasure	A playboy attired in silk dressing gown is welcoming an attractive blonde. "Come in, Miss Faversham. Looks like you're the only one to come to the party."

graduate students who were asked to sort the cartoon pool in terms of them, and those cartoons that were reliably assigned to the same category were retained. Finally, five cartoons corresponding to each of the six categories were selected for inclusion in the test booklet.

Subjects were 139 high school students (75 female and 64 male). aged 15–19. Such a group was thought to be well suited to a study of this kind because it is fairly homogeneous with respect to age, marital status, education and occupation, thus obviating the need to control for these demographic variables. The cartoon booklet was given to Ss with instructions to rate each cartoon according to the scale: (1) Not at all funny, (2) Slightly funny, (3) Moderately funny, (4) Very funny, (5) Extremely funny. Personality information was gathered by subsequent administration of the C-Scale and the E.P.I. (Eysenck and Eysenck, 1969).

The major results of this study are illustrated in Fig. I and Table II, in which the six categories of humour have been placed along an *a priori*

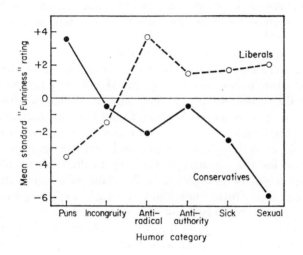

Humor category

TABLE II

Product-moment correlations between conservatism scores and "funniness" ratings
for each of six humour categories
(From Wilson and Patterson, 1969)

Ss	Puns	In-congruity	Anti-radical	Anti-authority	Sick	Sexual
Males	0·35†	0·14	−0·29*	−0·08	−0·10	−0·28*
Females	0·26*	0·08	−0·20	−0·03	−0·15	−0·23*
Total group	0·27†	0·10	−0·22†	−0·10	−0·18*	−0·24†

Note: For males, $N = 64$; for females, $N = 75$; total $N = 139$. $*p < 0.05$.
$†p < 0.01$.

dimension of tendentiousness ranging from the purely formal to the overtly libinal. Puns and incongruity jokes are "safe" and respectable in content, while the sick and sexual categories represent the outright expression and indulgence of aggressive and sexual impulses respectively. The antiradical and antiauthority categories are both forms of social satire involving the ridicule of certain classes of persons and institutions (a type of indirect, inter-personal aggression).

Figure 1 compares humour preference profiles for the thirty subjects scoring highest on the C-Scale (conservatives) and the thirty subjects scoring lowest (liberals). The general pattern of the profiles is very much as predicted, with conservatives tending to prefer the "safe", "non-tendentious" types of humour and liberals expressing a greater liking for the more openly "libinal" or "tendentious" types of humour. Using a t test these differences were all shown to be significant beyond the 0·01 level except for the incongruity and anti-authority categories, which were not significant. Correlations between C-scores and humour ratings on each of the cartoon categories are given for males and females separately, and for the total group, in Table II.

Certain complex differences between the humour preferences of males and females were detected but these were independent of the effects of conservatism since neither age nor sex was significantly related to conservatism with the present sample. In fact, the close similarity between males and females in the correlations between C and humour preferences shown in Table II may be taken as an indication that the results of this study are highly reliable, even though the actual correlations are quite low.

The failure for the incongruity category to discriminate liberals and conservatives might be interpreted as the result of a cancellation of two opposing processes. On the one hand, we might expect conservatives to express a liking for incongruity jokes because they are free of sexual and aggressive content; however, on the other hand, they might be threatened by them because they involve considerable disruption of the established order (certainly more than puns) and therefore comprise cognitively complex or "uncertain" stimulus configurations (Wilson et al., 1973). Apparently the "puns" category is the only one of the six that is both sufficiently respectable and sufficiently simple for the conservatives to show a significant preference relative to liberals.

The one deviation from the expected ordering of differences between liberals and conservatives, the partial reversal on the anti-radical and anti-authority categories, is interesting. Satire directed at radical targets (e.g. beatniks, artists, protest demonstrations) was rated higher by liberals than conservatives, even though it is conservatives who are supposedly more antagonistic towards these phenomena. However, there was no significant difference between liberals and conservatives in their ratings of satire directed at conservative institutions such as the Church and the Law. Psychoanalysts would doubtless interpret this finding as suggesting that conservatives, although superficially respectful of authority, actually harbour a certain amount of unconscious resentment which is expressed and revealed in their unexpectedly high appreciation of anti-authority humour. This expression of antiauthority feelings through enjoyment of humour would presumably only be possible because the joke mechanism provides an effective distraction from the real source of enjoyment (the anti-social content of the cartoons). Trait theorists, on the other hand, would be more inclined to argue that conservatives like jokes about conservative people and institutions simply because the subject matter is more familiar and relevant to their life style. The present results do not allow us to choose between these two hypotheses.

With reference to the Freudian notion that the function of humour is that of providing a socially acceptable setting for the partial expression of normally prohibited impulses, Wilson and Patterson conclude that their results suggest the importance of individual differences in the extent to which it is necessary for the libidinal content of a joke to be disguised before humorous affect is evoked. With very liberal persons there is apparently little or no necessity for any such veiling or "mitigation" of impulse expression. In other words, the Freudian theory of humour may today apply only to conservative people (whether or not it had universal application at the time it was first devised).

III. Video-Taped Responses

One of the possible limitations of the Wilson and Patterson study is the use of a self-report technique for measuring humour preferences. It might be argued that this method is susceptible to "social desirability" response bias, and that such a factor may have mediated the relationship found between conservatism and "funniness" ratings. Wilson and Patterson argued against this interpretation by noting that the E.P.I. "Lie Scale", which is essentially a measure of "faking good", did not relate to the humour scores to any appreciable extent (the only significant correlation being that with puns; $r = 0.18$, $p < 0.05$). In any case, we have previously pointed out that the concept of social desirability to some extent overlaps with that of conservatism, since "desirability" is defined in terms of the values of "middle-class respectability".

Another way of controlling for the possible biases in self-report measures is to observe actual behaviour in non-laboratory settings. This, of course, presents many practical difficulties, but is at least useful as a means of cross-validating results obtained by other methods. A good example of such a study is that of Thomas et al. (1971) who tested the hypothesis that conservatives would react less favourably to humour having a sexual theme using video-taped reactions to a serial cartoon.

The stimulus was a cartoon sequence of twelve pictures showing a nude female "growing" out of a doorbell, and the startled response of a male caller. The nature of the cartoon was such that it was difficult to see the point until all the pictures in the sequence were scanned. It was placed on the outside of a glass pane next to a side entrance door of the social sciences building at the University of Queensland, Australia. All persons who stopped to look at the cartoon (mostly education, psychology and sociology students on their way to lectures) were, unbeknown to them, video-taped from inside the entrance foyer. Shortly after their reactions to the cartoon had been recorded they were approached by two experimenters who asked them to complete the C-Scale under the pretext of "a random survey of the attitudes of people passing through the building". In this way thirty-nine subjects were obtained who had both looked at the cartoon and filled in the questionnaire. Only one person refused to complete the C-Scale, giving lack of time as a reason. None of the subjects gave any indication that they had connected the questionnaire with the cartoon.

The video-taped responses were rated for "favourability" by five psychology graduates who were unaware of the C-scores of the subjects. Inter-rater reliability coefficients were very high (ranging from 0·75 to 0·92) so the ratings of the five judges were combined to give a single index of favourability for each subject.

The product-moment correlation between conservatism and favourability of reaction to the cartoon was -0.44 ($p < 0.005$), indicating a significant tendency for conservatives to react less favourably than liberals. Reaction to the cartoon was also more favourable for males than females (point biserial correlation of 0·36), and since the females were significantly more conservative than the males, a partial correlation between favourability and conservatism was computed, with the effects of sex partialled out. The resulting correlation was -0.35, indicating that the tendency for conservatives to react unfavourably to the cartoon was independent of sex differences.

Thomas *et al.* concluded that their results support the validity of the C-Scale as a measure of general conservatism, as well as the finding of Wilson and Patterson that conservatives are less appreciative of sexual humour than liberals. It would now be interesting to see how video-taped responses of liberals and conservatives would compare on some of the other categories of humour, especially puns.

IV. Risqué Postcards

Since sexual or "risqué" humour is apparently the type that most markedly differentiates liberals and conservatives, Wilson and Brazendale

(1973) decided to investigate the relationship between conservatism and preferences among various types of risqué humour. For this purpose they used a set of forty-two colour slides of postcards collected from the seaside resorts of England. Nearly all of them were based upon sexual innuendo, but in order to ensure variety of content they were selected such that six cartoons represented each of the following areas: (a) the penis, especially erections, (b) testicles, (c) breasts, (d) the female pudendum, (e) intercourse, (f) pregnancy and maternity, (g) excretion, especially urination. A further restriction imposed on the selection of cartoons was that no cartoonist was represented more than once within each of the seven categories.

Subjects were 358 teachers' college students (269 females and 89 males), aged 17 to 30. Testing was carried out in group setting over a course of several sessions. The forty-two slides were shown in a fixed order that cycled through the different categories of humour, and each cartoon was rated according to the same five-point scale as that used by Wilson and Patterson.

The first analysis of results that was conducted concerned the question of how liberals and conservatives would compare in their overall ratings of the postcards. Surprisingly, the average ratings over the entire humour test were not significantly related to conservatism. In fact, exactly half of the postcards were preferred by liberals and half by conservatives. This finding might at first sight appear to contradict the findings of the previous two studies which showed that sexual humour is generally preferred by liberals. It might be explained, however, in the same way that Wilson and Patterson suggested that the conservative preference for puns and incongruity could have arisen. They hypothesized that because it is socially desirable to exhibit some "sense of humour" the conservatives react to the experimental situation by exaggerating their appreciation of the most innocuous jokes that are available, thus providing overall ratings that are as high as those of the liberals. Obviously, then, the next step is to look at the particular postcards that are most preferred by liberals and compare them to those most preferred by conservatives.

The six postcards that were most liked by liberals relative to conservatives are described in Table III and the six most liked by conservatives are given in Table IV. It is important to note that these are selected on the basis of covariance with C, not absolute levels of rated "funniness", so it is possible for them to have received generally low ratings. Examination of the content of the cartoons in these tables reveals that those preferred by liberals tend to refer fairly directly to sexual intercourse of a lustful and hedonistic type, while the preferences of conservatives include "lavatorial" jokes and oblique references to "the privates". One other difference between these two sets of cartoons may also be detected: the liberal jokes

TABLE III

Cartoons preferred by liberals

Correlation with C	Description of Postcard
−0·13†	Two men discussing attractive girl: "She's a nice girl. Doesn't drink or smoke, and only swears when it slips out!"
−0·13†	Two male swimmers admiring female sunbather: "She just lies in the sun all day, but she's lively enough once it goes in!"
−0·10*	Woman raising skirt in fear of mouse, to male companion: "Don't sit there laughing like a fool. Get up and drive it into the hole again!"
−0·10*	Two men lecherously surveying bikini-clad females: "Do you like fat or thin legs?" "Oh, I prefer something in between."
−0·10*	Scotsman in kilt up a ladder posting a bill advertising "Mint balls". One girl to another: "They look too small from here Kathleen!"
−0·10	Colonel sitting up in bed: "What's all the noise downstairs?" Hotel manager: "They're holding an Oddfellows Ball, Sir." Colonel: "Well if he makes all that row about it, why the devil don't they let him have it back?"

Note: df = 356;   *p < 0·05;   †p < 0·01.

TABLE IV

Cartoons preferred by conservatives

Correlation with C	Description of Postcard
0·14†	Man: "He died after eating jam, ma'am". Woman: "How did the doctor know?" Man: "He found the pot under the bed!"
0·14†	Attractive girl attending to back of motor-car; garage men running across to her. "Would someone have a look at my rear end?"
0·13†	Driving instructor to female learner: "That madam, is not the gear stick."
0·12†	Burglar to colleague emerging from toilet: "Blimey, Bert! No need to pull the ruddy chain and wake the whole house up."
0·11*	Newlyweds in bed: bridegroom drunk asleep; bride reading book entitled "Do it yourself".
0·09	Angry man wiping his trouser leg: "Is that your dog madam? Well you can pull the chain . . . he's finished."

Note: df = 356;   *p < 0·05;   †p < 0·01.

tend to include a greater degree of female sexual initiative, and sometimes even degradation of the male, whereas the conservative cartoons feature relatively naïve females. Thus, besides supporting the previous finding that conservatives are less favourable towards the overt expression of sexual desires than liberals, these results also suggest that they are less accepting of female equality in sexual relationships.

To ensure that the relationship between C and the postcard preferences could not have been mediated by age, sex, or intelligence, the effects of each of these variables on the humour ratings was also examined. Age did not significantly predict any of the humour ratings, nor did intelligence as measured by the Raven Progressive Matrices. (Samples less homogeneous on these factors might, however, yield some significant relationships.) Several of the postcards did significantly differentiate males and females, but not in such a way that sex could have mediated the association between C and the humour ratings. In any case, the correlation between C and sex (female) was only 0·17.

When the C-Scale was scored for attitude subfactors (Chapter 5) it was found that the anti-hedonism factor was the strongest predictor of the postcard preferences. The pattern of correlations was very similar to that of general C with the postcards, subjects scoring high on anti-hedonism showing a particular dislike for jokes referring to intercourse and sex organs but significantly appreciating jokes about urination and pregnancy relative to Ss scoring low on anti-hedonism. The other three subfactors, militarism-punitiveness, ethnocentrism, and religion-puritanism, showed a similar pattern of correlations but of much lower magnitude. Apparently, the anti-hedonism subfactor was the major contributor to the relationship of C with the postcard preferences.

V. Sexual Attractiveness, Attitudes and Humour

The last study to be discussed here was concerned with the extent to which attitude profiles and preferences among different kinds of risqué humour are predictable on the basis of rated sexual attractiveness. Wilson and Brazendale (1973) conducted the study in order to test the hypothesis of Wilson and Patterson (1970) that conservative attitudes may develop as a result of "perceived disadvantage in the new, permissive society", i.e. as a kind of "dynamic defence" which averts or rationalizes painful jealousy feelings. As examples, they suggested that "an unattractive girl may become a nun in order to deny the value of sexuality, or an aging father may vigorously protect his daughter's virtue as a means of resolving his unacceptable attraction to young girls".

Subjects were ninety-seven female student teachers, aged 18 to 21, such a sample being regarded as ideal because it is homogeneous in terms of age, sex, and occupation. The tests used were the C-Scale, a new form of the Eysenck Personality Inventory that includes a measure of psychoticism (Eysenck and Eysenck, 1969), and the set of forty-two seaside postcards described above. All tests were administered in a group setting.

Sexual attractiveness was rated without the Ss' knowledge by two male lecturers from a *different* teachers' college. This was thought necessary in order to avoid possible contamination of the attractiveness ratings by extraneous factors such as personality or intelligence. The two raters worked independently of each other and without knowledge of the girls' performance on the other measures. A five-point rating scale was used: (1) Not at all attractive, (2) Slightly attractive, (3) Moderately attractive, (4) Very attractive, (5) Extremely attractive. Their instructions were to "use this scale to indicate to what extent you think that each girl would be *attractive, on average, to most members of the opposite sex.* Try to disregard any peculiar preferences of your own and the way in which they are dressed or presented at the moment, i.e. rate them only on *native* attractiveness."

The interjudge reliability coefficient was 0·60, which indicates a fair amount of agreement between the two men as to which girls were the most attractive. Personality as measured by the Eysenck inventory showed no significant correlations with the attractiveness ratings, but social attitude scores showed low, consistent relationships (Table V). The overall pattern

TABLE V

Product-moment correlations of sexual attractiveness ratings with six attitude variables (N = 97).

	Rater 1	Rater 2
Conservatism (*vs.* Liberalism)	−0·14	−0·12
Realism (*vs.* Idealism)	0·18*	0·20†
Militarism-punitiveness	0·02	−0·01
Anti-hedonism	−0·11	−0·17*
Ethnocentrism	0·02	0·05
Religion-puritanism	−0·19*	−0·11

*p < 0·05 (one-tailed).   †p < 0·05 (two-tailed).

suggests that, compared to attractive girls, the unattractive girl tends to be idealistic (rather than realistic), anti-hedonistic (opposed to the "Playboy philosophy") and religious (particularly in a fundamental and puritanical way). On the other hand, there is no evidence that they differ with respect to militarism-punitiveness or ethnocentrism, and the correlation with general C fails to reach significance.

This pattern of associations between attractiveness and attitudes could be interpreted as supporting the hypothesis that opposition to sexual free-dom and pleasure-seeking may serve the ego-defensive purpose of denying the value of sexual attractiveness in people who perceive their own disadvantage in this area. That is, if sex can be repressed or classified as "sinful", then there is less need to feel jealous of those who have greater opportunity to indulge. Furthermore, adopting a system of beliefs that is idealistic and religious rather than practical and selfish would lend further, more "rational" support to anti-pleasure attitudes.

TABLE VI

Cartoons relatively liked by unattractive girls.

| | Correlation with attractiveness | |
Description of cartoon	Rater 1	Rater 2
2. Boy admiring large breasts of attractive girl. Fruitvendor: "Nice juicy *pear* there young fellow!"	$-0.33\dagger$	$-0.23*$
30. Man feeling under an inflated tube worn around the bust by an attractive girl. "I know it's soft, but that isn't my life belt!"	$-0.27\dagger$	$-0.21*$
23. Busty pet-shop girl showing man two birds in cage labelled tits. "They're baby ones sir, but I can show you a fully grown pair!"	$-0.28\dagger$	-0.12
28. Two men lecherously observing bikini-clad women on beach. "Do you like fat or thin legs?" "Oh, I prefer something between".	$-0.25*$	-0.16
18. Boy observing father's pot belly in bathroom. "The last time Mummy looked like that, I had a baby sister".	$-0.23*$	-0.15
14. Scantily clad girl bending over back of car, three garage men sprinting across to her. "Would someone have a look at my rear end?"	$-0.22*$	-0.04
42. Female shop assistant in short dress climbing ladder so as to display knickers to male customer. "Could I show you anything more, sir?" "No thanks, miss—*that's quite enough!*"	$-0.21*$	-0.04

*$p < 0.05$. $\dagger p < 0.01$ (two-tailed).

Although this theory is attractive, however, we cannot exclude the possibility that the two raters were, despite instructions, influenced by the dress, make-up, and general presentation of the girls, in addition to their basic attractiveness. Then it might be argued that their attractiveness was a reflection of their attitudes and beliefs rather than the other way about.

The results for the humour test are rather more difficult to explain in this way, however. Table VI describes the seven postcards that were significantly preferred by the unattractive girls according to the ratings of at least one of the two judges. (Correlations with the ratings of the other judge were consistent in direction even though only two of them reached statistical significance.) With one exception (Postcard No. 18), these cartoons have in common the theme of attractive women as the centre of male attention. Postcards preferred by attractive girls, on the other hand, showed no common characteristics. They referred to a variety of topics ranging from testicles and erections to intercourse, pregnancy and urination.

This fairly striking finding lends itself readily to an interpretation in terms of vicarious gratification through fantasy identification. In this view, the unattractive girl is deprived of male attention, and therefore imagines herself in the place of the girl in the cartoon so as to share in the kind of pleasure that in real life is available only to attractive girls. According to the psychoanalytic theory of humour (Freud, 1905) she would remain unconscious of the real source of pleasure, interpreting it to herself only as "funniness". The vagaries of this type of explanation are well-known, however (see Eysenck and Wilson, 1973), and it would be just as logical to argue that the attractive girl gives relatively low ratings to these cartoons because she is fed up with crude male approaches such as those illustrated in the postcards.

VI. Conclusions

The most consistent finding to emerge from the studies outlined in this chapter is that conservatives prefer humour that is relatively free from sex, aggression and anti-social sentiment. Therefore, these results appear to support the trait theory view that people derive the most enjoyment from humour dealing with subject matter that is familiar to them and consistent with their conscious attitudes and interests. Thus the liberal, who is generally more favourably disposed towards hedonistic sex, also enjoys sex jokes more than the conservative. Psychoanalytic theory, on the other hand, might have predicted that individuals who repress sex most strongly (presumably the conservatives) should be the ones to find sex jokes funniest because they have a greater need for the "safety valve" provided by the humour medium.

Certain other findings, however (particularly those concerning the interrelationships among sexual attractiveness, attitudes and humour preferences), would appear to be most parsimoniously accounted for in terms of "dynamic" concepts such as "denial" and "fantasy gratification". Nevertheless, it should be remembered that these explanations were generally *ad hoc*, and as many writers have pointed out, the greatest weakness of Freudian theory is its apparent facility to explain *any* outcome. As usual then, these studies raise many more questions than they are able to answer.

Whatever they fail to prove, the results that have been reviewed do demonstrate the relevance of the conservatism variable to the area of humour response. True, the actual correlations that emerged tended to be low in magnitude, but this was probably partly due to the fact that very homogeneous samples were employed. In these studies, age and intelligence showed no power to predict humour responses; sex and other personality variables such as extraversion and neuroticism were relatively poor predictors. Thus the present results may be taken as further evidence supporting the construct validity of the C-Scale and the argument concerning the pervasiveness of the conservatism factor throughout social behaviour.

References

Eysenck, S. B. G. and Eysenck, H. J. (1969). Scores of three personality variables as a function of age, sex and social class. *Brit. J. soc. clin. Psychol.* **8**, 69–76.

Eysenck, H. J. and Wilson, G. D. (1973). "The Experimental Study of Freudian Theories." Methuen, London.

Freud, S. (1960). "Jokes and their Relation to the Unconscious." (J. Strachey, ed.). Norton, New York. (Orig. publ. 1905).

Thomas, D. R., Shea, J. D. and Rigby, R. G. (1971). Conservatism and response to sexual humour. *Brit. J. soc. clin. Psychol.* **10**, 185–186.

Wilson, G. D., Ausman, J. and Mathews, T. R. (1973). Conservatism and art preferences. *J. Pers soc. Psychol.* in press.

Wilson, G. D. and Brazendale, A. H. (1973). Sexual attractiveness as a predictor of social attitudes and response to risqué humour. *Europ. J. Soc. Psychol.*

Wilson, G. D. and Patterson, J. R. (1969). Conservatism as a predictor of humour preferences. *J. consult. clin. Psychol.* **33**, 271–274.

Wilson, G. D. and Patterson, J. R. (1970). "Manual for the Conservatism Scale." N.F.E.R. Publishing Co., Windsor, England.

12 | The Temperamental Basis of Attitudes

GLENN D. WILSON

Institute of Psychiatry, University of London

I. Introduction

There are many theoretical reasons to expect that social attitude patterns and belief systems will partly reflect temperamental and personality factors. For example, Eysenck (1954) found that Fascists and Communists had in common high scores on a social attitude factor called Toughmindedness, and that this factor was related to extraversion and aggressiveness as measured by questionnaires. Similarly, many social psychologists have argued that racial prejudice may arise as a response to frustration or fear (e.g., Adorno *et al.*, 1950; Bagley, 1972). Some confirmation of this hypothesis may be found in the evidence concerning the connections between certain religious attitudes and behaviours and racial prejudice reviewed by Wilson and Bagley in Chapter 7. Wilson, Ausman and Mathews (1973) have hypothesized that the conservatism factor in social attitudes is a reflection of a generalized fear of uncertainty, whether *stimulus uncertainty* (complexity, ambiguity, novelty, change, etc., as states of the physical and social environment) or *response uncertainty* (freedom of choice, need conflict, etc., originating from within the individual).

This chapter will outline three studies that bear on these issues. They are concerned, respectively, with the extent to which social attitude and belief patterns are related to: (1) questionnaire measured temperamental traits; (2) projectively assessed styles of aggression and modes of response to frustration; (3) a self-report measure of the fear of death.

Finally, the theoretical implications of the results of these studies will be considered.

II. Personality

The first study to be outlined was concerned with the relationship between Eysenck's personality variables and social attitudes. It is fully reported in Wilson and Brazendale (1973).

Subjects were 97 female student teachers aged 18 to 34. As with several previous studies reported in this volume, it was argued that such a sample is well suited to a study of this kind because it is homogeneous in age, sex and occupation, thus obviating the need to allow for the effects of these variables. It does, however, mean that the results cannot necessarily be generalized beyond this group of people; eventually replications would be needed with other homogeneous groups.

The P.E.N. (Eysenck and Eysenck, 1969) and the C-Scale were administered in a group setting. The P.E.N. is a modified version of the Eysenck Personality Inventory which contains, in addition to the Extraversion (E), Neuroticism (N) and Lie (L) scales, a measure of a relatively new dimension labelled Psychoticism (P). The high P-scorer is described as emotionally cold, impersonal, anti-social, hostile and cruel. Each of these personality dimensions (except perhaps L) is presumed to have some kind of constitutional basis (Eysenck, 1967). The C-Scale was scored for the six attitude factors described in Chapter 5.

TABLE I

Product-moment intercorrelations among personality and attitude variables
$(N = 97)$.
(From Wilson and Brazendale, 1973).

	Conservatism (vs. Liberalism)	Realism (vs. Idealism)	Militarism –punitiveness	Antihedonism	Ethnocentrism –intolerance	Religion –puritanism
P	0·23*	−0·02	0·08	0·13	0·18	0·18
E	−0·35†	0·33†	−0·14	−0·36†	−0·11	−0·30†
N	0·03	0·17	0·12	−0·03	0·23*	−0·12
L	0·26†	−0·26†	0·03	0·24*	0·02	0·37†

*p < 0·05.   †p < 0·01.

Intercorrelations among the four personality variables and six attitude factors are shown in Table I. Extraversion shows significant correlations with Liberalism, Realism, Hedonism, and the absence of Religion-puritanism, while the Lie scale shows exactly the reverse pattern. Psychoticism has a low but significant association with general Conservatism, and Neuroticism relates to Ethnocentrism and intolerance of minority groups.

How do these results fit with theoretical expectations and previous empirical findings? The association of E with Liberalism is consistent with the hypothesis of Wilson *et al.* (1973) that conservatism represents a generalized fear of uncertainty, and the finding of Kish (Chapter 13) that conservatism is inversely related to sensation-seeking. In accord with Eysenck's description of the typical extravert, these results suggest that high E-scorers are not averse to novelty, change, excitement and risk, but may even value them positively. The correlations with Anti-hedonism and Religion-puritanism imply that the major part of the correlation between E and Liberalism is due to the extravert's relative freedom from religious beliefs and sexual inhibition; Militarism-punitiveness and Ethnocentrism do not correlate with E in the present sample. Finally, the correlation of E with Realism is consistent with Eysenck's (1961) finding that extraverts are more toughminded than introverts. (We have already noted the similarity between Realism as measured by the C-Scale and Eysenck's Toughmindedness factor.)

The Lie scale was included in the P.E.N. Inventory as a measure of social desirability rather than as a personality variable in its own right. There has, however, been increasing interest in the nature of the variable measured by the L scale, and the present results may throw some light on this question. The correlation of the Lie score with general C has been noted previously (e.g. Wilson and Patterson, 1969) and probably reflects the fact that "desirability" is defined in the context of the values of "middle-class respectability", thus overlapping conceptually with conservatism. (Paradoxically, "middle-class" values are actually more prevalent among the working classes; Eysenck, 1972.) The correlation with Idealism could be interpreted as supporting the suggestion of Eysenck, Nias and Eysenck (1971) that L may partly reflect a "lack of insight". The correlation with Religion-puritanism might imply that some part of L is associated with actual "good" behaviour, apart from the desire to "come out looking good".

Psychoticism correlates significantly only with general Conservatism, this relationship being contributed fairly evenly by the four different attitude content areas. This finding is very tentative, but it might be compared with the Stewart and Webster (1970) finding that in a sample of clergy, Conservatism was associated with a lack of Feeling Reactivity, Self-acceptance and Capacity for Intimate Contact as measured by the Personal Orientation Inventory. Apparently, Conservatism and Psychoticism have in common a reluctance to accept and express inner feelings, particularly those of a "positive" nature such as warmth and love. The findings upon which this hypothesis rests need replication, however.

The finding that Neuroticism is positively related to Ethnocentrism and the intolerance of minority groups would appear to support a "scapegoating" interpretation of prejudice. The argument, which also needs a great deal more empirical support, is that "free floating" anxiety in the neurotic is crystallized as perceived threat from a particular source, and that generalized frustration is manifested as aggression directed towards a suitable, vulnerable target.

While the interpretation of many of the particular correlations given above may be questioned, the overall results of this study strongly suggest that social learning effects, such as exposure to religious groups, are not in themselves sufficient to account for all the variation in attitude and belief patterns; they are apparently also a function of constitutional personality factors.

III. Projective Aggression

One possible criticism of the Wilson and Brazendale study is that the correlations between attitudes and temperament as measured by questionnaires might have occurred as a result of response styles common to both self-report measures. A study by Wilson (1973) was designed to investigate the relationship between different types of aggression, assessed *projectively* with the Rosenzweig Picture-Frustration Study, and the various attitude and belief factors measured by the C-Scale.

The P-F Study (Rosenzweig *et al.*, 1947) consists of 24 line drawings each depicting two people involved in a more or less frustrating situation. One character in the cartoon is shown saying something to the other, and the subject's task is to supply the response of the second person. Response protocols are scored for three *directions* of aggression: (1) Extrapunitiveness (aggression directed outwards), (2) Intrapunitiveness (aggression directed inwards towards the self), and (3) Impunitiveness (aggression evaded altogether). They are also scored for three *types* of aggression: (1) Obstacle-dominance (emphasis on the frustrating object), (2) Ego-defence (emphasis on protection of the self-image), and (3) Need-persistence (emphasis on finding a solution to the problem. It is also possible to score the P-F Study for certain more complex "patterns" and "trends", but these were not employed in the present investigation.

The P-F Study was administered along with the C-Scale to a sample of 91 students at California State University, Los Angeles. There were 47 females and 44 males, with a mean age of 25 years. This sample could not be claimed as representative of any larger group, but this is relatively unimportant when one is concerned only with covariance.

Intercorrelations between aggression scores and attitude factors are shown in Table II. Extrapunitiveness is significantly related to Realism, and apparently by corollary, Intrapunitiveness is related to Idealism. Impunitiveness does not predict any of the attitude factors. Of the aggression *types*, Obstacle-dominance relates to Idealism, Ego-defensiveness with

TABLE II

Intercorrelations among aggression and attitude variables (N = 91)
(From Wilson, 1973)

	Conservatism (vs. Liberalism)	Realism (vs. Idealism)	Militarism —punitiveness	Anti- hedonism	Ethnocentrism —intolerance	Religion —puritanism
Extrapunitiveness	0·04	0·26†	0·06	−0·14	0·19	0·11
Intrapunitiveness	0·01	−0·24*	−0·06	0·09	−0·07	−0·02
Impunitiveness	−0·05	−0·13	−0·03	0·11	−0·15	−012
Obstacle-dominance	0·04	−0·24*	−0·08	0·14	−0·18	0·10
Ego-defensiveness	0·15	0·19	0·17	−0·04	0·35†	0·13
Need-persistence	−0·22*	−0·06	−0·16	−0·05	−0·28†	−0·23*

*p < 0·05.   †p < 0·01.

Ethnocentrism and the intolerance of minorities, and Need-persistence with general Liberalism, and low scores on Ethnocentrism-intolerance and Religion-puritanism.

The highest correlation in the matrix, that between Ego-defensiveness and Ethnocentrism ($r = 0.35$, $p < 0.01$), is also the most interesting, since it could be interpreted as further support for the scape-goating theory of prejudice. In this case it would be argued that the expression of prejudice against foreigners and minorities functions as a means of preserving self-respect (see Chapter 7). Such a theory has frequently been cited in connection with the finding that the people who have most to lose by minorities achieving equality (e.g. the "white trash") are the most prejudiced.

Another interesting finding is the connection between Extrapunitiveness-Intrapunitiveness and Realism-Idealism. This is consistent with Eysenck's (1954) finding of a relationship between Toughmindedness and aggressiveness, and also the finding above that Realism is related to Extraversion (assuming that extrapunitiveness is characteristic of extraverts). Together these findings argue that people who project aggression outwards rather than inwards towards themselves are likely to express a toughminded, practical and expedient pattern of attitudes on most social issues.

The correlation between Liberalism and Need-persistence ($r = 0.22$, $p < 0.05$) also deserves comment. According to the description of the N-P factor given by Rosenzweig et al., it would suggest that liberals are more concerned than conservatives about finding solutions to the problems that confront them. This in turn may be seen as consistent with the view that conservatives lack self-reliance, preferring to accept a rigid external control of their feelings and behaviour. Examination of the correlations with each of the four attitude content factors reveals that it is the Ethnocentrism-intolerance and Religion-puritanism components of general Conservatism that are primarily responsible for its association with N-P. It is not clear why this should be so, although both tendencies could be regarded as "unreasonable" and dogmatic in the sense that they are not conducive to flexible, adaptive responses to new problems.

The effects of the demographic variables age and sex were also examined in this study. Age correlated significantly with general Conservatism and each of the four components but could not have mediated the relationships with aggression variables because it did not correlate significantly with any of them. There were sex differences on Realism (females more idealistic, $p < 0.01$), Anti-hedonism (males more hedonistic, $p < 0.01$) and Religion-puritanism (females more religious, $p < 0.01$). The females also tended to be relatively impunitive ($p < 0.01$) and less extrapunitive ($p < 0.05$).

The results of this study provide further support for the hypothesis that temperamental factors are involved in the development of social attitudes and beliefs. The actual correlations that were found are admittedly low, but they show a substantial degree of consistency both with theoretical predictions and previous empirical findings. This is all the more surprising when it is remembered that the P-F Study is a very indirect measure of aggression, and slightly suspect in terms of validity. One of the main problems with the test is that many respondents treat it as an opportunity to exercise their wit, and since the relationships among aggression, humour and attitudes are very complex (see Chapter 11), this could be a source of considerable error.

IV. Fear of Death

Nash (1972), in an unpublished study, hypothesized that if fear of uncertainty and "the unknown" were characteristic of the conservative, then this should extend to the fear of death. A Fear of Death Scale (Table IV) was constructed by selecting twenty questions concerned with death and its associations. Ten of these were intuitively keyed as indicating high fear of death if a positive response was given, and ten were keyed in the opposite direction. The possible response categories were "yes", "?" and "no" (as for the C-Scale) and each item was scored on a simple 0, 1, 2 system depending on the direction of keying. This F.O.D. Scale was given, along with an American modification of the C-Scale, to 74 students at California State University, Los Angeles (41 males and 33 females, ages ranging from 18 to 30). The two questionnaires were administered individually, with the F.O.D. Scale always completed first.

TABLE III

Product-moment correlations of social attitude factors with fear of death
(After Nash, 1972)

	r with F.O.D.	p
General conservatism	0·54	< 0·001
Males	0·55	< 0·001
Females	0·54	< 0·01
Realism	−0·17	n.s.
Militarism-punitiveness	0·40	< 0·001
Anti-hedonism	0·45	< 0·001
Ethnocentrism	0·42	< 0·001
Religion-puritanism	0·42	< 0·001

Note: For males, $N = 41$; for females, $N = 33$; total group, $N = 74$.

Correlations of the six attitude factors with the overall F.O.D. score are shown in Table III. General Conservatism correlated 0·54 with F.O.D. for the total group of 74 students, and the breakdown by sex showed that this result applied equally to males and females. The four subfactors of

H

Conservatism all correlated fairly evenly with F.O.D. (coefficients ranging from 0·40 to 0·45), while the Realism-Idealism factor showed no significant correlation.

The finding that all four oblique components of conservatism correlate with the fear of death is particularly interesting in connection with the "fear of uncertainty" hypothesis. Since several of the items in the F.O.D. scale relate directly or indirectly to religious beliefs it might have been argued that the Religion-puritanism component in the C-Scale had

TABLE IV

Differences between liberals and conservatives on each item of a
Fear of Death Scale.
(After Nash, 1972)

	t	p
1. Do you believe in afterlife?	3·28	<0·01
2. Should children be taken to funerals?	0·78	n.s
3. Do you believe in spirits?	0·66	n.s
4. Would you like to know the exact hour of your death?	−0·55	n.s.
5. Would you use a safety belt for a trip under two miles?	1·38	n.s.
6. Would you prefer to die rather than endure the worst pain you know for six months?	0·40	n.s.
7. Would you consider having your body frozen after death in the event that science will later be able to restore you to life and health?	1·00	n.s.
8. Do you ever wish that you were dead?	0·37	n.s.
9. Are you afraid of what might happen to your body after death?	3·94	<0·001
10. Would you attend a lecture on the meaning of death?	0·62	n.s.
11. Would you work ten hours a day at hard labour if it would extend your life ten years?	1·82	n.s.
12. Would you enter the "Indianapolis 500" for a year's salary?	−1·25	n.s.
13. Are you superstitious?	1·11	n.s.
14. If it were a simple medical procedure, would you ever consider sterilization for yourself?	0·12	n.s.
15. On a plane trip, would you choose your seat with your safety in mind?	2·67	<0·01
16. Would you ever consider cremation for yourself?	2·78	<0·01
17. If your doctor had determined that a habit of yours was injurious to your health, would you give it up immediately?	2·36	<0·05
18. Do you ever visualize yourself as dead?	0·00	n.s.
19. Do stories concerning death disturb you?	2·73	<0·01
20. During your lifetime would you, for £100, sell your body to medical science to be dissected after your death?	2·71	<0·01

Note: A positive *t* means that conservatives showed greater fear of death on the item according to the intuitive scoring of the scale.

mediated the correlation between C and Fear of Death. The equally high correlations with each of the other three components of C (Militarism-punitiveness, Anti-hedonism, and Ethnocentrism) however, indicates clearly that this is not the case, and the general fear of uncertainty hypothesis is thus supported.

In a more detailed analysis of results, Nash divided her sample into low and high C-Scale scorers by splitting them at the median score of 33·5. She then conducted t-tests to see which items in the F.O.D. scale were the strongest discriminators of the liberals and conservatives (Table IV). Several of the items that most strongly discriminated the conservatives from the liberals were concerned with possible events after death (belief in an afterlife, cremation, medical dissection, etc.). Other items showing a significant difference between the liberal and conservative groups referred to choosing a safe seat on an aeroplane, abstaining from habits that might be injurious to health, and being disturbed by stories concerning death. It is not easy to see why these particular items should have been the strongest discriminators. Perhaps they are just the "best items" in the sense that they are most central to the Fear of Death factor.

V. Conclusions

In this chapter we have outlined three studies concerned with the psychological basis of social attitude patterns as measured by the C-Scale. The results of them may be summarized as follows:

1. Correlations between attitudes and Eysenck's major personality factors suggest that temperamental factors may underlie some variance in social attitudes. For example, the tendency for the extravert to show liberal attitudes may be attributable to his need for higher levels of stimulation (e.g. excitement, change, and risk). Similarly, the tendency for high N-Scorers to be ethnocentric could be interpreted as an attempt to rationalize, and thus reduce, high levels of generalized anxiety.

2. Aggression scores on the Rosenzweig P-F Study also showed correlations with social attitudes that were consistent with theoretical expectations. Perhaps the most interesting finding here was the correlation of 0·35 between Ego-defensiveness on the P-F Study and Ethnocentrism, since this might also have been predicted by the "scape-goating" theory of prejudice.

3. The study by Nash showed that fear of death is positively related to Conservatism to a remarkable degree, and that this relationship is due not just to religious beliefs, but each of the major components of Conservatism about equally. This finding was taken as supporting the theory of Wilson et al. (1973) that the common psychological basis of all the attitudes comprising the conservatism "syndrome" is a generalized susceptibility to

feeling fear in the face of uncertainty. This theory is discussed more fully in the final chapter.

The link between these three studies is that they each point to the conclusion that social attitude and belief patterns cannot be explained entirely in terms of social learning processes (imitation, reference groups, etc.). Some amount of variance apparently arises from more fundamental (probably constitutional) personality factors such as aggressiveness, extra-version, and anxiety. It has already been suggested that motivational or "dynamic" factors are necessary to explain the "irrationality" of attitude patterning (Chapter 7). The study of individual differences in temperament provides one of the most satisfactory means of investigating the operation of such processes.

References

Adorno, T. W., Frenkel-Brunswick, E., Levinson, D. J. and Sanford, R. N. (1950). "The Authoritarian Personality." Harper, New York.

Bagley, C. (1972). Social prejudice and the adjustment of people with epilepsy. *Epilepsia*. **13**, 33–45

Eysenck, H. J. (1954). "The Psychology of Politics." Routledge and Kegan Paul, London.

Eysenck, H. J. (1961). Personality and social attitudes. *J. soc. Psychol.* **53**, 243–248.

Eysenck, H. J. (1967). "The Biological Basis of Personality." C. C. Thomas, New York.

Eysenck, H. J. (1972). "Psychology is About People." Allen Lane, The Penguin Press, London.

Eysenck, S. B. G. and Eysenck, H. J. (1969). Scores of three personality variables as a function of age, sex and social class. *Brit. J. soc. clin. Psychol.* **8**, 69–76.

Eysenck, S. B. G., Nias, D. K. B. and Eysenck, H. J. (1971). The interpretation of children's Lie Scale scores. *Brit. J. educ. Psychol.* **41**, 23–31.

Nash, M. E. (1972). "Conservatism and the Fear of Death." Unpublished MS. Cal. State Univ., Los Angeles.

Rosenzweig, S., Fleming, E. E. and Clarke, H. J. (1947). Revised scoring manual for the Rosenzweig Picture-Frustration Study. *J. Psychol.* **24**, 165–208.

Stewart, R. A. C. and Webster, A. C. (1970). Scale for theological conservatism and its personality correlates. *Percept. mot. Skills.* **30**, 867–870.

Wilson, G. D. (1973). Projective aggression and social attitudes. *Psychol. Rep.* in press.

Wilson, G. D., Ausman, J. and Mathews, T. R. (1973). Conservatism and art preferences. *J. Pers. soc. Psychol.* in press.

Wilson, G. D. and Brazendale, A. H. (1973). Social attitude correlates of Eysenck's personality dimensions. *Soc. Behav. Pers.* in press.

Wilson, G. D. and Patterson, J. R. (1969). Conservatism as a predictor of humor preferences. *J. consult. clin. Psychol.* **33**, 271–274.

13 | Stimulus-Seeking and Conservatism

GEORGE B. KISH

Roanoke College, Salem, Virginia U.S.A.

I. Introduction

This chapter reports some data and ideas comparing the concepts of "stimulus-seeking" and "conservatism". The research was stimulated by Wilson's analysis of conservatism as a pervasive general factor which permeates social attitudes and seems to be a tendency to *"resist change"*. It seemed, to this author, that conservatism was the obverse of a personality variable in which he was primarily interested, namely the tendency to *seek* change and novelty. Some research was, therefore, carried out in order to examine the relationship between these traits.

The material below will: (a) present a general introduction to the stimulus-seeking construct, (b) compare stimulus-seeking and conservatism conceptually and empirically and (c) examine some ideas regarding the genesis of these traits.

The general thesis of the argument will be that stimulus-seeking and conservatism to some degree share a common dimension, i.e. attitude towards change. It will be postulated that whether a person is a stimulus-seeker or a conservative may derive from the balance between two opposing primitive responses to novel, changing stimulation, namely fear and curiosity (exploratory motivation) and that this balance may be affected by both genetic and experiential factors.

Since the conservatism construct has been thoroughly elaborated in previous chapters we will assume that the reader is familiar with it and will not repeat this material here.

II. Stimulus-Seeking

Intensive research was carried out during the decades of the 1950s and 1960s investigating the reinforcing and motivating properties of stimulation (see reviews by Berlyne, 1960; Kish, 1966; and others). It now seems reasonably clear that organisms require and seek out stimulation for its own sake.

A number of theoretical attempts have been made to derive stimulus-seeking behaviour from more basic processes. Berlyne (1960), for example, has examined stimulus-seeking in the context of physiological arousal. Other attempts, at perhaps a lower level of generalization, have postulated processes such as curiosity, exploratory drive, and sensory reinforcement. Leuba (1955) integrated the early data on both the aversive consequences of intense stimulation and the reinforcing and motivating consequences of mild stimulation under the concept of "optimal level of stimulation". Under this principle, organisms are postulated to strive to maintain an optimal level of stimulation by withdrawing from excessive stimulation and seeking out additional stimulation when input levels are relatively low.

In general, these theoretical and empirical efforts were attempting to gain understanding of the process characteristics of organisms' responses to stimulation.

More recently, attention has turned to the examination of stimulus-seeking as a personality trait variable. In the context of Leuba's theory of "optimal stimulation," Zuckerman et al. (1964) postulated that individuals differed in their preferred level of stimulational input; more specifically, that some individuals preferred a relatively low input of stimulation whereas others seemed to require higher levels of input for optimal functioning. A self-report instrument called the "Sensation-Seeking Scale" (S.S.S.) was devised to measure this trait. Most of the research on stimulus-seeking has utilized this instrument (Form II) (Zuckerman et al., 1964) although more recent research has utilized a revised and expanded version (Form IV) (Zuckerman, 1971). Form IV discriminates a number of subfactors of the general stimulus-seeking trait (see below for more detailed description of these scales). Other instruments for measuring stimulus-seeking have been developed but have, in general, not generated the amount of research that the Sensation-Seeking Scale has generated (e.g. Garlington and Shimota, 1964).

Examination of the sensation-seeking scales, which have demonstrated reasonable degrees of reliability and construct validity, suggests the dimensions of stimulation which are sought by stimulus-seekers. These dimensions correlate fairly well with Berlyne's (1960) analysis of the characteristics of stimuli which arouse curiosity and include such dimensions as: complexity, intensity, novelty, change, and variety.

Research on stimulus-seeking to date has primarily studied the structural relationship between stimulus-seeking and a variety of personality traits. On the basis of this research, the high stimulus seeker has been characterized as tending to be: (a) field independent (Zuckerman *et al.*, 1964; Zuckerman and Link, 1968); (b) better educated, showing average or better than average intelligence and younger than the low stimulus-seeker (Blackburn, 1969; Kish and Busse, 1968); (c) low on measurable psychopathology (Blackburn, 1969; Brownfield, 1966; Kish, 1970; Kish and Busse, 1969); (d) interested in scientific occupations or those which are unstructured, have changing demands and require a problem-solving approach (Kish and Donnenwerth, 1969); (e) more creative than the low stimulus-seeker (Kish, 1970); (f) independent of others, exhibitionist, and needing change in his environment. (Zuckerman and Link, 1968); (g) unconventional, nonconformist and not valuing order and routine (Kish and Donnenwerth, 1969; Zuckerman and Link, 1968); (h) more likely to volunteer for esoteric psychological experiments (Zuckerman *et al.*, 1967); (i) impulsive, active, and outgoing (Blackburn, 1969, Kish and Busse, 1969, Zuckerman and Link, 1968.)*

III. Conservatism and Stimulus-Seeking

If conservatism is most simply defined as resistance to change, we might expect the conservative to favour the *status quo* in a variety of situations and towards a variety of issues. He may furthermore be rather closed minded and conforming to traditional authority. Wilson has noted the relationship of conservatism to such constructs as Dogmatism (Rokeach, 1960) and Authoritarianism (Adorno *et al.*, 1950).

Examination of the trait clusters suggested by the constructs of Conservatism, Dogmatism, and Authoritarianism contrasted with the cluster defining stimulus-seeking suggests that to some degree these traits lie at opposite poles of a continuum in which interest or attitude towards change, novelty, variety, etc., is the major dimension.

Such considerations suggest that measures of conservatism and stimulus-seeking should be negatively correlated. Since, in all likelihood, both stimulus-seeking and conservatism are factorially complex, one would not expect a perfect correlation between measures of these traits, however.

*Zuckerman (1972) has recently compiled a manual describing the development of the Sensation-Seeking Scale which includes a comprehensive review of the findings to April 1972, and provides a more complete characterization of the stimulus-seeker.

Furthermore, these considerations would suggest that some of the various correlates of stimulus-seeking should also prove to be negatively correlated with conservatism. For example, whereas the Sensation-Seeking Scale (S.S.S.) is negatively correlated with age, the Conservatism Scale (C-Scale) should be positively correlated with age. Of course, everyday observation would also suggest this. Older individuals seem to resist change to a greater extent than younger people.

The author and his co-workers examined some of these relationships in a short series of studies (Kish *et al.*, 1973). In one study 186 male and female college freshmen were administered both the C-Scale and Form II of the S.S.S. in a classroom setting. The group was relatively homogeneous in age with a modal age of 18 years. In a second study, the C-Scale and Form IV of the S.S.S. were adminstered to several extension classes in Social Work (N = 51). Mean age of this group of males and females was 37·8 with a much greater variability than for the freshman group. This was a more heterogeneous group both in age and in educational level (average educational level 15·2 years).

Form II of the S.S.S. consists of 34 forced choice items tapping the general trait of sensation-seeking by asking for preferences for such activities as (a) motor-cycle riding versus not motor-cycle riding (b) mountain climbing versus not mountain climbing.

Form IV is a seventy-two-item version in a similar format which taps four subfactors of sensation-seeking in addition to the general factor. These factors include (1) General Sensation-Seeking (Gen), (2) Thrill and Adventure-Seeking (TA), (3) Experience-Seeking (ES), (4) Disinhibition (Dis) and (5) Boredom Susceptibility (BS). The BS scale was found to be applicable only to males and was not included in the subsequent analyses.

In the first study, the C-Scale and Form II of the S.S.S. were found to be significantly negatively correlated (r = −0·33, p < 0·01, df. 184). No sex differences in degree of correlation were found.

In Study II, Form IV of the S.S.S. and the C-Scale yielded the correlations presented in Table I.

TABLE I

Pearson *rs* relating scales of S.S.S. to C-Scale and age*
(N = 51)

S.S.S. Scale	C-Scale	Age
Gen	−54†	−47†
TA	−29‡	−41†
ES	−52†	−42†
Dis	−26	−39†

*Decimals omitted. †p < 0·01. ‡p < 0·05.

The correlation with the General Sensation-Seeking factor, was greater in Study II than in Study I probably because both scales (C and S.S.S.) were tapping a broader range of individual differences in Study II. The correlation with Experience Seeking is theoretically most interesting. The description of this factor suggests "the need for a broad variety of inner experience through drugs, travel, music, art, and an unconventional life style. It also contains an element of resistance to irrational authority and conformity". (Zuckerman *et al.*, 1973). Such unconventionality and resistance to conformity and to authority in the high sensation-seeker would lead to a more anti-establishment stance towards the controversial issues of the C-Scale. This logic was substantiated by the correlation coefficient.

A correlation between age and the C-Scale was calculated with the heterogeneous age group of Study II and yielded an r of $+0.31$ ($p < 0.05$, df 49). Since the S.S.S. and age are negatively correlated, the prediction of a positive relationship between conservatism and age was confirmed.

To determine to what degree the common factor of a relationship with age was influencing the relationships between the C-Scale and the S.S.S. factors, partial correlations were performed as indicated in Table II.

TABLE II

Partial correlations among S.S.S. Scores, C-Scale, and age*

S.S.S. Scale	S.S.S.-C Age Constant	Age-C S.S.S. Constant	S.S.S.-Age C Constant
Gen	−46	+08	−37
TA	−18	+22	−35
ES	−45	+12	−32
Dis	−16	+24	−34

*Decimals omitted.

Interestingly, removal of age had only a slight effect upon the relationship between S.S.S. and C, whereas removal of the S.S.S. factors produced a significant drop in the relationship between the C-Scale and age. It seems that the factor of age enters into conservatism primarily via the vehicle of stimulus-seeking.

Apparently, one of the factors contributing to the conservatism of the older person is a reduction in his level of optimal stimulation.

All in all, the findings of these studies tended to confirm the interpretation that at least one important dimension of conservatism is stimulus-seeking.

This raises an interesting chicken and egg problem as to which trait is more basic. The author was inclined to consider stimulus-seeking to be the primary trait because of the extensive literature demonstrating stimulus-needs in a variety of lower organisms. However, there is also considerable evidence to the effect that novel stimulation also tends to arouse fear in both lower organisms and man. Observations of organisms in novel situations suggests the simultaneous arousal of fear and curiosity creating an approach-avoidance conflict with respect to novel stimulation. Novel situations are indeed fraught with uncertainty and, as any administrator will attest, changes produce considerable resistance on the part of employees in a variety of work settings.

Whether conservatism is to some degree a reflection of this tendency to fear novelty awaits further theoretical and empirical analysis .Superficially, such an analysis does not seem unreasonable, however, and suggests that conservatism and stimulus-seeking may be different aspects of a two-pronged reaction to novel situations and that a determinant of the individual's optimal level of stimulation may be the relative strength of these two processes.

The chicken and egg problem still remains but since it has not yet been solved in the chicken's case, it is unlikely to be solved in this case either.

IV. Further Considerations and Data

The finding that stimulus-seeking and conservatism are related concepts receives added support from the literature regarding stimulus-seeking.

Kish and Donnenwerth (1972) studied the relationships between authoritarianism and dogmatism and stimulus-seeking. They reported negative correlations between the S.S.S. and the California F-Scale which were particularly high for males ($r = -0.81$). The correlation between the S.S.S. and the Rokeach D-Scale was -0.38 (again for males). In both studies, the correlations for females were lower than for males (in the case of the S.S.S.-D correlation, it was zero for females).

Although these findings are consistent with the relationship between the S.S.S. and C-Scale, they raise the interesting possibility that, as for stimulus-seeking (see Kish and Donnenwerth, 1972), the interrelationships between conservatism and other personality characteristics may differ for males and females. Although the difference is slight, females tend to be more conservative than males (Wilson and Patterson, 1968; Kish et al., 1973). More importantly, however, studies are needed to explore for possible differences in the mode of expression of conservatism in females as contrasted to males.

Kish and Donnenwerth (1972) also reported data indicating that stimulus-seekers tend towards more liberal attitudes towards at least one controversial issue—namely, premarital intimacy. The S.S.S. and a measure of intimacy permissiveness correlated $+0.49$ for males and $+0.55$ for females. In this case, no sex difference was apparent.

Actual sexual practices and variety of sexual practices have been reported to be related to sensation-seeking by Zuckerman *et al.*, 1973. This paper also reported similar relationships with drug experience.

Further evidence consistent with this analysis of conservatism comes from a study of interest patterns and stimulus-seeking by Kish and Donnenwerth (1969). Conservatives might be expected to be more traditionalistic in their outlook and their interest patterns than those low on conservatism. One might predict that conservatives would gravitate towards occupations which are traditional for *their* sex or which are valued by the culture. The relationship between stimulus-seeking and conservatism would predict similar findings for the low sensation seeker. Kish and Donnenwerth (1969) examined the relationship between Form II of the S.S.S. and males' and females' scores on the Strong Vocational Interest Blank. In females, the S.S.S. tended to correlate negatively with such traditional female occupational scales as housewife, elementary teacher, home economics teacher and dietitian and postively with such nontraditional occupations as lawyer, life insurance saleswoman, author and psychologist. In males, the S.S.S. correlated negatively with the entire group (Group VIII) of business-detail occupations and positively with psychologist, social worker, minister, etc. In terms of the masculine role stereotype and the values of a capitalist culture, the business occupations are indeed more traditional while the helping professions may be a bit "far out".

It is interesting to note in this regard, that a study by Kish and Stage (1973) found that former students who had majored in economics and business scored more authoritarian on an Opinions of Mental Illness Scale than did former psychology and sociology majors.

Wilson and Patterson (1968) found that the mean C-Scale of liberal and conservative student groups were significantly different, with the conservatives scoring higher on the C-Scale. Several recent studies using measures of stimulus-seeking have reported similar, though inverse, results. Looft (1971) found that self ratings on a liberal-conservative continuum correlated positively with the S.S.S. and the Change-Seeker Index (+0·38 and +0·41 respectively) with stimulus-seekers rating themselves more liberal. Similarly, Stock and Looft (1969) found that self-perceived liberalism correlated with high scores on the Change-Seeker Index (+0·35).

All in all, the correlates of various indices of stimulus-seeking seem consistent with the assumption (and findings) that low sensation-seeking is correlated with high conservatism. The data, therefore, support the construct validity of the C-Scale as a measure of resistance to change and tendency to conform to the prevailing customs, norms, and authority of the culture.

V. Genesis of Stimulus-Seeking and Conservatism

An important question which can be asked regarding any personality trait concerns its developmental history. If people do indeed differ on such traits as stimulus-seeking or conservatism, how did these differences develop? Both genetic and historical variables can be conceptualized as influencing the final product.

With regard to genetic variables, there is evidence to suggest that exploratory behaviour in mice is a heritable trait (McClearn, 1959). Hall's (1951) classic experiment demonstrated the inheritance of fear or emotionality generated by novel situations in rats.

If exploratory motivation and/or fear of novel situations do indeed provide the primitive base for the more complex traits of conservatism and stimulus-seeking, then a hereditary contribution to these traits would be reasonable to postulate. The methodological problems involved in providing empirical support for such an hypothesis at the human level would be formidable indeed, however.

A first approximation to such empirical support would be the examination of family resemblances on these traits. Kish and Donnenwerth (1972) recently examined the problem for stimulus-seeking and found a modest correlation between parents and their male and female offspring ($+0.27$) on their S.S.S. scores. There was evidence of a possible sex difference in this data also, with females showing a greater resemblance to their parents than did the males.

Similarly Kish et al., 1973 examined parent-child resemblances on the Conservatism Scale, and found, with a rather small sample, a coefficient of $+0.41$. Interestingly, in both studies there were significant correlations between the husbands' and wives' scores (S.S.S. $+0.19$, C-Scale $+0.35$).

Since husbands and wives are not genetically related, but do resemble each other in these traits, the question is immediately raised regarding the bases for the parent–child resemblances. Although we cannot discount an hereditary influence completely, the findings seem also consistent with a learning hypothesis. People who live together for some time may develop certain consistencies in their attitudes towards controversial issues and in their interests regarding preferred activities. Alternately, with regard to spouses, the initial attraction and mutual choice may have been influenced by a degree of common outlook. Studies of interpersonal attraction, have shown it to be related to some extent to degree of agreement on various issues (Byrne, 1966). As usual, these studies of family resemblance have raised more questions than they have answered.

A more dynamically oriented analysis of developmental factors affecting conservatism and stimulus-seeking might postulate early learning experiences which would inhibit or enhance the child's exploratory behaviour and/or fears of novel stimulation. For example, consider a child with a normal degree of curiosity and tendency to explore his environment but with an over-anxious, perhaps over-protecting, parent. Such a parent, through his or her anxiety for the child's safety may condition anxiety responses to the child's exploratory tendencies and by generalization create a general suspicion, if not fear, of change and novelty.

Taking another tack, a child's exploratory forays are usually attempted from a secure emotional base. In other words, the conflict over exploring new situations tends to be attenuated if there is a parent available to provide comfort and security to help the child overcome his fear of new situations. Conceivably, then, a child in a precarious or insecure parent–child relationship may find novelty threatening and environmental stability comforting. Hence, another budding young conservative.

Kish *et al.* (in press) tried to take an exploratory look at the parental relationship variables for both conservatism and stimulus-seeking. They administered Form II of the S.S.S., the C-Scale, and the Family Relations Inventory /FRI) to eighty-five male and female college freshmen. The FRI was originally developed to measure some of the parental attitude variables contained in Roe's theory of vocational choice. It contains 202 items of the true-false variety, consisting of such parental relationship items as Item 36 "Only occasionally did my mother kiss or hug me". The inventory is scored for three dimensions for mother and three for father: (1) acceptance; (2) concentration (control, protection); and (3) avoidance. (Brunkan and Crites, 1968).

Unfortunately, this attempt to retrospectively examine the possible effects of parent–child relationship variables upon conservatism and stimulus-seeking yielded no significant findings. Hence, this theoretical account of the possible early learning influences upon these traits has no direct support at this time on the human level at least. Harlow's observation regarding the infant monkey's fearful reactions to novel stimulation in the absence of the surrogate or real mother provide some presumptive support, however (Harlow *et al.*, 1971). Similar observations have also been reported in human children. These data, of course, raise the important question of how such experiences might ultimately affect adult traits.

VI. Summary and Conclusions

The available evidence reviewed in this chapter supports the proposition that conservatism and stimulus-seeking are to some extent at opposite poles of a common dimension, namely—attitude towards changing, novel, complex, varied stimulation. Individuals low on the tendency to seek varied stimulation tend to be high on conservatism and vice versa.

A theoretical analysis of conservatism-stimulus-seeking was proposed in the form of a two-process reaction to novelty; fear and exploratory tendencies. In this analysis, the position of the individual on the continuum of attitudes towards stimulation is determined by the relative strengths of these opposing processes. It was hypothesized that conservative individuals may have such a balance that aversion to novelty is dominant over the approach tendencies, whereas in stimulus-seekers the exploratory tendencies would be dominant.

Hypotheses were also presented concerning the genesis of conservatism-stimulus-seeking. Both genetic and experiential factors are probably involved. Possible learning histories which could conditions anxiety to novel situations—such as an overprotective, anxious parent or a rejecting parent—were examined.

References

Adorno, T. W., Frenkel-Brunswick, E., Levinson, D. J. and Sanford, R. N. (1950). The Authoritarian Personality. Harper and Row, New York.

Berlyne, D. E. (1960). "Conflict, Arousal and Curiosity." McGraw Hill, New York.

Blackburn, R. (1969). Sensation-seeking, impulsivity, and psychopathic personality. *J. consult. clin. Psychol.* **33**, 571–574.

Brownfield, C. A. (1966). Optimal stimulation levels of normal and disturbed subjects in sensory deprivation. *Psychologia.* **9**, 27–318.

Brunkan, R. J. and Crites, J. O. (1968). An inventory to measure the parental attitude variables in Roe's theory of vocational choice. *J. counsel Psychol.* **32**, 633–667.

Byrne, D. (1966). "An Introduction to Personality: A Research Approach." Chapter 2. Prentice Hall, Englewood Cliffs, N.J.

Garlington, W. K. and Shimota, H. E. (1964). The Change Seeker Index: A measure of the need for variable stimulus input. *Psychol. Rep.* **14**, 919–924.

Hall, C. S. (1951). The Genetics of Behavior. In "Handbook of Experimental Psychology". (Stevens, S. S., ed.). John Wiley and Sons, New York.

Harlow, H. F., Harlow, M. K. and Suomi, S. J. (1971). From thought to therapy: Lessons from a primate laboratory. *Am. Sci.* **59**, 538–549.

Kish, G. B. (1966). Studies of Sensory Reinforcement. In "Operant Behavior: Areas of Research and Application". (Honing, W. K., ed.). Appleton-Century-Crofts, New York.

Kish, G. B. (1970a). Reduced cognitive innovation and stimulus-seeking in chronic schizophrenia. *J. clin. Psychol.* **26**, 170–175.

Kish, G. B. (1970b). Cognitive innovation and stimulus-seeking. A study of the correlates of the obscure figures test. *Percept. mot. Skills.* **31**, 839–847.

Kish, G. B. and Busse, W. (1968). Correlates of stimulus-seeking: Age, education, intelligence, and aptitudes. *J. consult. clin. Psychol.* **32**, 633–637.

Kish, G. B. and Busse, W. (1969). M.M.P.I. correlates of sensation-seeking in male alcoholics: A Test of Quay's Hypothesis Applied to Alcoholism. *J. clin. Psychol.* **25**, 60–62.

Kish, G. B. and Donnenwerth, G. V. (1969). Interests and stimulus-seeking. *J. counsel. Psychol.* **16**, 551–556.

Kish, G. B. and Donnenwerth, G. V. (1972). Sex differences in the correlates of stimulus-seeking. *J. consult. clin. Psychol.* **38**, 42–49.

Kish, G. B. Netterberg, E. E. and Leahy, L. (1973). Stimulus-seeking and conservatism. *J. clin. Psychol.* **29**, 17–20.

Kish, G. B. and Stage, T. (1973). College student mental hospital volunteers: Any benefits to the student or society? *J. Community Psychol.* **1**, 13–15.

Leuba, C. (1955). Toward some integration of learning theories: The concept of optimal stimulation. *Psychol. Rep.* **1**, 27–33.

Looft, W. R. (1971). Conservatives, liberals, radicals, and sensation-seekers. *Percept. mot. Skills.* **32**, 98.

McClearn, G. E. (1959). Genetics of mouse behaviour in novel situations. *J. comp. physiol. Psychol.* **52**, 62–67.

Rokeach, M. (1960). "The Open and Closed Mind." Basic Books, New York.

Stock, W. A. and Looft, W. R. (1969). Relationships among several demographic variables and the change seeker index. *Percept. mot. Skills.* **29**, 1101–1014.

Wilson, G. D. (1970). Is there a general factor in social attitudes? Evidence from a Factor Analysis of the Conservatism Scale. *Br. J. soc. clin. Psychol.* **9**, 101–107.

Wilson, G. D. and Patterson, J. R. (1968). A new measure of conservatism. *Br. J. soc. clin. Psychol.* **7**, 264–269.

Zuckerman, M. (1971). Dimensions of sensation-seeking. *J. consult. clin. Psychol.* **36**, 45–52.

Zuckerman, M. "Manual and Research Report for the Sensation-Seeking Scale (S.S.S.)". Unpublished manuscript.

Zuckerman, M., Bone, R. N., Neary, R., Mangelsdorff, D. and Brustman, B. What is the sensation-seeker? Personality trait and experience correlates of the Sensation-Seeking Scales. *J. consult. clin. Psychol.* **39**, 308–321.

Zuckerman, M., Kolin, E. A., Price, L. and Zoob, I. (1964). Development of a Sensation-Seeking Scales. *J. consult. clin. Psychol.* **28**, 477–482.

Zuckerman, M. and Link, K. (1968). Construct validation for the Sensation-Seeking Scale. *J. consult. clin. Psychol.* **32**, 420–426.

Conservatism Within Families: A Study of the Generation Gap*

14

ROGER BOSHIER

University of Auckland, New Zealand

I. Introduction

The "generation-gap" concept, invoked to account for the apparent rebellion of young people, commands the attention of various groups of social scientists. One group considers the "generation-gap" too wide to be bridged (e.g. Friedenberg, 1965, 1969; Feuer, 1969) and predicts that tension between an exploitative older generation and youth will escalate into open conflict before long. Bettelheim (1965) goes so far as to say that rebellion is a necessary concomitant of personal growth. He argues that factors that traditionally mitigate generational conflict have become moribund or weak; the older generation is no longer a powerful resource for coping with the world. To become an adult a young person simply has to rebel. Feuer (1969) argues that gerontocratic power structures and the failure of the older generation to resolve current problems makes inter-generational conflict almost inevitable. Similarly, Musgrove (1965, 1970) maintains that because of high survival rates positions of power and respon-

* The initial impetus for this study came from the N.Z. broadcasting corporation who provided the expenses. The programme arising from the study entitled "Bridging the Gap" was screened by N.Z.B.C. in November, 1971.

sibility are not quickly vacated. The demand and opportunities for young people are thus reduced, so there is a "power struggle" between young and old.

A second group is sanguine and considers there is more harmony than disharmony between generations (cf. Larson and Myerhoff, 1965; Douvan and Adelson, 1968; Kandel and Lesser, 1969). These writers generally accept that there is a "generation-gap" but argue that attitudinal continuity within families out-weighs attitudinal discontinuity.

A third group of social scientists declare the "generation-gap" to be a misnomer. They suggest that the thrust of fresh activity from young people is the translation of parental ideals into substantive action (e.g. Kenniston, 1968). However, this third orientation is considered by Bengston to be a rather uninspiring compromise. "That some things change, and some things stay the same, is simply irrefutable; and to say that there is neither a great gap nor a complete congruence between generations may be points worth emphasizing in order to allay anxieties of parents and taxpayers" (1969, p. 11), but unless investigators can show what points of difference exist, and which kinds of attitudes and values exhibit the greatest variation between various age groups, then additional data can do little but reinforce already entrenched speculations.

Whether the "generation-gap" is wide, inevitable, or merely a misnomer, authoritarian personality researchers (Adorno et al., 1950) were adamant that family background is a powerful determinant of personality development. They predicted that despite age-related differences in attitude, autocratic family structures would be associated with the development of authoritarian personality patterns and that equalitarian family structures would be associated with the development of democratic personality patterns in children.

Hart (1957), for example, found that authoritarian parents in contrast to equalitarian parents, select non-love oriented disciplinary techniques. In a series of studies (Levinson and Huffman, 1955) the *Traditional Family Ideology* scale was found to correlate positively with F-scores. Similarly, Block (1955) found that F-scores correlated with the holding of restrictive versus permissive child-rearing attitudes among a group of military officers. Zuckerman and Oltean (1959), using the *Parental Attitude Research Inventory* found high and positive correlations between F-scores and authoritarian control of child behaviour.

The TFI and the F-Scale used in the above studies are open to methodological criticism (see Chapter 3 of this volume). Nevertheless, Boshier and Izard (1972), using the C-Scale and a shortened P.A.R.I. found conservative mothers in New Zealand to be more inclined than liberal mothers to "dominate", "reject" and "indulge" their children. A circular pattern of cause and effect may therefore be postulated as operating with respect to child-rearing practices and the development of conservative–liberal attitudes in children.

The aims of the present study were to:

(1) Ascertain the degree to which attitudes of parent child dyads are in accord.

(2) Ascertain the extent to which children are aware of parental attitudes towards major social issues.

(3) Identify attitudinal areas where inter-generational agreement and disagreement is greatest.

In pursuing these objectives an attempt was made to obtain respondents more typical of their generational cohort than the atypical radicals who have provided the focus of most previous "generation-gap" research.

II. Method

The first sample consisted of 34 boy and 42 girl high school students aged 17–19 years, who were at a residential course in Wellington as applicants for *Volunteer Service Abroad* (New Zealand's mini Peace Corps). They had a mean Otis I.Q. of 127 and above average records of physical and social achievement. Although they came from all parts of New Zealand and a wide variety of social and economic circumstances it is not contended they were a cross section of New Zealand 17–19-year-olds.

This sample (hitherto referred to as the "children")* accepted an invitation to take part in a research project under the auspices of the University and the New Zealand Broadcasting Corporation, the first step of which consisted of their completing a modified C-Scale. Some items were replaced on the basis of a rotated factor analysis of the original scale; Boshier, 1972.

Subsequently the "children" completed the scale a second time, on behalf of their mothers (mother estimates) and a third time on behalf of their fathers (father estimates). The requests were made to them as follows:

> From time to time you will have noticed that your parents hold attitudes and opinions that are different from your own. You will also have noticed that you and your parents share certain attitudes and opinions. We want you now to fill in the questionnaire as you think your *mother* would fill it in. Remember, think of your mother, and fill it in for her. We want an accurate picture of what you think are your mother's attitudes.

After the three questionnaires had been completed the children were informed that the data just gathered was to be used in a television pro-

---

*It is accepted that 17–19-year-olds are not "children" and may be more appropriately described as "young adults". However, as we compared in-family attitudes (i.e. attitudes of parents and their children) we retained the term "children" so as clearly to distinguish the samples under study.

gramme in connection with which they were asked to give their parents' names, addresses and telephone numbers. All the children consented to their parents being approached. The parents, except for those who were overseas, were sent the following letter before the children could return home and possibly contaminate results by discussing the research with their parents.

> Your son/daughter has taken part in a New Zealand wide survey of social attitudes that we are conducting, and has agreed to our contacting you to ask if you would play a similar part. In some cases we are writing to both parents, and if this is so in your family, would you please complete the questionnaire sheets separately? Later, you will no doubt enjoy sharing your views with each other.
>
> This survey is being conducted ... in an attempt to assess the social attitudes of significant New Zealand families. No information will be presented or released in a way which could lead to your identification.
>
> The results will be analysed by computer, and will form the basis of a 'Survey" television studio programme later this year. Some of those completing questionnaires will be invited to take part in a discussion of the results to be recorded at W.N.T.V.1. early in October.
>
> Please complete and return the form promptly. We depend on your co-operation for the success of this research programme.

The parents (like their children) were co-operative, with 87 per cent responding within ten days and a further 9 per cent responding after a reminder by telephone. The non-response rate of 4 per cent was far below that which other researchers have received in postal surveys (cf. Travers, 1969, p. 199).

In the "parent" cohort men were significantly ($t = 4 \cdot 0$, $p < 0 \cdot 001$) older than the women. The mean age of men was $50 \cdot 12$ years (S.D. $= 5 \cdot 89$) for women $46 \cdot 24$ years (S.D. $= 4 \cdot 81$).

III. Results

A. Inter-Generational Attitudes

C-Scale means for each of the sample groups are shown in Table I.

Both boys and girls estimated their mothers and fathers to be more conservative than they really were. There were slight differences between the mean conservatism scores of boys and girls and the mean scores of fathers and mothers, but they were not statistically significant. However, the differences between the C-Scores of girls and their mothers ($t = 4 \cdot 7$), of girls and their fathers ($t = 4 \cdot 6$), of boys and their fathers ($t = 3 \cdot 7$), and boys and their mothers ($t = 4 \cdot 7$), were all statistically significant ($p < 0 \cdot 005$). Overall, the children were significantly more liberal than their

TABLE I

Conservatism Scale means and S.D.s for various groups.

	N	Mean	S.D.
Boys	34	33·75	11·15
Girls	42	34·64	12·59
Fathers	72	43·95	13·82
Mothers	71	46·69	13·86
Boys' estimates of their father	33	54·81	10·87
Girls' estimates of their father	40	56·57	13·73
Boys' estimates of their mother	33	52·40	14·32
Girls' estimates of their mother	42	52·33	12·30

parents, whilst the parents were significantly more liberal than their children estimated them to be.

A "whole scale" conservatism-discrepancy score was then calculated for each dyad (boy/father, boy/mother, girl/mother, girl/father, etc.) by subtracting the "whole scale" C-score obtained by, for example, Billy Gilbert, from that obtained by Mr Gilbert, Snr., to obtain a boy/father discrepancy score, and Billy Gilbert's "whole scale" C-score from Mrs Gilbert's "whole scale" C-score to obtain a boy/mother discrepancy score. These scores were summed for each pair of comparison groups across all the families involved in the study. The resultant mean "Conservatism discrepancy scores" are presented in Table II.

TABLE II

"Whole-scale" conservatism discrepancy scores for several sample pairs.

	Boys		Girls	
	M	S.D.	M	S.D.
Father	12·21	10·60	17·49	10·50
Mother	16·93	13·07	15·45	11·69
Father/Father estimate	11·87	8·91	14·41	8·5
Mother/Mother estimate	11·18	8·22	11·57	8·07

This shows that the "generation-gap", as measured by "whole scale" Conservatism scores is greatest between children and the opposite sexed parent. In other words, boys are attitudinally closer to their father than their mother, whilst the girls are attitudinally closer to their mother. Mother/father attitude discrepancies averaged 10·07, which is significantly lower than the discrepancies between any of the parent child pairs. Of all the comparison groups considered, the "gap" was greatest between girls and their fathers.

"Father/father estimate" discrepancy scores were calculated by sub-tracting each father's C-score from the estimated C-score provided for him by his son or daughter; likewise for "Mother/mother estimate" discrepan-cies. These show that boys are as well informed about their mother's attitudes as about their father's attitudes. Girls estimate their mother's attitudes with about the same degree of inaccuracy as do the boys, but make more errors when estimating their father's attitudes. In short, there was a "whole scale" attitudinal "generation gap" and also a "communication-gap" within the families studies, the greatest gap being between fathers and daughters.

To test the notion that conservative parents nurture conservative children, product-moment correlations among the C-scores of boys, girls, fathers, mothers, "children" and "parents" were calculated.

TABLE III

Correlation coefficients between the conservatism scores of children and their parents.

	N	Fathers	Mothers	"Parents"
Boys	28	0·31*	0·17	0·27
Girls	31	0·17	0·33*	0·30
"Children"	59			0·27†

*p < 0·05 (one-tailed test).   †p < 0·02 (one-tailed test).

Seventeen parent/child dyads were excluded from the above analysis because one or more members of the family were absent (deceased, separ-ated or divorced). These results show that conservative mothers tend to nurture conservative daughters ($r = 0.33$, $p < 0.05$) and conservative fathers tend to nurture conservative sons ($r = 0.31$, $p < 0.05$) which suggests that parents have less control over the attitudinal development of opposite-sexed offspring than same-sexed offspring. Overall, the presence of con-servative/liberal social attitudes in "parents" is associated with the presence of similar attitudes in their "children" ($r = 0.27$, $p < 0.02$).

Kenniston (1965, 1967, 1968) described how alienated youth em-pathized and identified with their mothers in a reaction against weak father images. Left-wing activists he describes in a similar way. The dominant ethos of families producing activist males was equalitarian, permissive and individuated. The mother, rather than the father, was most likely to epitomize these values. Male activist youth, in Kenniston's samples, were most likely to identify with, and take on the characteristics of their mothers rather than their fathers. Our child respondents, more typical of their generational cohort than Kenniston's radicals, hold attitudes that more closely resemble those of the same-sexed parent than the opposite-sexed parent.

B. MEAN ITEM SCORES

The above conclusions were based on *total* C-Scale scores. To identify the "social issues" where inter-generational agreement and disagreement was greatest, *item* means were calculated for each of the comparison groups. These results, presented in Tables IV and V, show parents to be significantly more inclined than children to favour the death penalty, school uniforms, sabbath observance, patriotism, self denial, military drill, divine law, white superiority, licensing laws, chastity, royalty, conventional clothing, censorship, birching, strict rules, austere prisons, and Bible truth. They are significantly more inclined than their children to disapprove of evolution theory, striptease shows, beatniks, modern art, cousin marriage, student demonstrators, electronic music, nudist camps, disarmament, mixed marriage and coloured immigration. Children, however, were more inclined to "favour, approve of, or believe in", masculine superiority, and were more against trade unions; in these respects they could be described as more conservative than their parents.

The fact that "replacement" items (trade unions, masculine superiority, and security police) failed to discriminate between the "generations" calls into question the justification for their use in the scale. However, two "replacement" items, austere prisons and electronic music, were among the best discriminators. The most powerful discriminators (viz. beatniks, electronic music, disarmament, student demonstrators, modern art) are high loading items on an "intolerance of youth" factor (Boshier, 1972).

C. "CHILDREN'S" ESTIMATES OF SEPARATE PARENTAL ATTITUDES

Children (boys and girls combined) made accurate estimates of their mothers' attitudes on thirty-three items, and inaccurate* estimates on the remaining seventeen. They considered their mothers to be significantly more conservative than they really were with regard to modern art, self denial, masculine superiority, missionaries, student demonstrators, legalized abortion, empire building, student pranks, electronic music, conventional clothing, church authority, jazz, Chinese restaurants and divorce. Some of these are "peripheral" issues; the inability of the "children" to correctly estimate their mothers' attitudes may simply be a reflection of the fact that these issues are not important. Mothers were more conservative than the children estimated them to be on disarmament and austere prisons.

Children estimated their father's attitude correctly on only twenty-four items. Overall, they estimated their fathers to be significantly more conservative than they really were. They overestimated their fathers'

---

*Defined as a significant difference ($p < 0.05$) between the parent's mean item response and the children's estimate of their parent's response to that item.

TABLE IV

Conservatism Scale item means, per cent making the conservative response, and S.D.s

Item	Boys			Girls			Children			Fathers		
	Item mean	%	S.D.	Item mean	%	S.A.	Item mean	%	S.D.	Item mean	%	S.D
Death penalty	0·44	(22·0)	0·82	0·33	(16·5)	0·75	0·38	(19·0)	0·78	0·82	(41·0)	0·96
Evolution theory	0·05	(02·5)	0·34	0·31	(15·5)	0·68	0·20	(10·0)	0·57	0·54	(27·0)	0·86
School uniforms	1·20	(60·0)	0·97	1·38	(69·0)	0·93	1·30	(65·0)	0·95	1·62	(81·0)	0·78
Striptease shows	0·61	(30·5)	0·92	1·40	(70·0)	0·82	1·05	(52·5)	0·95	1·31	(65·5)	0·90
Sabbath observance	1·00	(50·0)	0·95	1·16	(58·0)	0·98	1·09	(54·5)	0·97	1·36	(68·0)	0·89
Beatniks	0·58	(29·0)	0·85	0·76	(38·0)	0·79	0·68	(34·0)	0·82	1·35	(67·5)	0·89
Patriotism	1·44	(72·0)	0·89	1·59	(79·5)	0·79	1·53	(76·5)	0·84	1·76	(88·0)	0·61
Modern art	0·32	(16·0)	0·72	0·09	(04·5)	0·37	0·20	(10·0)	0·57	0·82	(41·0)	0·94
Self denial	1·23	(61·5)	0·95	1·35	(67·5)	0·87	1·30	(65·0)	0·91	1·69	(84·5)	0·72
Working mothers	0·82	(41·0)	0·99	0·47	(23·5)	0·80	0·63	(31·5)	0·91	0·98	(49·0)	0·95
Masculine superiority	1·23	(61·5)	0·98	0·69	(34·5)	0·92	0·93	(46·5)	0·98	0·46	(23·0)	0·81
Birth control	0·26	(13·0)	0·66	0·23	(11·5)	0·65	0·25	(12·5)	0·66	0·27	(13·5)	0·68
Military drill	0·76	(38·0)	0·98	0·90	(45·0)	0·93	0·84	(42·0)	0·95	1·02	(51·0)	0·99
Co-education	0·26	(13·0)	0·66	0·00	(00·0)	0·00	0·12	(0·60)	0·46	0·16	(08·0)	0·54
Divine law	0·67	(33·5)	0·87	1·09	(54·5)	0·87	0·91	(45·5)	0·90	1·16	(58·0)	0·96
Socialism	0·76	(38·0)	0·92	0·81	(40·5)	0·94	0·79	(39·5)	0·93	0·71	(35·5)	0·90
White superiority	0·05	(02·5)	0·34	0·00	(00·0)	0·00	0·03	(00·1)	0·23	0·33	(16·5)	0·69
Cousin marriage	1·11	(55·5)	0·97	1·04	(52·0)	0·96	1·08	(54·0)	0·96	1·36	(68·0)	0·83
Missionaries	1·35	(67·5)	0·91	1·33	(66·5)	0·90	1·34	(67·0)	0·90	1·38	(69·0)	0·89
Student demonstrators	0·26	(13·0)	0·66	0·47	(23·5)	0·80	0·38	(19·0)	0·75	0·84	(42·0)	0·94
Security police	1·11	(55·5)	1·00	1·28	(64·0)	0·89	1·21	(6·05)	0·94	1·02	(51·0)	0·99
Legalised abortion	0·88	(44·0)	0·97	1·02	(51·2)	0·97	0·96	(48·0)	0·97	0·96	(48·0)	0·96
Empire building	0·47	(23·5)	0·82	0·45	(22·5)	0·77	0·46	(23·0)	0·79	0·27	(13·5)	0·62
Student pranks	0·29	(14·5)	0·71	0·69	(34·5)	0·89	0·51	(25·5)	0·84	0·56	(28·0)	0·83
Licensing laws	1·70	(85·0)	0·71	1·50	(75·0)	0·86	1·59	(79·5)	0·80	1·69	(84·5)	0·69
Electronic music	0·47	(23·5)	0·86	0·28	(14·0)	0·70	0·37	(18·5)	0·78	0·96	(48·0)	0·92
Chastity	1·23	(61·5)	0·98	1·45	(72·5)	0·86	1·35	(67·5)	0·92	1·60	(80·0)	0·74
Fluoridation	0·44	(22·0)	0·78	0·23	(11·5)	0·65	0·33	(16·5)	0·72	0·44	(22·0)	0·79
Royalty	1·05	(52·5)	1·01	1·14	(57·0)	0·95	1·10	(55·0)	0·97	1·38	(69·0)	0·91
Women judges	0·23	(11·5)	0·65	0·14	(07·0)	0·52	0·18	(09·0)	0·58	0·38	(19·0)	0·76
Conventional clothing	1·00	(50·0)	0·98	0·95	(47·5)	0·96	0·97	(48·5)	0·97	1·64	(82·0)	0·75
Trade unions	0·67	(33·5)	0·94	0·76	(38·0)	0·90	0·72	(36·0)	0·92	0·16	(08·0)	0·50
Apartheid	0·20	(10·0)	0·59	0·19	(09·5)	0·55	0·20	(10·0)	0·57	0·26	(13·0)	0·62
Nudist camps	0·23	(11·5)	0·60	1·02	(50·1)	0·97	0·67	(33·5)	0·92	0·96	(48·0)	0·94
Church authority	0·58	(29·0)	0·82	0·86	(47·5)	0·92	0·74	(37·0)	0·88	0·85	(42·5)	0·97
Disarmament	0·35	(17·5)	0·77	0·19	(09·5)	0·55	0·26	(13·0)	0·66	0·58	(29·0)	0·88
Censorship	0·94	(47·0)	1·01	1·02	(51·0)	0·97	0·99	(49·5)	0·99	1·15	(57·5)	0·95
Workers' strikes	1·02	(51·0)	0·96	1·14	(57·0)	1·00	1·09	(54·5)	0·98	0·85	(42·5)	0·95
Birching	0·47	(23·5)	0·86	0·40	(20·0)	0·76	0·43	(21·5)	0·81	0·67	(33·5)	0·92
Mixed marriage	0·26	(13·0)	0·66	0·04	(00·02)	0·30	0·15	(07·5)	0·51	0·65	(32·5)	0·89
Strict rules	0·67	(33·5)	0·94	0·52	(26·0)	0·83	0·59	(29·5)	0·88	0·87	(43·5)	0·96
Jazz	0·50	(25·0)	0·86	0·52	(26·0)	0·86	0·51	(25·5)	0·86	0·42	(21·0)	0·79
Straitjackets	0·64	(32·0)	0·88	0·47	(23·5)	0·74	0·55	(27·5)	0·81	0·60	(30·0)	0·81
Chinese restaurants	0·20	(10·0)	0·53	0·04	(00·2)	0·21	0·12	(06·0)	0·40	0·18	(09·0)	0·51
Peacetime conscription	0·82	(41·0)	0·99	0·73	(36·5)	0·96	0·78	(39·0)	0·97	0·71	(35·5)	0·96
Divorce	0·52	(26·0)	0·88	0·61	(30·5)	0·88	0·58	(29·0)	0·88	0·56	(28·0)	0·88
Austere prisons	0·55	(27·5)	0·86	0·45	(22·5)	0·80	0·50	(25·0)	0·83	0·87	(43·5)	0·96
Coloured immigration	0·41	(20·6)	0·78	0·11	(05·5)	0·45	0·25	(12·5)	0·63	0·80	(40·0)	0·95
Bible truth	0·35	(42·5)	0·95	0·92	(46·5)	0·92	0·90	(45·0)	0·93	1·25	(62·5)	0·91
Welfare legislation	0·17	(08·5)	0·57	0·04	(00·2)	0·30	0·10	(05·0)	0·45	0·13	(06·5)	0·47

or sample groups.

Mothers			Parents			Fathers (Chn's estimates)			Mothers (Chn's estimates)		
Item Mean	%	S.D.	Item Mean	%	S.D.	Item Mean	%	S.D.	Item Mean	%	S.D.
0·67	(33·5)	0·91	0·74	(37·0)	0·93	0·83	(41·5)	0·95	0·43	(21·5)	0·82
0·61	(30·5)	0·84	0·58	(29·0)	0·85	0·49	(24·5)	0·78	0·54	(27·0)	0·79
1·80	(90·0)	0·57	1·72	(86·0)	0·68	1·80	(90·0)	0·55	1·78	(89·0)	0·60
1·72	(86·0)	0·69	1·53	(76·5)	0·82	1·16	(58·0)	0·90	1·83	(91·5)	0·47
1·54	(77·0)	0·85	1·46	(73·0)	0·87	1·16	(58·0)	0·94	1·38	(69·0)	0·91
1·49	(74·5)	0·77	1·42	(71·0)	0·83	1·77	(88·5)	0·59	1·59	(79·5)	0·73
1·79	(89·5)	0·55	1·78	(89·0)	0·58	1·74	(87·0)	0·63	1·72	(86·0)	0·62
0·41	(20·5)	0·78	0·60	(30·0)	0·88	1·39	(69·5)	0·87	1·10	(55·0)	0·96
1·84	(92·0)	0·55	1·77	(88·5)	0·64	1·33	(66·5)	0·88	1·45	(72·5)	0·84
0·66	(33·0)	0·89	0·81	(40·5)	0·93	1·07	(53·5)	0·95	0·51	(25·5)	0·87
0·54	(27·0)	0·87	0·50	(25·0)	0·84	1·40	(70·0)	0·86	0·90	(45·0)	0·93
0·15	(07·5)	0·51	0·21	(10·5)	0·60	0·71	(35·5)	0·89	0·46	(23·0)	0·79
1·34	(67·0)	0·93	1·19	(59·5)	0·97	1·50	(75·0)	0·83	1·18	(59·0)	0·90
0·13	(06·5)	0·47	0·15	(07·5)	0·50	0·33	(16·5)	0·67	0·28	(14·0)	0·67
1·31	(65·5)	0·92	1·24	(62·0)	0·94	1·06	(53·0)	0·93	1·29	(64·5)	0·88
1·08	(54·0)	0·94	0·90	(45·0)	0·93	1·23	(61·5)	0·87	1·26	(63·0)	0·87
0·18	(09·0)	0·56	0·25	(12·5)	0·63	0·27	(13·5)	0·66	0·12	(06·0)	0·46
1·59	(79·5)	0·76	1·48	(74·0)	0·80	1·49	(74·5)	0·74	1·53	(76·5)	0·74
1·47	(73·5)	0·83	1·43	(71·5)	0·86	1·51	(75·5)	0·81	1·79	(89·5)	0·60
0·87	(43·5)	0·90	0·85	(42·5)	0·92	1·46	(73·0)	0·88	1·34	(67·0)	0·92
1·25	(62·5)	0·92	1·14	(57·0)	0·96	1·37	(68·5)	0·90	1·24	(62·0)	0·92
0·97	(48·5)	0·98	0·97	(48·5)	0·97	1·49	(74·5)	0·74	1·35	(67·5)	0·86
0·44	(22·0)	0·79	0·36	(18·0)	0·72	0·81	(40·5)	0·82	0·70	(35·0)	0·82
0·75	(37·5)	0·91	0·66	(33·0)	0·87	1·47	(73·5)	0·86	1·33	(66·5)	0·93
1·84	(92·0)	0·52	1·77	(88·5)	0·61	1·59	(79·5)	0·77	1·70	(85·0)	0·71
0·77	(38·5)	0·92	0·86	(43·0)	0·92	1·57	(78·5)	0·77	1·41	(70·5)	0·87
1·82	(91·0)	0·53	1·72	(86·0)	0·64	1·80	(90·0)	0·58	1·83	(91·5)	0·53
0·43	(21·5)	0·81	0·42	(21·0)	0·79	0·21	(10·5)	0·53	0·30	(15·0)	0·65
1·57	(78·5)	0·81	1·48	(74·0)	0·86	1·57	(78·5)	0·77	1·70	(85·0)	0·69
0·11	(05·5)	0·45	0·24	(12·0)	0·63	0·77	(38·5)	0·87	0·20	(10·0)	0·57
1·33	(66·5)	0·93	1·47	(73·5)	0·86	1·89	(94·0)	0·47	1·64	(82·0)	0·76
0·51	(25·5)	0·81	0·35	(17·0)	0·70	0·63	(31·5)	0·85	0·59	(29·5)	0·85
0·16	(08·0)	0·45	0·21	(10·5)	0·54	0·11	(05·5)	0·44	0·18	(09·0)	0·56
1·33	(66·5)	0·87	1·15	(57·5)	0·92	1·44	(72·0)	0·79	1·28	(64·0)	0·90
0·93	(46·5)	0·96	0·90	(45·0)	0·96	1·11	(55·5)	0·97	1·49	(74·5)	0·84
0·88	(44·0)	0·95	0·74	(37·0)	0·92	0·79	(39·5)	0·92	0·38	(19·0)	0·73
1·64	(82·0)	0·73	1·40	(70·0)	0·88	1·79	(89·5)	0·56	1·80	(90·0)	0·57
1·34	(67·0)	0·89	1·11	(55·5)	0·95	1·16	(58·0)	0·96	1·30	(65·0)	0·92
0·61	(30·5)	0·90	0·64	(32·0)	0·91	0·99	(49·5)	0·95	0·62	(31·0)	0·89
0·69	(34·5)	0·90	0·67	(33·5)	0·89	0·67	(33·5)	0·91	0·66	(33·0)	0·92
1·20	(60·0)	0·89	1·04	(52·0)	0·94	1·33	(66·5)	0·88	1·01	(50·5)	0·94
0·41	(20·5)	0·74	0·41	(20·5)	0·76	1·36	(68·0)	0·92	1·35	(67·5)	0·89
0·54	(27·0)	0·79	0·57	(28·5)	0·79	0·87	(43·5)	0·88	0·67	(33·5)	0·84
0·08	(04·0)	0·38	0·13	(06·5)	0·45	0·30	(15·0)	0·67	0·33	(16·5)	0·70
1·02	(51·0)	0·97	0·87	(43·5)	0·97	1·30	(65·0)	0·91	1·04	(52·0)	0·94
0·64	(32·0)	0·88	0·60	(30·0)	0·87	0·99	(49·5)	0·97	1·01	(5·05)	0·99
0·90	(45·0)	0·99	0·89	(44·5)	0·98	0·74	(37·0)	0·91	0·62	(31·0)	0·86
0·57	(28·5)	0·87	0·68	(34·0)	0·91	0·70	(35·0)	0·87	0·57	(28·5)	0·81
1·43	(71·5)	0·83	1·35	(67·5)	0·87	1·06	(53·0)	0·93	1·42	(71·0)	0·82
0·08	(04·0)	0·38	0·10	(0·50)	0·42	0·14	(07·0)	0·49	0·12	(06·0)	0·43

TABLE V

Conservatism Scale item means, significance of differences between sample groups.

	I	II	III	IV	V
				Mothers/	Fathers/
	Boys/	Parents/	Fathers/	Mothers	Fathers
	Girls	Children	Mothers	(Chn's est)	(Chn's est)
Death penalty	0·59	2·88*	0·84	1·59	−0·06
Evolution theory	−2·09*	3·74*	−0·39	0·48	0·40
School uniforms	−0·79	3·27*	−1·44	0·27	−1·46
Striptease shows	−3·87*	3·56*	−2·75 *	−1·05	0·94
Sabbath observance	−0·75	2·66*	−1·09	1·06	1·26
Beatniks	−0·91	6·08*	−0·05	−0·77	−3·07*
Patriotism	−0·78	2·27*	−0·21	0·63	0·19
Modern art	1·67	3·88*	2·52*	−4·67*	−3·45*
Self denial	−0·57	3·87*	−1·21	3·26*	2·53*
Working mothers	1·65	1·32	1·90*	0·94	−0·52
Masculine superiority	2·46*	−3·16*	−0·55	−2·30*	−6·30*
Birth control	0·18	−0·46	1·11	−2·80*	−3·15
Military drill	−0·63	2·46*	−1·82*	1·01	−2·90*
Co-education	2·32*	0·41	0·35	−1·50	−1·52
Divine law	−2·07*	2·47*	−0·84	0·14	0·63
Socialism	−0·21	0·85	−2·19*	−1·16	−3·26*
White superiority	1·00	3·49*	1·24	0·69	0·46
Cousin marriage	0·31	3·04*	−1·53	0·50	−0·86
Missionaries	0·10	0·68	−0·58	−2·49*	−0·85
Student demonstrators	−1·25	3·90*	−0·19	−3·03*	−3·78*
Security police	−0·76	−0·52	−1·28	0·06	−2·05*
Legalized abortion	−0·63	0·03	−0·02	−2·43*	−3·33*
Empire building	0·10	−0·88	−1·30	−1·85*	−4·19*
Student pranks	−2·14*	1·20	−1·18	−3·65*	−5·94*
Licensing laws	1·14	1·62*	−1·27	1·32	0·80
Electronic music	0·01	3·99*	1·13	−4·14*	−3·92*
Chastity	−1·01	2·98*	−1·83*	−0·10	−1·65*
Fluoridation	7·14*	0·92	0·07	0·96	1·79*
Royalty	−0·37	2·75*	−1·20	−0·94	−1·23
Women judges	0·67	0·64	2·28*	−0·94	−2·67*
Conventional clothing	0·21	3·66*	1·97*	−2·15*	−2·15*
Trade unions	−0·40	−3·06*	−2·78*	−0·59	−3·80*
Apartheid	−0·12	0·12	0·90	−0·23	1·44
Nudist camps	−4·31*	3·58*	−2·15*	0·34	−3·02*
Church authority	−1·34	1·18	−0·44	−3·53*	−1·48
Disarmament	1·03	4·17*	−1·79*	3·41*	−1·27
Censorship	−0·36	3·00*	−3·11*	−1·44	−4·43*
Workers' strikes	−0·50	0·14	−2·85*	0·26	−1·76*
Birching	0·35	1·63*	0·39	−0·07	−1·85*
Mixed marriage	1·75	5·20*	−0·20	0·20	−0·10
Strict rules	0·73	3·38*	−1·87*	1·17	−2·73*
Jazz	−0·12	−0·82	0·06	−6·79*	−6·16*
Straitjackets	0·90	0·14	0·40	−0·93	−1·79*

	I	II	III	IV	V
				Mothers/	Fathers/
	Boys/	Parents/	Fathers/	Mothers	Fathers
	Girls	Children	Mothers	(Chn's est)	(Chn's est)
Chinese restaurants	1·61	0·18	1·19	−2·63*	−1·12
Peacetime conscription	0·38	0·66	−1·71*	−0·14	−3·51*
Divorce	−0·44	0·18	−0·46	−2·35*	−2·55*
Austere prisons	0·56	2·96*	−0·16	1·76*	0·77
Coloured immigration	1·94	3·86*	1·33	0·06	0·60
Bible truth	−0·35	3·36*	−1·06	0·04	1·20
Welfare legislation	1·17	−0·03	0·56	−0·52	−0·18

*p < 0·05.

conservatism on beatniks, modern art, masculine superiority, military drill, socialism, student demonstrators, security police, legalized abortion, empire building, student pranks, electronic music, chastity, women judges, conventional clothing, trade unions, nudist camp censorship, workers, strikes, birching, strict rules, jazz, straitjackets, peacetime conscription and divorce, and made underestimates on self-denial and fluoridation. Many of these are "core" issues. The fact that "children" made inaccurate estimates reflects the fact that there is no bisexual symmetry in socialization processes. One suspects that our "child" sample, like the "young American male" studied by Braugart (1971) typically has more exposure to female than male adult figures.

D. "CHILDREN'S" ESTIMATES OF INTER-PARENT ATTITUDINAL DIFFERENCES

Boys considered that their parents shared the same attitudes on no less than forty-five of the fifty items. On three of the five remaining items they considered their fathers were more conservative than their mothers: the death penalty, working mothers, and women judges but their mothers to be more conservative on striptease shows and missionaries.

Girls considered that their parents shared the same attitudes on thirty-two items. They estimated that their fathers were significantly more conservative than their mothers on patriotism, self-denial, masculine superiority, military drill, socialism, legalized abortion, chastity, royalty, conventional clothing, workers strikes, straitjackets, Bible truth, and their mothers more conservative on evolution theory, striptease shows, co-education, white superiority, fluoridation and apartheid. There were also real inter-parental differences on a number of items (Table V).

E. INFAMILY ATTITUDES—ITEM DISCREPANCY SCORES

Following another approach to infamily differences boy/father, boy/mother, girl/father and girl/mother discrepancy scores were than calculated for each item. It will be recalled that a conservative response to each item is scored 2, a "?" is scored 1, whilst a liberal response is scored 0. Infamily attitudes on each item were calculated by counting the number of $+2$, $+1$, 0, -1 and -2 item-discrepancy scores. These data were then added to show the per cent of families manifesting a "generation-gap", and intergenerational attitudinal "congruence" for each item.

While confirming the existence of a "generation-gap" the results also indicated substantial congruence between the attitudes of the parents and "children" under study.

(i) *Father/son item-discrepancy scores*

On forty-two items the percentage of father/son dyads manifesting attitudinal "congruence" exceeded the percentage where the son was more liberal than the father. Only on eight items (striptease shows, sabbath observance, beatniks, modern art, cousin marriage, student demonstrators, electronic music and austere prisons) did the per cent of father/son dyads in which the son was more liberal than the father exceed the per cent of dyads manifesting father/son congruence.

The greatest father/son disagreement (i.e. items for which more than 40 per cent of the dyads showed the son as more liberal than his father) occurred on high loading "religious" items (sabbath observance, divine law), "retributive conservatism" (death penalty, austere prisons) "sexual" items (striptease shows, nudist camps) and "intolerance of youth" (beatniks, modern art, student demonstrators, electronic music, conventional clothing). It is noteworthy that these items do not range over all the social issues measured by the C-Scale. Indeed, much father/son disagreement concerns "peripheral" matters (e.g. striptease shows, electronic music, etc.); substantial disagreement concerning controversial "core" issues (e.g. race, foreign affairs) was absent.

Over 60 per cent of father/son dyads manifested congruence on "core" "racial" items (white superiority, apartheid, mixed marriage, coloured immigration), "militarism" (patriotism, socialism, empire-building, security police, disarmament, peacetime conscription), "women's liberation" items (birth control, co-education, women judges, divorce, welfare legislation), and "socio-religious" items (evolution theory, censorship, strict rules, Bible truth). The remaining items where "congruence" occurred in more than 60 per cent of father/son dyads were on relative New Zealand non-issues (school uniforms, student pranks, licensing laws, fluoridation, royalty, trade unions, Chinese restaurants).

(ii) *Father/daughter item-discrepancy scores*

On forty-eight items the percentage of father/daughter dyads manifesting attitudinal "congruence" equalled or exceeded the percentage where the daughter was more liberal than her father. The greatest father/daughter agreement (more than 60 per cent of dyads manifesting "congruence") occurred on "racial" items (white superiority, apartheid, mixed marriage), "women's liberation" items (co-education, women judges, divorce, birth control, chastity, welfare legislation), two "foreign affairs" items (patriotism, disarmament), one "religiosity" item (church authority), licensing laws, fluoridation, jazz and Chinese restaruants.

The greatest father/daughter disagreement (more than 40 per cent of dyads manifesting "incongruence") occurred on beatniks, cousin marriage, student demonstrators, nudist camps, austere prisons, coloured immigration, and Bible truth. Four of these seven items load highly on an "intolerance of youth" factor but generally, father/daughter disagreement does not exceed father/daughter attitudinal "solidarity" and occurs on items which represent most of the main C-Scale factors. No strong single source of disagreement emerges.

On five items (striptease shows, empire-building, socialism, fluoridation, trade unions) the per cent of dyads in which the father was more liberal than his daughter actually exceeds the per cent in which the daughter was more liberal than her father. On seven other items (legalized abortion, licensing laws, apartheid, church authority, censorship, Chinese restaurants, divorce) the number of dyads in which the father was more liberal than his daughter was equal to the number in which the daughter was more liberal than her father.

(iii) *Mother/daughter item-discrepancy scores*

On each of the fifty items the per cent of mother/daughter dyads manifesting "congruence" was greater than the per cent where the daughter was more liberal than the mother (or the mother more liberal than the daughter). On missionaries, security police, trade unions and divorce, the per cent of dyads where the mother was more liberal exceeds the per cent where the daughter was more liberal. Overall mother/daughter attitudinal solidarity far exceeds mother/daughter "incongruence".

The greatest mother/daughter disagreement (daughter more liberal in more than 40 per cent of dyads) occurred on items that characteristically load on an "intolerance of youth" factor (beatniks, electronic music, conventional clothing, nudist camps, and strict rules).

The greatest mother/daughter agreement (60 per cent of dyads manifesting "congruence") occurred on "core" issues: "racial" items (white superioritv, apartheid, mixed marriage, coloured immigration), "religiosity" (sabbath observance, divine law, divorce), "women's liberation" (birth control, women judges, co-education), "retributive conservatism" (death penalty, austere prisons, welfare legislation), and "militarism" items (patriotism, military drill). Other items showing a high degree of mother/daughter congruence appeared to be "peripheral" (and somewhat dated) non-issues (school uniforms, modern art, licensing laws, fluoridation, jazz).

(iv) *Mother/son item-discrepancy scores*

On forty-three items the percentage of mother/son dyads manifesting attitudinal "congruence" exceeded the percentage where the son was more liberal than the mother. Over 75 per cent of mother/son dyads manifested "congruence" on birth control, co-education, white superiority, licensing laws, fluoridation, women judges, apartheid, Chinese restaurants and welfare legislation.

The greatest "incongruence" (more than 40 per cent of dyads showing the son as more liberal than his mother) occurred on "sexual" items (striptease shows, nudist camps, chastity), "socio-religious rigidity" (sabbath observance, church authority, Bible truth, censorship, self denial, strict rules), "intolerance of youth" (student demonstrators, student pranks, beatniks), and also, military drill, royalty and cousin marriage.

Items on which the percentage of dyads where the mother was more liberal than the son exceeded the percentage where the son was more liberal, were masculine superiority, jazz and straitjackets.

VI. Conclusion

Examination of item means revealed the parents to be more conservative than the children on forty-three of the fifty items, twenty-seven of these differences being statistically significant. Children were significantly more conservative than parents on only two items (masculine superiority and trade unions). These results, derived from "whole-scale" and "item mean" data, support the notion that an attitudinal "generation-gap" exists within the sample studied.

However, examination of "within family" data reveals a considerable amount of congruence. On all but a few items there were more in family dyads where attitudes were "congruent" than dyads in which the child was more liberal than the parent (or the parent more liberal than the child). Items on which the percentage of dyads in which the parents was more liberal than the child, were, in many cases, "replacements" for original C-Scale items; the justification for their inclusion is therefore doubtful. A "generation-gap" *was* found in the families studied. Nevertheless parent/child agreement outweighs parent/child disagreement.

Concerning the inter-generational differences that were identified, it could be argued that the latter arise as a function of age-group behavioural differences in maturation. The needs, "dominant concerns", and cognitive mechanisms of 17–19-year-olds are simply different to those of 40–45-year-olds, as is suggested in the theorizing of ego and life-cycle theorists. According to a "social-structural" model (e.g. Musgrove, 1965) power accrues to a person as he grows older and inter-generational conflict stems from a demand for power at an earlier age than society presently allows.

No doubt, some inter-generational conflict in attitude can be thus accounted for, but the present data is best explained by a "cohort-historical" model. According to this model the socialization environment is different for different generations. Since each cohort "comes of age" in different eras their experiences with various social institutions and people (schools, teachers, policemen, politicians, etc.) will vary, producing a set of attitudes unique to each generation. Crises (e.g. wars, depressions), sudden intellectual or technological advances (e.g. new art forms, the atomic age, television) modifications in the social structure (e.g. "baby booms", urbanization) force those coming of age during the period to develop "styles of life" and attitudes that differ from those developed by older people. Thus, our parent sample, most of whom reached adulthood during or just after World War II, hold social and political attitudes different from those of their children, most of whom were born around 1953.

The changing nature of child-rearing behaviour is probably also critical. In this regard Kenniston (1968) goes so far as to say that young radicals are the prototype of children that can be expected to emerge from the permissive, non-authoritarian atmosphere recommended by Dr Spock.

Infamily social attitudes such as those studied may also be mediated by factors such as the magnitude and direction of attitudinal differences between parents, dominance-submission patterns of the husband and wife, the presence/absence for long periods of one or both parents (or one or more children), birth order (see Boshier and Walkey, 1972), and the differential amount of day to day contact between father and child as compared to mother and child.

References

Adorno, T. W., Frenkel-Brunswik, E., Levinson, D. J. and Sanford, R. N. (1950). "The Authoritarian Personality." Harper and Row, New York.

Bengston, V. (1969). The generation-gap: differences by generation and by sex in the perception of parent-child relations. *Paper presented to the Pacific School. Assoc.* Seattle.

Bettelheim, B. (1965). The problem of generations. In "The Challenge of Youth." (Erikson, E., ed.). Anchor Book Co., New York.

Block, J. (1955). Personality associated with fathers' attitudes towards child-rearing. *Child Dev.* **26**, 41–48.

224   R. BOSHIER

Boshier, R. W. (1972). To rotate or not to rotate: the question of the Conservatism Scale. *Brit. J. soc. clin. Psychol.*

Boshier, R. W. and Izard, A. (1972). Do conservative parents use harsh child-rearing practices? *Psychol. Rep.* **31**, 734.

Boshier, R. W. and Walkey, F. H. (1972). Birth order and conservatism: an Adlerian myth? *Psychol. Rep.* **29**, 392–394.

Braugart, R. G. (1971). Parental identification and student politics. *Sociol. Educ.* **44**, 463–475.

Douvan, E. and Adelson, J. (1968). "The Adolescent Experience." Wiley, New York.

Feuer, L. (1969). "The Conflict of Generations: the Character and Significance of Student Movements." Basic Books, New York.

Friedenberg, E. (1965). "Coming of Age in America." Vintage Books, Random House, New York.

Friedenberg, E. (1969). The generation-gap. *Annals. Amer. Acad. pol. soc. Sci.* **382**, 32–42.

Hart, I. (1957). Maternal child-rearing practices and authoritarian ideology. *J. abnorm. soc. Psychol.* **55**, 232–237.

Kandel, D. and Lesser, A. (1969). Parental and peer influences and educational plans of adolescents. *Amer. sociol. Rev.* **34**, 212–223.

Kenniston, K. (1965). "The Uncommitted." Harcourt, Brace and World, New York.

Kenniston, K. (1967). The sources of student dissent. *J. soc. Issues.* **23**, 108–137.

Kenniston, K. (1968). "Young radicals: notes on committed youth." Harcourt, Brace and World, New York.

Larson, W. R. and Myerhoff, B. (1965). Primary and formal family organization and adolescent socialization. *Sociol. soc. Res.* **50**, 63–71.

Levinson, D. J. and Huffman, P. E. (1955). Traditional family ideology and its relation to personality. *J. Pers.* **23**, 251–273.

Musgrove, F. (1965). "Youth and the social order." Indiana University Press, Bloomington, Indiana.

Musgrove, F. (1970). "The generation-gap." Chancellor's lectures presented at Victoria University of Wellington, New Zealand.

Travers, R. M. W. (1969). "An Introduction to Educational Research." Macmillan, London.

Wilson, G. D. and Patterson, J. R. (1970). "Manual for the Conservatism Scale." N.F.E.R. Publishing Co. Windsor.

Zuckerman, M. and Oltean, M. (1959). Some relationships between maternal attitude factors and authoritarianism, personality needs, psychopathology, and self-acceptance. *Child Dev.* **30**, 27–36.

15 Conservatism, Psychiatry, and Mental Distress

FRANCIS J. LILLIE

Queen Elizabeth II Hospital, Welwyn Garden City

I. Introduction

In the last decade the increasing concern with social factors in psychiatric illness, whether from an aetiological or treatment point of view, has led to recognition of the importance of attitude variables in the treatment of patients and in the selection and training of psychiatric staff. Since publication of the C-Scale (Wilson and Patterson, 1970) there have been several empirical studies on the relationship between conservatism and psychiatric treatment. It is the purpose of this chapter to review these studies, which have particularly concentrated on correlating conservatism with attitudes to treatment, in nurses, psychiatric patients and psychiatrists. After data on these groups have been examined a study relating conservatism to students' reporting of emotional distress will be discussed.

II. Attitudes to Psychiatric Treatment

A. THE ATTITUDES TO TREATMENT QUESTIONNAIRE

Caine and Smail (1969) summarized their work to date on the attitudes of staff and patients to their roles and to the treatment given in psychiatric hospitals. They have argued that treatment decisions, at the present time,

I

are dominated by patient and staff attitudes as to the nature of psychiatric illness rather than by more objective criteria. In the course of their work Caine and colleagues have developed a seventy-five item Attitudes to Treatment Questionnaire (A.T.Q.) which patients and staff complete to reveal ward attitudes and the degree to which particular treatments are endorsed.

Principal components analyses of the attitudes of patients, nurses and doctors to psychiatric treatment revealed three statistically important components. Component I emphasized physical treatments (electro-convulsive therapy, drugs), the need for hygiene, strict discipline and maintenance of the staff's image as idealized omnipotent people. Component II stressed the therapeutic value of honest, non-professional communication between staff and patients in a group situation, as opposed to the traditional doctor–patient relationship. The third component, more difficult to interpret in most of Caine's studies, also stresses a therapeutic approach but unlike Component II there is a reliance on the doctor as an omnipotent individual rather than an emphasis on the group. The emphasis on omnipotence in the third component is more like traditional individual therapy while the second component Caine sees as representing the therapeutic community approach.

The relationship between these different components and conservatism is the concern of many of the studies quoted in this chapter. An attempt will be made to discuss the findings systematically according to the professional roles of the individuals studied.

B. Nurses' Attitudes

Psychologists have increasingly found intelligence tests of poor predictive value in selecting nurses (Singh, 1972, for instance) and it would appear that attitudinal factors may be at least as relevant as intelligence in successful assessment in this area. Hall (1973) who is currently using the C-Scale in attempting to choose nursing staff for a token economy ward has made this point.

As a follow-up to a finding (Caine, 1970) which suggested a conservatism continuum ranging from general nurses with traditional values at one end through psychiatric nurses to therapeutic community nurses with more liberal views at the other end. Caine and Leigh (1972) attempted to correlate nurses attitudes to treatment with their scores on the C-Scale. They gave the A.T.Q. and the C-Scale to three groups associated with nursing. Groups A and B (N.s. of 75 and 94) were heterogeneous mixtures of administrators, tutors, trained ward staff and nursing students. Group C was more homogeneous and comprised seventy-two psychiatric nurses attending a conference. Table I shows the conservatism/A.T.Q. correlation with age partialled out (in Group C age had correlated with conservatism,

TABLE I

Correlations between C-Scale scores and attitudes to treatment in three groups of psychiatric staff.
(Adapted from Caine and Leigh, 1972.)

Group	N	Correlation (with age partialled out)
A. Mixed hospital staff	75	0·50†
B. Mixed hospital staff	94	0·22*
C. Psychiatric nurses	72	0·44†

*p < 0·05. †p < 0·01.

$r = 0.31$). These results suggest that the conservative nurse tends to have traditional views of hospital ward organization, emphasizing formal staff/patient relationships as opposed to the more "revolutionary" (Caine's word) approach of group psychotherapy or the therapeutic community.

Caine and Leigh also examined differences in response to the one directly political item in the C-Scale ("Socialism") to see if political allegiance had implications for psychiatric treatment. No significant differences in treatment attitudes were found between those nurses endorsing or rejecting socialism.

C. PATIENT ATTITUDES

In the same paper Caine and Leigh investigated the attitudes to treatment of eighty-five neurotic out-patients attending a day hospital, using the C-Scale and a "Composite Group/Behaviour Therapy Attitude Scale". The latter scale examines a patient's assumptions about his illness and treatment expectations, with individual items chosen by group and behaviour therapists to represent their respective approaches. Although the scale is only at a developmental stage, analysis showed that it significantly differentiated patients in group therapy from those in behaviour therapy. The most powerfully discriminating eight items were then correlated with the C-Scale, with age again being partialled out. This correlation ($r = -0.37$, $p < 0.01$) was in the predicted direction; attitudes favourable to group therapy were associated with a liberal outlook and attitudes favourable to behaviour therapy were associated with a more traditional, authoritarian orientation.

Although no significant differences were found between nurses endorsing or rejecting the "Socialism" item, there were significant differences between the patient groups. Patients assigned to behaviour therapy had more negative attitudes to socialism (i.e. they were more conservative) than those assigned to group therapy (Table II). This suggested to Caine and Leigh that the conservative patient presented his problem in a way that demanded a more authoritarian type of therapy.

TABLE II

Differences between "Socialist", "Non-Socialist" and "Don't know"
neurotic patients in overall conservatism and attitudes to treatment
(Adapted from Caine and Leigh, 1972)

	N	Mean	S.D.			N	Mean	S.D.		
	\multicolumn{3}{c}{Conservatism Scale}				\multicolumn{3}{c}{Composite Group/Behaviour Therapy Attitude Scale}		
Socialists	33	35·27	12·36			30	21·60	4·27		
Non-Socialists	37	43·16	12·81	n.s.	t = 3·0 / p < 0·001	33	17·93	4·00	n.s.	t = 3·9 / p < 0·001
Don't know	24	43·46	10·17			22	17·73	4·00		

In their discussion Caine and Leigh point out that subjects who responded "?" to the "Socialism" item in the C-Scale are aligned with the conservatives rather than with the liberals in their attitude to psychiatric treatment (Table II), and they speculate about the possibility that the neutral responder is basically a conservative person. It needs to be remembered, however, that out of statistical necessity, neutral responses will tend to correlate with total C-Score in any group that has a mean C-Score of less than 50.

In line with their findings of a positive correlation between conservatism and assignment to behaviour therapy rather than to group therapy, Caine and Leigh suggest that in presenting their case conservative patients may have laid greater emphasis on symptomatology than on interpersonal difficulties and so be more likely to be assigned to behaviour therapy. The patient's attitude may, then, have been a partial determinant of the doctor's choice of treatment. The notion of the conservative denying the seriousness of his difficulties or admitting only to the less mysterious of psychiatric symptoms (those most closely allied to physical illness) is consistent with the findings of Robertson and Kapur (1972) which are to be discussed later.

D. PSYCHIATRISTS' ATTITUDES

The work now to be described relates psychiatrists' attitudes and experience to Caine's three A.T.Q. Components; i.e. preference for physical treatments (I); a preference for group therapy (II) ;and a preference for individual psychotherapy (III). Panayotopoulos* and Stoffelmayr (1973) compared two groups of psychiatrists and hypothesized that those with formal training in psychotherapy would favour psychological treatments (as indicated by a preference for Components II and III rather than I) and would have more liberal social attitudes than those psychiatrists without such training. Doctors in Group A had received at some stage either psychoanalytic training or a specialized course of psychotherapy

* This author has since shortened his name to Pallis.

lasting at least one year. Those in Group B had received no such training. The tests used for the comparison were the C-Scale, the A.T.Q. and Eysenck's Social Attitude Inventory (Eysenck, 1954) with its two dimensions, one of radicalism/conservatism and the other of tough/tendermindedness.

TABLE III

Attitudes to treatment and General Social Attitudes of Psychiatrists trained in Psychotherapy and Psychiatrists without such training.

(Adapted from Panayotopoulos and Stoffelmayr, 1972.)

Variables	A. Psychiatrists trained in psycho- therapy (N = 20)	B. Psychiatrists untrained in psycho- therapy (N = 20)	t	p
A.T.Q. component I	35·9	44·4	−3·39	<0·005*
A.T.Q. component II	43·6	41·9	1·09	n.s.
A.T.Q. component III	37·5	37·1	0·29	n.s.
Conservatism (C-Scale)	28·4	37·7	−1·93	<0·05*
Radicalism (S.A.I.)	9·7	7·7	1·75	<0·05
Tendermindedness (S.A.I.)	17·2	13·7	2·21	<0·05

* One tailed tests.

In addition, Panayotopoulos and Stoffelmayr collected personal data, but no significant differences related to age and length of psychiatric experience were found. The main results in Table III show that, as predicted, psychotherapy-trained psychiatrists (Group A) were less conservative than those without training in psychotherapy, and tended to favour psychological treatments rather than physical (see difference on A.T.Q. Component I). Group A is also significantly more tenderminded than Group B. The latter finding of a correlation between tendermindedness and psychotherapy preference is supported by evidence that doctors who are "thinking introverts" (very similar to Eysenck's tenderminded category) have a preference for psychotherapy (Kreitman, 1962; Walton, 1966).

Panayotopoulos and Stoffelmayr conclude: "Although the present findings do not indicate the underlying casual relationship between social attitudes and training preferences, it would seem unlikely that the psychiatrists' social attitudes could change as a result of a short term psychiatric training experience. This suggests that psychiatrists choose their particular training because of the attitudes they hold, but this needs further empirical testing" (p. 217).

This hypothesis was subjected to more extensive testing in a later study by the same authors (Pallis and Stoffelmayr, 1972). They were principally interested in how different kinds of training experience in psychiatrists would relate to their different treatment approaches and their social attitudes. As in their previous study, the A.T.Q., the C-Scale, and the Eysenck inventory were used. Forty-two psychiatrists were sampled including nine in the first year of psychiatric training (four of these being uncertain as to their choice of speciality).

TABLE IV

Intercorrelations of social and treatment attitude measures.
(From Pallis and Stoffelmayr, 1973.)

Variables	1	2	3	4	5	6
1. A.T.Q. component I	—					
2. A.T.Q. component II	−0·11	—				
3. A.T.Q. component III	0·48†	0·16	—			
4. Conservatism (C-Scale)	0·44†	−0·04	0·12	—		
5. Radicalism (S.A.I.)	−0·59‡	0·16	−0·22	−0·83‡	—	
6. Tendermindedness (S.A.I.)	−0·32*	0·01	−0·19	0·14	0·15	—

$*p < 0.05$; $†p < 0.01$; $‡p < 0.001$

The results are presented in Table IV. The C-Scale and the R-Scale of the Social Attitudes Inventory are highly correlated ($r = -0.83$) and both scales correlate with A.T.Q. Component I in such a way as to suggest that conservatism is associated with a preference for physical treatments. Tendermindedness has a negative correlation with Component I, which confirms Panayotopoulos and Stoffelmayr's finding that tenderminded psychiatrists prefer psychological rather than physical treatments.

Also in support of the Panayotopoulos and Stoffelmayr study was the finding that Components I and III are significantly correlated ($r = 0.48$) suggesting that these are not separate treatment approaches. The lack of discriminability amongst the three components in this study casts doubt on the validity of separating these treatment approaches.

Pallis and Stoffelmayr also studied the effect of length of previous medical experience on social attitudes and treatment orientation. Psychiatrists were grouped according to the time they had spent in medicine after the minimum period required for registration (Group A: 1 year's medical training, $N = 9$; Group B: 2–5 years' training, $N = 21$; Group C: 6 years plus, $N = 8$). There were no differences in their attitudes to treatment except that Group A differed from Groups B and C in terms of Eysenck's radicalism ($F = 3.45$, df 2/53, $p < 0.05$). But when Groups B and C were combined, Group A differed significantly in conservatism ($F = 5.42$, df 1/36, $p < 0.025$) being less conservative as a group.

This finding, that the less conservative doctor chooses his psychiatric career earlier than the more conservative doctor, is supported by a study showing that social attitudes are related to certainty of choice of a psychiatric speciality (Sharaf et al., 1968).

TABLE V

Mean attitude scores and analysis of variance among three groups of psychiatrists. (From Pallis and Stoffelmayr, 1972.)

Variable	Means of Groups*			Grand Mean	F	p
	Group A (N = 5)	Group B (N = 4)	Group C (N = 8)			
A.T.Q. component I	39·0	54·5	36·4	41·4	14·43	<0·001
A.T.Q. component II	44·2	43·2	43·7	43·8	0·26	n.s.
A.T.Q. component III	36·0	39·0	37·5	37·4	0·50	n.s.
Conservatism (C-Scale)	26·6	57·7	23·9	32·6	8·01	<0·01
Radicalism (S.A.I.)	10·2	4·5	10·6	9·0	5·40	<0·025
Tendermindedness (S.A.I.)	10·6	14·0	15·7	13·8	1·81	n.s.

*Groups A and B had experience in psychiatry not exceeding 1½ years; Group C had 3–5 years' experience. Group A had made a definite choice of psychiatric career whereas Group B were still undecided.

If the length of the doctor's general medical experience is ignored and only his present status in psychiatry considered, it can be seen from Table V that no differences were found in attitudes between senior psychiatrists (consultants and senior registrars) and junior psychiatrists. However, the subgroup of junior doctors undecided as to a psychiatric career were more conservative ($p < 0.01$), less radical ($p < 0.025$), and more in favour of physical treatments (Component I of the A.T.Q., $p < 0.001$) than their junior colleagues who had firmly opted for a psychiatric career.

In the total group, psychiatrists who did not practice psychotherapy at all ($N = 8$) were found to be significantly more conservative ($F = 4.32$, df 4/39, $p < 0.01$) and less radical ($F = 7.06$, df 2/39, $p < 0.01$) as well as having higher scores on the physical treatment component of the A.T.Q. (F 9·36, df 2/39, $p < 0.001$) than those of colleagues who did sometimes practice psychotherapy. It is important to emphasize that although 80·4 per cent of the sample said, when asked, that they were practising psychotherapy, only 19·9 per cent had a "predominant psychotherapeutic orientation". The term "psychotherapy" is notoriously difficult to define, and it must be remembered that most psychologists, psychiatrists and other psychiatric personnel, favour use of a variety of approaches. Therefore, it is not surprising that the group of eight in Pallis and Stoffelmayr's study who said that they did not practice psychotherapy at all were more conservative and physically orientated in treatment.

Emphasizing the lack of mutually exclusive treatment categories in clinical practice, Pallis and Stoffelmayr further examined the validity of the A.T.Q. components by asking the psychiatrists in their sample to characterize their *actual* treatments by one of five categories including the three from the A.T.Q. The categories and their percentage allegiances were as follows: Eclectic 50 per cent; Community therapy 11·9 per cent; Individual psychotherapy 19 per cent; Physical treatments 4·8 per cent; Uncommitted 4·2 per cent. The breakdown shows that most psychiatrists in this sample prefer an eclectic approach. No significant differences were found between senior and junior psychiatrists with regard to self-reported treatment orientation, which confirms the similarly negative findings of their first study.

TABLE VI

Mean attitude scores for self-reported "Eclectics" "Psychotherapists" and the total sample.
(From Pallis and Stoffelmayr, 1973.)

Variables	"Eclectic" group (N = 21)	"Individual psychotherapy" and "Community therapy groups combined (N = 13)	Total sample (N = 42)
A.T.Q. component I	41·5	34·8	40·2
A.T.Q. component II	43·2	43·9	43·1
A.T.Q. component III	38·7	35·8	37·5
Conservatism	33·0	29·4	33·0
Radicalism	8·9	9·8	8·9
Tendermindedness	14·8	16·8	15·2

To further investigate this self-reported orientation the five groups above were compared on the three A.T.Q. components and the social attitude factors. The Physical treatments category, however, was so small that it was excluded, leaving four groups. Analysis of variance revealed no significant differences for any of the attitude variables. However, when the three main groups (Eclectic, Individual psychotherapy, and Community therapy) were collapsed into two groups (Table VI) significant differences in the A.T.Q. Component I (Physical treatments) were demonstrated between Group 1 (Electic) and Groups 2 and 3 combined (F = 6·33, df 1/32, p < 0·025). Thus the first A.T.Q. component discriminates between a mixed eclectic-organic approach and that of a psychotherapeutically orientated psychiatrist, while Components II and III do not to the same extent. In fact, Table VI shows that psychiatrists who call themselves eclectic can be distinguished from those describing themselves as psychotherapeutic, but, once again, the group and individual orientations are not discriminated by the A.T.Q. Components II and III. The attitudinal measures, however, did not discriminate between the eclectic and psychotherapeutic psychiatrists.

The results discussed here, as well as the findings of several other studies (Kreitman, 1962; Strauss *et al.*, 1964), suggest a clear discrimination between only two broad approaches—a psychological and an organic one.

III. Conservatism and Mental Distress

A recent study by Robertson and Kapur (1972) showed that students who reported they had been "emotionally or nervously unwell" but who had not consulted a doctor were less conservative (i.e. more radical) than students who had not been unwell. The authors of this study characterize low scores on Wilson's conservatism dimension as "radicalism" and couch their findings and discussion in terms of a sociological analysis of radicalism and existentialism. In this discussion "liberal" will be used interchangeably with "radical".

The study started from a finding that at Edinburgh University between 1961 and 1967 there had occurred an increase in students answering the following question affirmatively:

"Have you been emotionally or nervously unwell during the past six months?"

The significant increase in reported distress was confined to working class males and middle class female students. Robertson and Kapur were able to rule out internal bias and suggested that the change was not artifactual either in the reporting or experiencing of distress. They hypothesized that there had been some change in a radical direction in students' value systems in these six years, operating differentially with sex and class. Because conservatism data from the 1961 students was unavailable, an indirect test of the hypothesis was adopted by postulating that students reporting emotional stress would show less conservatism than those who did not.

The question asked of students in the 1961 and 1967 studies was again used in 1969 with a random sample of 304 third year students who had been members of the first year class in the 1967 study. Besides being asked if they had been nervously unwell the students were asked to say whether they had consulted a doctor. These questions, along with the C-Scale questionnaire, were sent by post, the return being 84·5 per cent. The main results are presented in Table VII. Firstly, women are more conservative than men, which is, of course, a well substantiated finding.

TABLE VII A

Mean C-scores in relation to declared emotional distress
(From Robertson and Kapur, 1972.)

	N	Males Mean C	N	Females Mean C
(a) Emotional distress reported	15	27·87	36	34·86
(b) No emotional distress reported	66	34·74	139	38·95
(c) Emotional distress reported and a doctor consulted	3	33·33	13	39·62
(d) Emotional distress reported and a doctor *not* consulted	12	26·50	23	32·17

TABLE VII B

t values for differences among means in VII A.

	Males	Females
a *vs* b	1·91	1·63
b *vs* d	2·07*	2·24*
c *vs* d	1·31	1·65

*$p < 0.05$.

A more interesting finding is the difference between those students who reported an emotional problem but did not consult a doctor and those students who reported no emotional distress. The non-consulting distressed students are less conservative (more "radical") than those students who reported no distress (this result being consistent for males and females). Those students who did consult a doctor about their emotional problems were at the same level of conservatism as those who reported no problem.

Several hypotheses were offered to explain this phenomenon, but only the two most plausible explanations will be mentioned here. Firstly, it seems likely that the liberal person who is distressed is less likely to seek help from an "establishment" doctor, bearing in mind that Edinburgh University at that stage had no counselling or psychiatric service. Secondly, the more conservative person may interpret personal distress and psychiatric symptoms generally as a loss to his pride or self-esteem and report to a doctor (or a researcher) only in an extreme case. This second explanation is relevant to the earlier discussion on Caine's work, when it was suggested that the conservative patient might prefer to present physical symptoms rather than psychological ones.

Before leaving Robertson and Kapur's study an important methological point must be made. In their study, and in most studies concerned with attitudes to treatment, there will be subjects who will not respond to questionnaires. It seems likely from Patterson and Wilson's (1969) finding of a significant correlation between anonymity and conservatism, that the absence of these subjects represents not a random exclusion, but an *un*-conservative bias to this data.

IV. Discussion

At this stage it is necessary to emphasize three areas for discussion: (1) the difficulty of placing behaviour therapy on the conservative dimension, (2) the conservative's emphasis on the physical aspects of his psychiatric symptoms, and (3) the relevance of attitudinal factors, particularly conservatism, to psychiatry.

The increasing popularity and importance of the behaviour therapy approach within psychiatry means that several points about the position of behaviour therapy on the C dimension must be clarified. While Caine and Leigh (1972) have not made explicit the component they see behaviour therapy as following in terms of their A.T.Q., it is clear they conceptualize it as most like their first ("organic") component and their data, reported earlier, supported this. Aversion therapy, *one* type of behaviour therapy, can be easily caricatured as authoritarian, conservative and freedom destroying as Anthony Burgess has brilliantly done in "A Clockwork Orange". Nevertheless, some prominent aversion therapists see it as a last resort treatment to be given after all else has failed, and generally, behaviour therapy involves reward rather than punishment. Moreover, most behaviourists argue that their therapy is concerned with increasing an individual's control and understanding of his own learning processes and so making him less vulnerable to the vicissitudes of his environment. In this light behaviour therapy would seem to be an unconservative freedom-giving treatment.

Some behavioural treatments, such as token economies, are concerned with interpersonal aspects of the total environment. Nevertheless, behaviour therapy has emphasized symptom removal with a denial of the primary importance of the therapist–patient relationship. This does not mean, however, that behaviour therapists ignore the interpersonal aspects of therapy or that behaviour therapists are less understanding or sympathetic in terms of the conservative dimension. In fact, the ethics of behaviour therapy would suggest quite the reverse to the writer (e.g. see Bandura, 1970). However, in Caine's sample the patients receiving behaviour therapy as opposed to group therapy *are* a relatively conservative group. Obviously, the way a patient and therapist view each other and the treatment process has important implications for treatment outcome and would seem to be an area where more research is needed.

The second area for discussion centres on Robertson's and Kapur's data which suggests that the conservative may be unwilling to admit that he is unwell psychiatrically. Every clinician is aware of a group of psychiatric patients who prefer their symptoms to have a simple physical explanation, or to be carefully circumscribed in "physical" language. The patient is perhaps able in this way (consciously or unconsciously) to avoid blame for his illness or avoid its attribution to his family or personal circumstances. After all, as long as the aetiology of psychiatric illness remains relatively obscure the conservative who is psychiatrically ill may be constantly aware of the possibility that he and/or his family are "to blame" for his condition.

The conservative's preference for a physical illness model is shared by a large proportion of Western society and may have been contributed to culturally by a basically conservative medical profession, which, for historical reasons, has looked after the mentally, as well as physically ill. Szasz (1965) argues that the medical model of psychiatric illness has rescued the madman from psychological guilt and physical torture, but at the same time has imprisoned the psychiatric patient within a conceptual straitjacket. However extreme Szasz's total view may seem, it is reasonable to suggest that the medical model may have hindered the development of the investigation of social and attitudinal factors in the patient and staff who treat him. The historical perspective is apparently necessary to account for the paucity of research into staff and patient attitudes within psychiatry.

Thirdly, and in conclusion, the difficulty in characterizing psychiatric treatment approaches according to Caine's three components has been shown by Pallis and Stoffelmayr's data, which suggests that only two broad approaches (psychological and organic) are easily discriminable. However, the importance of the general factor of conservatism for psychiatry does emerge clearly from the studies reviewed in this chapter, e.g. Caine and Leigh's study showing a neurotic sample's expectations of treatment being correlated with conservatism in a similar way to the preferences of nursing staff. This suggests that the C-Scale is an instrument worth investigating further both from a theoretical and practical point of view.

References

Bandura, A. (1970). "Principles of Behaviour Modification." Holt, Rinehart and Winston, London.
Caine, T. M. (1970). "A Question of Attitudes". Appendix 1, Reprint No. 463, London: The Hospital Centre.
Caine, T. M. and Leigh, R. (1972). Conservatism in relation to psychiatric treatment. *Br. J. soc. clin. Psychol.* **11**, 52–56.
Caine, T. M. and Smail, D. J. (1969). "The Treatment of Mental Illness: Science, Faith, and the Therapeutic Personality." University Press, London.

Eysenck, H. J. (1954). "The Psychology of Politics." Routledge and Kegan Paul, London.

Hall, J. N. (1973). The relevance of formal selection methods and attitudes to the staffing of token economy programmes. Proceedings of the Third Annual Conference of the European Association for Behaviour Therapy, Munich (in press).

Kreitman, N. (1962). Psychiatric orientation: a study of attitudes among psychiatrists. *J. ment. Sci.* **108**, 317–328.

Pallis, D. J. and Stoffelmayr, B. E. (1972). Training preferences, social attitudes and treatment orientation among psychiatrists. *J. clin. Psychol.* **28**, 2, 216–217.

Panayotopoulos, D. J. and Stoffelmayr, B. E. (1973). Social attitudes and treatment orientations among psychiatrists. *Br. J. med. Psychol.* in press.

Patterson, J. R. and Wilson, G. D. (1969). Anonymity, occupation and conservatism. *J. soc. Psychol.* **78**, 263–266.

Robertson, A. and Kapur, R. L. (1972). Social change, emotional distress, and world view of students: an empirical study of the existentialist ethic and the spirit of suffering. *Br. J. Sociol.* **23**, 4, 462–477.

Sharaf, M. R., Schneider, P. and Kantor, D. (1968). Psychiatric interest and its correlates among medical students. *Psychiatry,* **31**, 150–160.

Singh, A. (1972). The predictive value of cognitive tests for selection of pupil nurses. *Nursing Times,* **68**, 23 (occasional papers).

Strauss, A., Schatzman, L., Bucher, R., Ehrlich, D. and Sabshin, M. (1964). "Psychiatric Ideologies and Institutions." Free Press, Glencoe, Illinois.

Szasz, T. S. (1965). "Psychiatric Justice." Macmillan, New York.

Walton, H. J. (1966). Differences between physically-minded and psychologically-minded medical practitioners. *Br. J. Psychiat.* **112**, 1097–1102.

Wilson, G. D. and Patterson, J. R. (1970). "Manual for the Conservatism Scale." N.F.E.R. Publishing Co., Windsor.

Attitudes to the Common Market: A Case Study in Conservatism

16

DAVID K. B. NIAS

Institute of Psychiatry, University of London

I. Hypotheses

The present study is concerned with the relevance of personality and social attitudes to a political issue, namely whether or not Britain should join the European Economic Community (the Common Market). Previous research in social psychology suggests a number of hypotheses that might be relevant to this particular issue.

(1) Opposition to change is assumed to be one of the prime characteristics of people who are conservative in personality (Adorno *et al.*, 1950). Thus our first hypothesis might be that British people who score highly on conservatism will tend to be more opposed to joining the Common Market. In addition, information concerning the nature of the conservatism dimension allows us to make certain more specific predictions.

(2) Of the various sub-factors of conservatism, ethnocentrism would seem the most relevant for predicting attitudes to the Common Market. Ethnocentrism involves a dislike for foreigners and strangers generally, and since joining would imply a closer identity with Europeans, the move

is unlikely to be welcomed by people who tend to be ethnocentric. Thus our second hypothesis might be that the primary contributor to the relationship between conservatism and opposition to the Common Market will be the ethnocentric component.

(3) Changes that involve an element of doubt or risk are likely to give rise to feelings of insecurity, and such feelings in turn are likely to give rise to pessimism. This generalization seems to apply even when people are given a choice between the known status quo and some potentially more attractive, if unknown, alternative. In evolution theory terms, it is as if the status quo is felt to have greater survival value. While such reactions to uncertainty may be characteristic of the conservative, they may also be related to the amount of knowledge that a person feels he has on the issue in question. The expression "fear through ignorance" may serve to illustrate this point. Thus our third hypothesis might be that people who feel they know relatively little about the Common Market will be more opposed to joining.

(4) A generalized opposition to change may also be motivated by feelings of loyalty for the past. Conservative people may resist changes in our way of life because they are more likely to identify with cultural traditions. However, because changes are always taking place anyway, it might be expected that such people would look back on the apparent advantages of the past with feelings of nostalgia ("the good old days"), and consequently regard life in Britain as deteriorating. Thus our fourth hypothesis might be that people who regard life in Britain as changing for the worse will be more opposed to joining the Common Market.

There may be many other factors related to feelings about the Common Market including non-psychological variables; the above hypotheses were chosen because they seem central to the concept of conservatism.

II. Effects of Political Allegiance

Eysenck (1954, 1972) has drawn attention to the paradox of social class and attitudes in relation to political affiliation. Results both in Britain and the U.S. indicate that the working class, as a group, are relatively conservative in their social attitudes, but liberal (radical) in relation to economic matters. Similarly, people in higher status occupations are liberal in their social attitudes, but conservative (reactionary) in relation to economic matters.

A paradox has arisen because the economic policies of the two main parties (Conservative and Labour in Britain; Republican and Democratic in the U.S.) run counter to their policies on most other issues. Thus the working class approve of the social policies of the Conservative (or Republican) party, but are relatively less likely to vote this way because they disapprove of the party's economic policies. Similarly, the middle and upper classes have social attitudes in keeping with the Labour (or Democratic) party, but are unlikely to vote this way for economic reasons. The net result of all this is that supporters of the Conservative party mainly consist of people who are in higher status occupations and people who are conservative in personality, while supporters of the Labour party mainly consist of people who are in low status occupations and people who are liberal in personality.

Eysenck suggests that the "social class or self-interest" theory formulated by Centers (1949) to account for economic attitudes, can be adapted to explain many of the other attitude differences between social classes. In particular, he suggests that the working class are likely to regard the social policies of the Conservative party as being in their interests, in much the same way that they regard the economic policies of the Labour party as being for their benefit. For example, the working class are more likely to develop racial prejudice because it is they (rather than the middle class) who will have to compete with immigrants for jobs, housing, schooling, etc. Other examples are given to explain various other attitudes held by working class people that are counter to the policies of the Labour party.

TABLE I

Perceived personal benefit from entry to the Common Market related to political affiliation, social class, and age.
(From Harris Poll results, The *Guardian*, 12 June 1972.)

"Do you think that Britain's entry to the Common Market would make you personally better off or worse off during the next ten years?"

	Better off %	Worse off %	Don't know %
All electors	27	50	23
Conservatives	42	29	29
Labour	16	67	17
Liberal	29	56	15
Class AB	36	42	20
Class C1	30	44	25
Class C2	27	51	23
Class DE	20	58	22
Age 18–24	36	40	23
Age 25–44	32	48	19
Age 45–64	24	54	21
Age 65 +	13	56	31

Joining the Common Market may provide another example of the clash between social attitudes and economic considerations. From the economic standpoint, results from a public opinion poll (Table I) indicate that young people, and people in higher status occupations, feel that they will be "better off" in the Common Market. Thus the decision to join may be interpreted as consistent with the economic policies of the Conservative party. (An alternative explanation for these poll results can, of course, be made in terms of conservatism, which may be related to a generally anti-Market attitude as well as to age and low occupational status. In other words, the poll results may merely reflect that conservative people, who tend to be older and more working class, are more opposed to joining.) From the social or personality standpoint, if our hypothesis about conservatism being related to opposition to the Common Market is correct, then it can be argued that the Conservative party are doing a non-conservative thing in seeking to join. Conservative voters are, therefore, likely to be in a conflict situation. On the one hand, economic considerations (assuming people have knowledge about the likely effects) and their loyalty to the party (or simply the belief that the party is the best judge of what is right) suggest that they should be in favour. On the other hand, their underlying conservative attitudes imply that they should be against joining.

Thus it seems that for a lot of people the effects of political allegiance are likely to act in the opposite direction to the effects of conservatism as a personality trait. If this is the case, then it will be desirable to control for the effects of party affiliation when investigating the relationship between conservatism and attitude to the Common Market. One way of doing this is to test our hypotheses for each party separately. Our first hypothesis would then be revised to predict that *within each political party*, conservative people will be more opposed to joining.

III. Method

It was decided to carry out the research on a sample of both students and the general population. The students were in their second or third year at a London College of Education; the females were specializing in one or more of various subjects, and the men were all specializing in physical education. The general population sample consisted of volunteers covering a wide range of ages and occupations.

Three questionnaires were administered: the C-Scale, a revised version of the Eysenck Personality Inventory (E.P.I.) and a specially constructed questionnaire (Table II). This latter questionnaire included statements relevant to the testing of our third and fourth hypotheses, i.e. those concerning the amount of perceived knowledge about the Common Market, and whether life in Britain is changing for the better or the worse. The C-Scale was scored for the standard six factors as outlined in Chapter 5. The scoring of the revised E.P.I. was based on a large series of factor analyses (S.B.G. Eysenck, unpublished), yielding scores for Psychoticism, Extraversion, Neuroticism, and the "Lie" scale. The ratings from the specially constructed questionnaire, together with age and occupational status, provided the remainder of the data for analysis. Occupation was graded according to the Registrar General's classification, using a score of 1 for the highest status jobs down to 5 for the lowest; housewives and retired people were assigned an intermediate score if their previous occupation was not given.

TABLE II

Opinion Scales on the Common Market and Political Parties

Occupation . . . . .Age . . . . Sex . . . . . .

A. Please circle which *one* of the following statements comes closest to your own feelings about Britain joining the Common Market:

　　1. I feel strongly that we should join.
　　2. I am inclined to feel that we should join.
　　3. I cannot decide whether or not we should join.
　　4. I am inclined to feel that we should not join.
　　5. I feel strongly that we should not join.

B. Please circle which *one* of the following statements comes closest to describing how much you know about the factors involved in joining:

　　1. I know quite a lot about the Common Market.
　　2. I know about as much as the average person.
　　3. I know relatively little about the Common Market.

C. Please circle which *one* of the following statements comes closest to describing how you see life, generally, in Britain as changing:

　　1. I feel that life in Britain is generally changing for the better.
　　2. I feel that life in Britain is about the same now as in the past.
　　3. I feel that life in Britain is generally changing for the worse.

D. Please circle which *one* of the following parties *comes closest* to being the one you would vote for in a general election:

　　1. Conservative.
　　2. Labour.
　　3. Liberal.

The data were analysed separately for the students and the general population, for males and females, and for each of the three main political parties. Means for the six C-Scale scores, the four personality scores, the three political ratings, age and occupational status (for the general population sample only) are presented in Table III. Intercorrelations among these fifteen variables were computed (Table VI); the correlations with an anti-Market attitude are presented in Table IV, and the correlations with conservatism are presented in Table V.

IV. Results

A. POLITICAL PARTY DIFFERENCES

The desirability of correlating conservatism with opposition to the Common Market for each political party separately becomes apparent from Table III. First, Conservative voters have obtained higher scores on conservatism in each of the four groups. The mean conservatism scores for the total sample are 50 for Conservative voters, 40 for Liberal, and 39 for Labour voters. Using analysis of variance, this overall difference is highly significant ($F = 14$, $p < 0.01$). Second, Conservative voters have tended to be relatively favourable towards joining the Common Market; scoring was in accordance with the statement numbers in Table II, therefore low scores signify being in favour of joining and high scores against. The mean scores for the total sample are 2·0 for Conservative, 2·3 for Liberal, and 2·6 for Labour voters ($F = 5.3$, $p < 0.01$). Thus we have evidence that relative to Labour and Liberal, Conservative voters tend to be generally conservative in their attitudes, and yet more in favour of joining the Common Market.

B. ANTI-COMMON MARKET CORRELATES

Hypothesis 1 : Conservatism is related to opposition to the Common Market. The conservatism correlations presented in Table IV indicate that this hypothesis has received partial support. For the general population sample, the coefficients tend to be positive. Although the coefficients are rather different, in view of the small sample sizes involved, averages were computed. A "pooled within groups" correlation matrix was used for this purpose, since it takes account of the raw scores unlike the alternative procedure of using Fisher's z transformation on the actual coefficients. The six conservatism coefficients average 0·16 which falls just short of significance (Fisher's method would have given a significant average of 0·20). Nevertheless, the direction of this result provides a striking contrast to the finding noted above that Conservative voters tend to be relatively favourable towards joining, and helps illustrate the conflict that must be facing Conservative voters.

The correlations for students tend to be negative, and give an average of −0·21 ($p < 0.05$). There are no immediate reasons to explain why this result is in the opposite direction to that obtained for the general population sample; we will return to this problem later.

Hypothesis 2 : Ethnocentrism is related to opposition to the Common Market. The ethnocentrism correlations presented in Table IV provide strong support for this hypothesis as regards the general population. The coeffi-

TABLE III

Means for each sub-group on the 15 variables

Gen. Pop.	Con.*	Rea.†	Mil.‡	He.§	Eth.**	Rel.††	P.*	E.†	N.‡	L.§	CM*	−K†	Br.‡	Age§	−Oc.**
Male															
23 Con.	47	34	14·8	11	11·1	8·1	4·8	12	7·9	8·2	2·0	1·9	1·7	43	2·3
22 Lab.	40	31	9·0	11	9·0	8·9	5·5	13	9·4	5·3	2·4	2·0	1·9	37	3·3
10 Lib.	40	30	11·2	12	8·5	6·9	4·5	14	12·1	9·0	1·8	1·9	2·2	36	3·1
Female															
32 Con.	54	28	13·8	15	11·6	10·6	3·5	12	10·2	9·0	2·2	2·2	2·2	42	2·9
17 Lab.	38	28	7·9	12	6·7	9·1	3·8	14	10·8	7·3	2·8	2·1	1·9	38	3·0
15 Lib.	43	27	11·1	12	8·3	9·5	3·3	12	10·3	8·5	2·7	2·2	2·2	38	2·9
Students															
Male															
8 Con.	46	27	12·8	13	8·3	10·5	5·8	17	8·1	2·8	2·0	1·9	1·4	25	
37 Lab.	40	27	7·9	12	7·8	11·1	6·6	15	10·1	4·4	2·5	2·0	2·4	21	
10 Lib.	38	28	9·3	12	6·5	9·6	6·2	14	11·2	5·0	2·4	2·1	2·2	22	
Female															
12 Con.	46	26	11·6	14	7·5	11·8	4·9	17	10·5	4·8	1·8	2·0	2·2	20	
21 Lab.	37	26	7·2	13	6·0	9·8	5·6	14	11·8	5·0	2·7	2·0	2·0	21	
7 Lib.	36	28	8·1	11	5·9	9·3	6·1	16	12·3	5·2	2·0	2·1	2·4	19	

* Conservatism
† Realism
‡ Militarism (Punitiveness)
§ Anti-Hedonism
** Ethnocentrism
†† Religiosity

* Psychoticism
† Extraversion
‡ Neuroticism
§ "L"-scale

* Opposition to the Common Market
† Little knowledge about the Common Market
‡ Britain changing for the worse
§ Age in years
** Low occupational status

TABLE IV

Correlations with opposition to the Common Market

	Con.	Rea.	Mil.	−He.	Eth.	Rel.	P.	E.	N.	L.	−K.	−Br.	Age	−Oc.
Gen. pop.														
Male														
23 Con.	0·32	0·13	0·09	0·19	0·43	0·30	0·06	−0·12	−0·09	−0·09	0·38	0·47	0·03	0·32
22 Lab.	0·03	0·19	0·06	−0·10	0·28	−0·01	−0·05	−0·28	0·12	0·07	0·13	0·35	−0·09	−0·30
10 Lib.	0·54	−0·06	0·62	0·24	0·55	0·34	−0·23	−0·35	0·04	0·24	0·56	0·27	−0·09	0·64
Female														
32 Con.	−0·07	0·38	−0·05	−0·25	0·20	−0·06	0·13	−0·11	0·54	−0·08	0·25	0·43	−0·30	0·22
17 Lab.	0·02	0·06	−0·12	0·04	0·39	−0·09	−0·49	0·04	0·25	0·24	−0·34	−0·30	0·28	0·29
15 Lib.	0·50	0·03	0·43	0·30	0·75	0·31	−0·23	0·02	0·03	0·27	−0·37	0·41	0·17	0·36
119 combined	0·16	0·18	0·09	0·01	0·36†	0·08	−0·05	−0·11	0·17	0·06	0·10	0·26†	−0·02	0·19*
Students														
Male														
8 Con.	−0·42	0·32	−0·78	−0·12	0·09	−0·47	0·53	−0·10	−0·10	−0·59	0·44	0·60	−0·37	
37 Lab.	−0·18	0·28	0·31	−0·25	−0·18	−0·24	0·11	0·28	0·20	−0·29	0·12	0·19	0·13	
10 Lib.	−0·44	−0·28	0·52	0·29	−0·08	0·36	−0·25	−0·05	0·03	−0·42	0·09	−0·60	−0·58	
Female														
12 Con.	−0·07	0·10	−0·24	0·02	0·34	0·21	0·25	−0·23	0·18	−0·24	0·79	−0·40	−0·06	
21 Lab.	−0·46	0·26	−0·28	−0·15	−0·20	−0·58	−0·11	−0·13	−0·11	−0·39	−0·17	0·64	−0·11	
7 Lib.	−0·41	0·09	−0·82	−0·44	−0·30	0·36	0·04	−0·15	0·71	−0·74	0·59	−0·26	0·43	
95 combined	−0·21*	0·18	0·01	−0·16	−0·12	−0·25*	0·05	0·06	0·11	−0·35†	0·16	0·17	−0·04	
214 total	0·00	0·18†	0·06	−0·06	0·18†	−0·06	−0·01	−0·05	0·15	−0·07	0·13*	0·22†	−0·02	

* = p < 0·05 (two-tail test).   † = p < 0·01 (two-tail test).

cients average 0·36, which is highly significant. Coefficients for the students average −0·12, which falls short of being significantly different from zero, but is again in the opposite direction to the general population result.

For the general population, the conflict facing the Conservative voters is again apparent. The means in Table III show that, compared with the other two parties, Conservative voters have obtained higher scores on ethnocentrism in each of the four groups. The mean scores for the total sample are 10 for Conservative, 7·5 for Labour, and 7·4 for Liberal voters ($F = 13$, $p < 0·01$). Thus we have evidence that ethnocentric people (in the general population sample) are *against joining* the Common Market, but are in support of the Conservative party, members of which otherwise tend to be *in favour of joining*.

Hypothesis 3: Perceived lack of knowledge about the Common Market is related to being against joining. The correlations in Table IV tend to be positive for both the general population and the students, thus supporting the hypothesis. The average of all the coefficients is 0·13 ($p < 0·05$). In the case of the present variables the means do not indicate any differences between the political parties.

Hypothesis 4: Feeling that life in Britain is changing for the worse is related to being against joining. The correlations in Table IV again tend to be positive for both samples, thus supporting the hypothesis. The average of all the coefficients is 0·22 ($p < 0·01$). Again the means do not indicate any differences between the parties.

Other factors related to opposition to the Common Market. In addition to the relationships that were hypothesized, there are four other significant results (Table IV).

Realism tends to be related to an anti-Market attitude for both the general population and the students; the coefficients average 0·18 ($p < 0·01$). Religiosity is related to a pro-Market attitude, but only for students; their coefficients average −0·25 ($p < 0·05$). High scores from the E.P.I. L-Scale are related to a pro-Market attitude, but again only for students; their coefficients average −0·35 ($p < 0·01$). Finally, low occupational status is related to an anti-Market attitude; the coefficients for the general population average 0·9 ($p < 0·05$).

C. Conservatism Correlates

It has already been noted that conservatism is significantly related to a preference for the Conservative party. The relationships between conservatism and the other variables are presented in Table V. Of particular interest are the correlations for the general population with (i) perceived lack of knowledge about the Common Market ($r = 0·21$, $p < 0·05$), and (ii) the feeling that life in Britain is changing for the worse ($r = 0·23$, $p < 0·05$). This provides evidence consistent with the rationale for our hypothesis that these two feelings are related to an anti-Market attitude *because* they tend to be characteristic of the conservative personality.

Conservatism is also associated with low occupational status ($r = 0.25$, $p < 0.01$), which supports Eysenck's (1972) finding that working class people tend to be conservative in personality, while those in higher status occupations tend to be liberal. The remaining correlations with age, personality, and the sub-factors of conservatism are, by and large, also consistent with previous findings (see Chapter 12).

D. SOCIAL CLASS CORRELATES

Apart from the relationship of low occupational status with opposition to the Common Market and with conservatism noted above, Table VI shows that the only other significant relationship is with ethnocentrism ($r = 0.30$, $p < 0.01$). Thus the aspect of conservatism most closely associated with social class appears to be ethnocentrism, cf. the "Alf Garnett" ("Archie Bunker") syndrome.

For the sake of completeness, the intercorrelations among all the fifteen variables are presented for the general population and the student sample in Table VI. The coefficients for the various sub-groups have been averaged for the purposes of this table; the coefficients for males and females and for the three political parties appeared, on the whole, sufficiently similar to justify averaging in this way (cf. the separate figures given for conservatism in Table V).

E. DIFFERENCES IN MEAN SCORES

Political party differences. Three differences between the parties have already been mentioned, namely that relative to Labour and Liberal, Conservative voters are more in favour of joining the Common Market, more conservative, and more ethnocentric. The remaining significant differences from Table III are for (i) Militarism, with Conservative voters scoring higher than Liberal and Labour ($F = 39$, $p < 0.01$), (ii) Age, with Conservative voters being older than Labour and Liberal ($F = 16$, $p < 0.01$), (iii) the L-scale, with Liberal voters scoring higher than Conservative and Labour ($F = 8.5$, $p < 0.01$), (iv) Occupation, with Conservative voters having higher status occupations than Liberal and Labour ($F = 4.6$, $p < 0.01$), and (v) Psychoticism, with Labour voters scoring higher than Liberal and Conservative ($F = 3.4$, $p < 0.05$).

Sex differences. For the student sample, the only significant sex difference is for age, with the males being older ($F = 6.9$, $p < 0.01$). For the general population sample, the males are higher on Realism ($F = 10$, $p < 0.01$) and Psychoticism ($F = 5.0$, $p < 0.05$), and lower on Religiosity ($F = 4.4$, $p < 0.05$). For both samples combined, there are two other significant

TABLE V

Correlations with conservatism

	Rea.	Mil.	–He.	Eth.	Rel.	P.	E.	N.	L.	–CM	–K.	–Br.	Age	–Oc.
Gen. pop.														
Male 23 Con.	–0·40	0·70	0·86	0·71	0·58	–0·50	–0·50	–0·06	0·27	0·32	0·33	0·33	0·57	0·21
22 Lab.	–0·31	0·74	0·81	0·65	0·72	–0·28	–0·35	0·39	0·34	0·03	0·29	0·09	0·37	0·34
10 Lib.	–0·53	0·63	0·79	0·75	0·72	–0·40	–0·60	0·23	0·14	0·54	0·57	0·27	0·14	0·49
Female 32 Con.	–0·29	0·83	0·82	0·72	0·74	–0·22	0·07	–0·09	0·32	–0·07	0·16	0·13	0·28	0·38
17 Lab.	–0·66	0·88	0·88	0·74	0·82	–0·09	–0·26	0·32	0·48	0·02	0·46	0·40	0·38	–0·06
15 Lib.	–0·49	0·93	0·78	0·79	0·77	–0·30	–0·37	–0·13	0·43	0·50	–0·52	0·32	0·72	0·17
119 combined	–0·39†	0·80†	0·82†	0·71†	0·72†	–0·29†	–0·26†	0·06	0·33†	0·16	0·21*	0·23*	0·37†	0·25*
Students														
Male 8 Con.	–0·48	0·59	0·84	0·46	0·92	0·08	0·46	–0·27	0·76	–0·42	0·01	–0·39	0·69	
37 Lab.	–0·40	0·46	0·82	0·66	0·78	–0·46	–0·29	0·46	0·24	–0·18	0·21	–0·17	–0·21	
10 Lib.	–0·39	0·77	0·67	0·48	0·39	–0·60	0·14	–0·19	0·05	0·44	–0·22	–0·05	0·38	
Female 12 Con.	–0·28	0·49	0·74	0·43	0·78	–0·12	–0·61	0·22	0·58	0·07	0·13	0·10	0·18	
21 Lab.	–0·40	0·82	0·70	0·65	0·78	–0·47	0·39	–0·08	0·50	–0·46	0·34	–0·30	0·01	
7 Lib.	–0·54	0·68	0·92	0·81	0·40	–0·28	0·38	–0·79	0·33	–0·41	–0·48	0·04	–0·06	
95 combined	–0·39†	0·60†	0·78†	0·62†	0·75†	–0·38†	0·04	0·10	0·32†	–0·21*	0·10	–0·16	–0·10	
214 total	–0·39†	0·73†	0·80†	0·68†	0·73†	–0·32†	–0·16*	0·08	0·33†	0·00	0·16*	0·09	0·31*	

TABLE VI

Intercorrelations among the 15 variables for the two samples

	Con.	Rea.	Mil.	−He.	Eth.	Rel.	P.	E.	N.	L.	−CM.	−K.	−Br.	Age	−Oc.
Con.	—	*−0·39*	*0·60*	*0·78*	*0·62*	*0·75*	*−0·38*	*0·04*	*0·10*	*0·32*	*−0·21*	*0·10*	*−0·16*	*0·10*	
Rea.	−0·39	—	*0·17*	*−0·67*	*0·19*	*−0·55*	*0·39*	*−0·00*	*0·09*	*−0·37*	*0·18*	*−0·02*	*0·23*	*−0·10*	
Mil.	0·80	−0·05	—	*0·21*	*0·38*	*0·19*	*−0·14*	*0·13*	*0·13*	*0·08*	*0·01*	*−0·03*	*−0·04*	*−0·08*	
−He	0·82	−0·65	0·52	—	*−0·08*	*0·05*	*−0·43*	*−0·09*	*0·02*	*0·29*	*−0·16*	*0·09*	*−0·26*	*0·05*	
Eth.	0·71	0·09	0·54	0·42	—	*0·22*	*−0·15*	*−0·08*	*0·10*	*0·04*	*−0·12*	*0·17*	*−0·01*	*−0·00*	
Rel.	0·72	−0·52	0·41	0·53	0·32	—	*−0·28*	*−0·02*	*0·10*	*0·33*	*−0·25*	*0·06*	*−0·18*	*0·23*	
P.	−0·29	0·36	−0·18	−0·38	−0·23	−0·05	—	*−0·04*	*0·13*	*−0·15*	*0·05*	*0·00*	*0·09*	*−0·12*	
E.	−0·26	0·23	−0·12	−0·31	−0·19	−0·18	0·18	—	*−0·35*	*−0·05*	*0·06*	*−0·13*	*−0·06*	*0·03*	
N.	0·06	0·00	0·01	0·04	0·04	0·16	0·10	−0·22	—	*−0·17*	*0·11*	*0·05*	*0·13*	*−0·14*	
L.	0·33	−0·15	0·27	0·30	0·30	0·09	−0·41	−0·25	−0·13	—	*−0·35*	*0·07*	*0·06*	*−0·08*	
−CM.	0·16	0·18	0·09	0·01	0·36	0·08	−0·05	−0·11	0·17	0·06	—	*0·16*	*0·17*	*−0·04*	
−K.	0·21	0·03	0·19	0·13	0·18	0·18	0·06	−0·17	−0·17	−0·05	0·10	—	*0·00*	*0·16*	
−Br.	0·23	0·04	0·18	0·13	0·26	0·18	−0·04	−0·19	0·11	0·03	0·26	0·20	—	*0·17*	
Age	0·37	−0·34	0·24	0·37	0·21	0·25	−0·13	−0·12	0·01	0·41	−0·02	−0·02	−0·02	—	*0·09*
−Oc	0·25	0·15	0·18	−0·08	0·30	0·17	0·01	0·05	0·15	−0·05	0·19	0·18	0·16	0·09	—

Note: Averaged coefficients are given in the lower left for the general population (N = 119), and in the upper right for the student sample (N = 95). Coefficients in italics are significant at the 0·05 level (two-tail test).

differences; males are lower on the L-scale ($F = 4{\cdot}0$, $p < 0{\cdot}05$) and on anti-Hedonism ($F = 3{\cdot}9$, $p < 0{\cdot}05$).

Differences between the two samples. Apart from being older, the general population sample score higher than the students on the "L"-scale ($F = 29$, $p < 0{\cdot}01$), Ethnocentrism ($F = 12$, $p < 0{\cdot}01$), Realism ($F = 8{\cdot}1$, $p < 0{\cdot}01$) and Militarism ($F = 7{\cdot}3$, $p < 0{\cdot}01$) and lower on Extraversion ($F = 15$, $p < 0{\cdot}01$), Psychoticism ($F = 10$, $p < 0{\cdot}02$) and Religiosity ($F = 6{\cdot}0$, $p < 0{\cdot}05$). Because of the age discrepancy, these differences between the general population and the students may be partly a reflection of age. In particular, the L-scale is correlated $0{\cdot}41$ with age for the general population sample, thus accounting for at least part of the difference in L-scores between the two samples.

V. Discussion

Our four hypotheses are supported with the exception of the first; the broad factor of conservatism shows a slight but not significant association with opposition to the Common Market (in the general population sample). The three aspects of conservatism, however, which were picked out for special attention are each related to an anti-Market attitude at a significant level. Ethnocentrism seems the most relevant of the five sub-factors measured by the C-Scale (for the general population sample). Perceived lack of knowledge, which was assumed to reflect heightened fear of uncertainty in conservatives, is related both to opposition to the Common Market and to conservatism (for the total sample). Similarly, the feeling that life in Britain is changing for the worse, which was assumed to be a reflection of conservatives' disappointment at the eroding of cultural traditions (of which joining the Common Market might be seen as yet another step on the downhill path) is related both to opposition to the Common Market and to conservatism.

An interaction of these hypotheses with political party is apparent. The results confirm that conservative personality types are more likely to vote for the Conservative party and paradoxically, that the middle and upper classes are less conservative than the working class. The interaction of conservatism with political party affiliation in predicting attitudes to the Common Market is consistent with this. Thus Conservative voters are in favour of joining, while conservatism tends if anything to be related to opposition to the Common Market. The finding that people in higher status occupations are more in favour of joining provides at least a partial explanation as to why Conservative voters are in favour.

Also apparent is an even clearer interaction with ethnocentrism. Ethnocentrics are more likely to vote Conservative, are more working class and more against joining. Even though ethnocentrism is closely related to conservatism (r = 0·71 for the general population), the closer relationship with attitude to the Common Market obtained with ethnocentrism, may serve to justify the practice of investigating separately the various (if highly correlated) sub-factors of conservatism.

There are two circumstances under which the present results might have been more clear-cut. First, a better method of controlling for political allegiance would have been to obtain a measure of degree of party preference and then to have statistically partialled this effect out. Such a method would correct for any tendency of Conservative voters to be in favour of joining on account of, for example, their conservatism acting to increase their loyalty to the party's decision, rather than acting to increase their "emotional" resistance to the idea. In this connection, it is noticeable that the association between the different variables and attitude to the Common Market (Table IV) tends to be clearer for Liberal voters, perhaps because they are relatively free from the "distorting" effects of party loyalty on this particular issue.

Second, the mean scores for opposition to the Common Market in Table III are all below 3·0 (the mid-point for the 5-point scale used); in fact, 20 per cent and 48 per cent of the total sample endorsed statements Nos. 1 and 2 respectively, in Table II. Thus most people were in favour of joining, so reducing the variance and consequently the size of the correlations. A bias in the attitude of our sample is indicated, since public opinion polls using various questions have consistently found that only a minority of

TABLE VII

Public opinion poll results on questions of the type "Are you for or against joining the Common Market?"

	% In favour	% Against	% Don't know
1971			
October	33	48	19
November	38	44	18
December	39	47	14
1972			
January	42	41	17
February	34	45	21
June	35	49	16
July	39	45	16
August	38	43	19
September	38	44	18
October	35	46	19

Note: These figures were obtained by averaging results published in newspapers over the past year by the following companies: British Market Research Bureau, Gallup, Harris, National Opinion Polls, and Opinion Research Centre.

people are in favour of joining (see Table VII). The bias may have occurred because our subjects were volunteers, and it is likely that people who are willing to fill in questionnaires (especially those on personality) are more likely to approve of joining the Common Market (cf. Patterson and Wilson, 1969; Boshier, Chapter 9).

An outstanding feature of the present results is the difference between the general population and the students in the correlates of opposition to the Common Market. The correlations are in the opposite direction to a significant degree in the case of conservatism, ethnocentrism, religiosity, and the L-scale. If the study had been carried out on this student sample alone, then a rather different set of conclusions to those outlined above would have been indicated. This provides a striking example of a situation in which results based on students cannot be generalized to the population at large.

How can we explain the students' idiosyncratic results? It was suggested in Chapter 6 that children's social attitudes are structured according to the principles of what they consider right and wrong, and that these principles which tend to be of a religious nature have probably been derived from their parents and teachers. The more complex pattern observed in adults was seen to develop following various "real-life" learning experiences, and with the accumulation of vested interests (wife, children, property, career, etc.), cf. the "social-class interest" theory. Adult attitudes are thus seen to be of a motivational or "dynamic" nature compared with the more "cognitively" derived attitudes of children.

Perhaps a similar explanation can be advanced in the present case; the hypothesis being that social desirability, idealistic notions, or just considerations of what is the "in thing", are more relevant in determining attitudes to the Common Market for students, while various emotional and motivational factors are the predominating influences for the general population. For example, students would seem more concerned with the pros and cons of a United Europe in the ideological sense, while the population at large would seem more concerned with the effect of practical matters, such as food prices, on their personal circumstances.

If motivational factors are less compelling for students in determining attitudes to the Common Market, then one prediction is that social desirability should play a greater part. The L-scale of the E.P.I. provides a means of checking on the role of this variable, since the scale appears to be more a measure of social desirability as a personality trait than that of lying, especially when there is little motivation for dishonesty such as when the questionnaire is answered anonymously (as in the present case), cf. Michaelis and Eysenck (1971). Anyway, the prediction is supported since the L-Scale is correlated −0·35 with opposition to the Common Market for students, whereas the correlation is 0·06 for the general population.

Now because of the negative association of the L-scale with opposition to the Common Market in students, it may be predicted that the correlates of this scale should likewise be negatively associated with an anti-Market attitude. This prediction receives some support since taking the five variables most closely associated with the L-scale in students, each is correlated in the predicted direction with opposition to the Common Market as follows: Realism (-0.37 with L) 0.18, Religiosity (0.33 with L) -0.25, Conservatism (0.32 with L) -0.21, Anti-Hedonism (0.29 with L) -0.16, and Neuroticism (-0.17 with L) 0.11. Thus we have evidence that social desirability has a fairly general association with attitude to the Common Market in students.

Moreover, if the attitudes of students are less influenced by motivational factors, then their criteria for social desirability should also be different from those of the general population. In particular, the hypothesis put forward implies that social desirability for students should be more closely associated with religion or idealism, if only because of the lack of opposing motivational factors. Apart from the correlations of L with opposition to the Common Market (-0.35 compared with 0.06 for the general population), three other examples that are consistent with this hypothesis are (i) Ethnocentrism (0.04 with L compared with 0.30 for the general population), (ii) Religiosity (0.33 compared with 0.09), and (iii) Realism (-0.37 compared with -0.15).

Thus while the results for attitude to the Common Market in the general population, and their views of what is socially desirable, seem to be readily explicable in terms of expediency and motivationally determined attitudes, the results for students seem to be explicable more simply in terms of the values and ideals they hold to be socially desirable.

The results on political party differences indicate that the C-Scale, even though it is not directly concerned with economic issues, does differentiate quite well between Conservative voters on the one hand and Labour and Liberal voters on the other. For the total sample, Conservative voters are significantly higher on conservatism, ethnocentrism, and militarism than supporters of the other two major parties.

In conclusion, it might be claimed that the present study has demonstrated the relevance of psychological factors to a political issue that might otherwise tend to be evaluated solely in terms of economics.

VI. Summary

The relevance of social attitudes and personality to the issue of joining the Common Market was investigated in a small sample of students and the general population. Hypotheses concerning the Common Market based on notions about the nature of conservatism, found partial support. For the total sample, opposition to the Common Market was positively related to Realism, *perceived* lack of knowledge about the Common Market, and a feeling that life in Britain is changing for the worse. For the general population sample, opposition to the Common Market was also positively related to Ethnocentrism and low occupational status.

It was necessary to control for political allegiance, which would otherwise have tended to obscure these relationships. This complication arose because voting behaviour is determined both by economic considerations and by social attitudes, two variables which are often at odds for our two main political parties. For example, the Conservative party in seeking to join the Common Market are acting in accordance with the wishes of people in high status occupations but not people who are ethnocentric, and it is both ethnocentric people and those in high status occupations who tend to support the Conservative party.

For students, certain variables were related to Common Market attitudes, but in the opposite direction to the corresponding results for the general population, e.g. conservatism, religiosity, and the E.P.I. L-scale were each associated with a pro-Market attitude only in students. This reversal is interpreted in terms of attitudes to the Common Market being determined more directly by considerations of social desirability in students. Moreover, their criteria for social desirability are apparently different from those of the general population, e.g. it appears socially desirable to be pro-Market, idealistic, and religious in students, while for the general population it appears socially desirable to be low on psychoticism, and ethnocentric.

A theory of attitudes being determined mainly by social desirability and associated concepts such as value judgments and idealistic notions, seems necessary to explain the students' results. For the general population results, the theory of attitudes being determined by complex motivational or "dynamic" factors seems the most appropriate interpretation.

References

Adorno, T. W., Frenkel-Brunswik, E., Levinson, D. J. and Sanford, R. N. (1950) "The Authoritarian Personality." Harper, New York.
Centers, R. (1949). "The Psychology of Social Classes." Princeton University Press, Princeton.
Eysenck, H. J. (1954). "The Psychology of Politics." Routledge and Kegan Paul, London.
Eysenck, H. J. (1972). "Psychology is About People." Allen Lane, London.
Michaelis, W. and Eysenck, H. J. (1971). The determination of personality inventory factor patterns and intercorrelations by changes in real life motivation. *J. genet. Psychol.* **118**, 223–234.
Patterson, J. R. and Wilson, G. D. (1969). Anonymity, occupation and conservatism. *J. soc. Psychol.* **78**, 263–266.

A Dynamic Theory of Conservatism

17

GLENN D. WILSON

Institute of Psychiatry, University of London

I. The Problem

The studies reviewed earlier in the book concerning the structure of attitudes and beliefs have clearly demonstrated the overwhelming import-ance of a general factor that is most appropriately labelled "conservatism". The conservatism syndrome was found to include religious dogmatism, right-wing political orientation (in Western countries), militarism, ethno-centrism, intolerance of minority groups, authoritarianism, punitiveness, anti-hedonism, conformity, conventionality, superstition and opposition to scientific progress. The consistency with which these characteristics were found to intercorrelate together led to the proposal that personality dynamics must be involved in the organization of social attitudes, i.e. that individual differences in motivational processes are partly responsible for this tendency for attitudes to arrange themselves around a general factor of liberalism versus conservatism. Many of the studies described in the latter half of this book are concerned with testing hypotheses based upon such an assump-tion. In this chapter a preliminary attempt will be made to integrate the currently available evidence concerning the correlates of conservatism within the context of a general theory of the psychological origins of the dimension.

With respect to the origins of conservatism, there are two questions that require answering. These are logically separate though often confused in the literature.

(1) What are the processes which lead some individuals to adopt a

K

generally conservative pattern of attitudes, values and beliefs, and others liberal? (the problem of *acquisition*).

(2) How do attitudes come to be organized (patterned) in the particular way that they do? e.g. Why does religious dogmatism tend to be positively related to ethnocentrism rather than negatively, and so on (the question of *organization*).

The first question is relatively easy to answer, and a great deal of pertinent evidence is already available (McGuire, 1969). Some of the factors affecting the acquisition and modification of attitudes are: (a) genetic temperamental traits such as aggressiveness, (b) simple learning processes, such as exposure to reference groups, imitation, and fear learning, (c) cognitive or rational considerations such as logic and expediency, and (d) unconscious, "dynamic" factors such as jealousy, ego-defence and dissonance reduction.

Adorno *et al.* (1950), in discussing the development of the "authoritarian personality, based their theory largely on the Freudian argument that the relationship of the child with its parents is prototypic of relationships with all authority figures in adult life. According to this view, the child raised in a very authoritarian household will maintain a childlike dependency, displaying obedience in a situation of institutional subservience, and identifying with the father when in a position of authority. God is presumed to be a projection of the father in adulthood and is therefore an object of fear and reverence. There is, in fact, substantial evidence that authoritarian parents tend to produce authoritarian children (e.g. Byrne, 1965) and similar findings have been obtained with the dimension of conservatism (Insel, 1971; Kish, *et al.*, 1973; Boshier, Chapter 14 this volume).

While an explanation along these lines may be adequate to account for the transmission of authoritarian attitudes from one generation to the next, it does little to explain how attitudes have come to be organized in the way that they have, i.e. the particular pattern of intercorrelations among various attitude and belief areas that emerges consistently from one culture to another, encompassing all areas of attitude and belief—not just those relating to authority. The model which follows constitutes an attempt to integrate the known correlates of conservatism into a theory of the psychological antecedents of the dimension that would account for its organization as well as its transmission.

II. Outline of the Theory

It would seem that the most logical way to approach the problem of attitude organization is to start with the empirically determined pattern of attitudes (the "conservatism syndrome") and work backwards in the hope of discovering something they have in common that might explain why they cluster together. Such a procedure might be expected to provide clues as to the psychological basis of the general factor of conservatism-liberalism.

Table I illustrates the central proposition of the present theory, that the common basis for all the various components of the conservative attitude syndrome is a *generalized susceptibility to experiencing threat or anxiety in the face of uncertainty*. The concept of uncertainty, is employed here in the information theory sense, and includes both *stimulus uncertainty* (innovation, complexity, novelty, ambiguity, risk, anomie, etc., as states of the physical and social environment), and *response uncertainty* (freedom of choice, conflicting needs and desires, etc., originating within the individual). Thus each component of the general conservatism factor has been identified with a specific kind of stimulus or response uncertainty which might constitute a source of threat to the individual who has a generalized proneness to feelings of vulnerability in "uncertain" situations.

It might be objected that in this scheme all that has been achieved is the translation of preferences into their opposites (aversions), producing a circular argument which does not add anything in terms of explanation. This is not the case, however, and something has been gained. The various attitude components have not been converted into precise and comprehensive antonyms; rather, some aspect of the physical, social or internal environment which relates to the information theory concept of uncertainty has been postulated as a *partial* determinant of the attitude cluster with which it is associated. In this way it has been shown that it is possible to reduce the several diverse attitude clusters down to a single hypothesized psychological antecedent. This might be expected to suggest a number of research studies and assist in tracing the origins of the conservatism syndrome back through other possible antecedents.

Figure 1 summarizes some hypothesized antecedents of the fear of uncertainty. Throughout this diagram the listed concepts refer to individual differences that should be regarded as continuous variables. They are all expressed in terms of the end of the dimension that theoretically predisposes towards conservatism rather than liberalism; this is done for the sake of convenience and ease of interpretation and no negative evaluation is intended.

The theory suggests that certain genetic factors such as anxiety proneness, stimulus aversion (sensitivity to strong stimuli), low intelligence, lack of physical attractiveness, old age, and female sex, and certain environmental factors such as parental coldness, punitiveness, rigidity and inconsistency, and membership of the lower classes, will give rise to feelings of insecurity and inferiority (low self-esteem). For example, a child continually subjected to harsh punishment might eventually accept or "internalize" the low evaluation of himself that he perceives his parents or teachers to hold. Feelings of insecurity and inferiority may be expected to result in a

TABLE I

Fear of uncertainty as the hypothesized basis of conservative attitudes

	Source of threat	Attitudinal manifestation	
FEAR OF UNCERTAINTY	Supernatural forces	Superstition	**GENERAL CONSERVATISM**
	Death	Religious dogmatism	
	The unknown and unpredictable		
	Ambiguity		
	Anarchy	Right-wing politics	
	Social disruption		
	Unfamiliar people	Ethnocentrism	
	Foreign influences	Militarism	
	Deviant behaviour	Intolerance of minorities	
	Anomie	Authoritarianism	
	Disorganization	Punitiveness	
	Dissent		
	Decisions	Rigid morality	
	Loss of control of own feelings and desires	Anti-hedonism	
		Adherence to external authority	
	Complexity	Conventionality	
	Novelty	Conformity	
	Innovation		
	Technological change	Anti-science	
	Erosion of traditional ideas		

ORIGINS

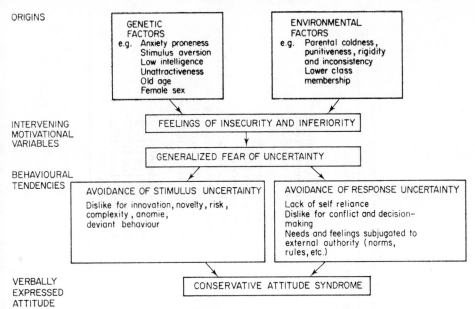

INTERVENING
MOTIVATIONAL
VARIABLES

BEHAVIOURAL
TENDENCIES

VERBALLY
EXPRESSED
ATTITUDE

Fig. 1. A theory of the psychological antecedents of conservatism

generalized fear of uncertainty, the insecure individual fearing stimulus uncertainty because he perceives the environment as complex, changeable, and treacherous, and the individual with low self-esteem fearing response uncertainty because he lacks confidence in his ability to control events in his environment or make autonomous decisions regarding his own behaviour.

At the behavioural level the fear of uncertainty would manifest itself as: (1) a tendency to dislike and avoid uncertain stimulus configurations—innovation, novelty, risk, complexity, social disorganization, etc., and (2) a tendency to dislike and avoid situations that involve a great deal of response uncertainty—need conflict, decision-making, etc. These two groups of tendencies would be differentiated to some extent, the fear of stimulus uncertainty being associated more strongly with insecurity and the fear of response uncertainty being more closely tied with inferiority feelings. There would, however, also be a positive correlation between them because of their common genetic and environmental origins. The last step in the model suggests that this dislike for and avoidance of stimulus and response uncertainty would be manifested as an organized pattern of attitudes—that which we have labelled "the conservatism syndrome".

Thus it is argued that conservative attitudes serve a defensive function. They arise as a means of simplifying, ordering, controlling, and rendering more secure, both the *external* world (through perceptual processes, stimulus preferences, etc.) and the *internal* world (needs, feelings, desires,

TABLE II

Empirical evidence relating conservatism to its hypothesized genetic and environmental origins

Variable	Measure	Correlation with C	Source
Genetic Factors			
Anxiety proneness	E.P.I. Neuroticism	0·20†	Bagley (1971, unpublished)
	E.P.I. Neuroticism	0·06	Nias (1972, unpublished)
	E.P.I. Neuroticism	0·03	Wilson and Brazendale (1973a)
Stimulus aversion	E.P.I. Extraversion	−0·35†	Wilson and Brazendale (1973a)
	E.P.I. Extraversion	−0·26†	Nias (1972, unpublished)
	Zuckerman S.S.S.	−0·33†	Kish (Chapter 13)
	Zuckerman S.S.S.	−0·46†	Kish (Chapter 13)
Intelligence	Remote Associates Test	−0·16	Anderson and Race (1972, unpublished)
Attractiveness	Ratings	−0·12	Wilson and Brazendale (1973b)
Age	—	0·23† to 0·61†	Wilson and Patterson (1970)
Sex (female)	—	0·31†	Wilson and Bagley (Chapter 7)
Environmental Factors			
Parental treatment	P.A.R.I. Total score	0·39†	Boshier and Izard (1972)
	P.A.R.I. Rejection	0·23*	Boshier and Izard (1972)
	P.A.R.I. Domination	0·44†	Boshier and Izard (1972)
	P.A.R.I. Indulgence	0·28*	Boshier and Izard (1972)
Social class	Occupational Status	−0·35†	Nias (Chapter 16)

*p < 0·05.   †p < 0·01.

TABLE III

Empirical evidence relating conservatism to hypothesized motivational variables

Variable	Measure	Relationship to C	Source
Insecurity			
Risk avoidance	Questionnaire	0·67*	Steiner and Parrish (1971, unpublished)
Anonymity	Giving name on C-Scale	p < 0·001	Patterson and Wilson (1969)
Occupational preferences	Holland Vocational Preferences Test	"Safe" occupations preferred (See Table IV)	Di Scipio (1968, unpublished)
Superstition	Avoidance of walking under ladders	p < 0·05	Boshier (Chapter 9)
Marital Status	—	Age × C correlation higher for unmarrieds	Wilson and Richman (1971)
Inferiority			
Self-concept	Bills I.A.V. Self-esteem	−0·51†	Boshier (1969)
	Bills I.A.V. Self-acceptance	−0·13	Boshier (1969)
	Bills I.A.V. Self/ideal discrepancy	−0·30*	Boshier (1969)
Power and achievement imagery	T.A.T. n. Power	−0·32†	Mack et al. (1971)
	T.A.T. n. Achievement	−0·24*	Mack et al. (1971)
Deference	E.P.P.S. n. Deference	−0·26*	Webster and Stewart (Chapter 8)
Autonomy	E.P.P.S. n. Autonomy	−0·30*	Webster and Stewart (Chapter 8)
Fear of Uncertainty			
Art preferences	Ratings of complex pictures	−0·56†	Wilson, Ausman and Mathews (1973)
Fear of death	Questionnaire	0·54†	Wilson (Chapter 12)
Need for order	E.P.P.S. n. Order	0·24*	Webster and Stewart (Chapter 8)
Dogmatism	Rokeach D-Scale	−0·58†	Webster and Stewart (Chapter 8)
Role conflict	Questionnaire	−0·24*	Webster and Stewart (Chapter 8)
Existentiality	Personal Orientation Inv.	−0·51	Webster and Stewart (Chapter 8)
Spontaneity	Personal Orientation Inv.	−0·32	Webster and Stewart (Chapter 8)

*p < 0·05.   †p < 0·01.

etc.). Order is imposed upon inner needs and feelings by subjugating them to rigid and simplistic external codes of conduct (rules, laws, morals, duties, obligations, etc.), thus reducing conflict and averting the anxiety that would accompany awareness of the freedom to choose among alternative modes of action.

III. The Empirical Evidence

The evidence most relevant to this theory of conservatism is summarized in Tables II and III. Table II shows a number of empirical relationships that could be interpreted as reflecting the effects of various genetic and environmental factors on Conservatism Scale scores; Table III shows the relationships between various operationalizations of the intervening motivational variables in the model and C-scores. Although some of the correlations (e.g. those with intelligence and physical attractiveness) fail to reach statistical significance, the relationships are all in the direction predicted by the model. It should be noted, however, that many of these results were available before the theory was constructed, and it was tailored to fit them. The theory should be regarded as a model which integrates the existing findings; the testing of future hypotheses derived from it may be expected to result in its modification and development.

The two studies that were based on the theory rather than contributing to its development appear to provide particularly strong support for its predictions. The first is the Wilson *et al* (1973) study outlined in Chapter 10 of this volume, which demonstrated that high C-scorers tend to dislike paintings that were judged beforehand as involving a great deal of stimulus uncertainty. The second is the study by Nash (1972) cited in Chapter 12, of this volume, in which it was shown that conservatives are fearful concerning what might happen to them after death, the correlation with fear of death applying not only to the religious subfactor in the C-Scale, but all of the four major attitude components equally.

The correlations of C-scores with preferences for different types of occupations (Table IV) have not been reported previously, and were calculated specifically to test the hypothesis derived from the present theory that high C-scorers would tend to prefer "safe and secure" occupations. The data were collected by Di Scipio (1968) using a sample of 22 male civil servants ranging in age from 23 to 47 years. The Vocational Preference Inventory (Holland, 1965) requires respondents to express their feelings about 160 different occupations which are classified in such a way that 10 scores are obtained. The hypothesis is clearly confirmed in the results: the conservatives prefer occupations labelled "Conventional" and "Realistic", while the liberals prefer "Artistic" and "Infrequent" (bizarre and unusual) occupations.

TABLE IV

Correlations of conservatism with Holland Vocational Preference scores
(N = 22)

Holland Scale	Correlation with C
Conventional	0·65†
Realistic	0·47*
Intellectual	0·45*
Sociable	0·18
Masculine	0·11
Enterprising	0·11
Self-control	−0·09
Status	−0·28
Infrequent	−0·28
Artistic	−0·47*

One other study listed in Table III that has not been previously reported is that of J. Steiner and J. Parrish (personal communication, 1971). Using a small sample of psychiatric staff they found that conservatism was inversely related to risk-taking as measured by their own questionnaire ($r = -0·67$, $df = 10$, $p < 0·02$). Most of the other findings cited in these tables have been reported either in journal articles or preceding chapters.

IV. Conclusion

As suggested previously, the major implication of this theory is that attitude and belief patterns cannot be explained purely in terms of rational processes and logical overlap among various content areas. Apparently it is necessary to postulate certain more fundamental personality processes as instrumental in determining the organization of attitudes—factors that may be characterized as motivational or "dynamic". In particular, it has been suggested that the conservative attitude syndrome serves an ego-defensive function, arising as a response to feelings of insecurity and inferiority, and a generalized fear of uncertainty (whether in terms of environmental complexity or the alternatives to action that are available).

This is primarily a theory of attitude *organization*; other processes may be necessary to account fully for the *transmission* and *modification* of attitudes and beliefs (e.g. imitation learning). Nevertheless, in so far as attitudes must be acquired in the process of being organized the theory may be regarded as having relevance to these areas as well. It is a descriptive theory in the sense that it integrates a large number of empirical findings, but hopefully, it will also be seen to have some explanatory power. Although constructed to fit the existing evidence, it is unlikely that future research will prove it totally wrong. Rather, apparent disconfirmations should lead to modification of the theory and clarification of the exact connections between the genetic and environmental origins of the conservatism dimension, the intervening motivational variables, and its behavioural and attitudinal manifestations.

References

Adorno, T. W., Frenkel-Brunswik, E., Levinson, D. J. and Sanford, R. N. (1950). "The Authoritarian Personality." Harper, New York.

Boshier, R. (1972). An empirical investigation of the relationship between conservatism and superstitions. *Brit. J. soc. clin. Psychol.* in press.

Boshier, R. and Izard, A. (1972). Do conservative parents use harsh child-rearing practices? *Psychol. Rep.* **31**, 734.

Byrne, D. (1965). Parental antecedents of authoritarianism. *J. pers. soc. Psychol.* **1**, 369–373.

Di Scipio, W. (1968). Conservatism and vocational preferences. Unpublished results.

Holland, J. L. (1965). "The Vocational Preference Inventory." Educational Research Associates.

Insel, P. M. (1971). "Family similarities in personality, intelligence and social attitudes." Ph.D. thesis, Univ. London.

Kish, G. B., Netterberg, E. E. and Leahy, L. (1973). Stimulus-seeking and conservatism. *J. clin. Psychol.* **29**, 17–20.

McGuire, W. J. (1969). The nature of attitudes and attitude research. In "Handbook of Social Psychology". (Lindzey, G. and Aronson, E., eds.). (2nd edn.). Addison-Wesley, London.

Mack, D., Powell, J. R., Lehmann, A. D. and Wendt, H. W. (1971). The influence of aggression, anxiety, liberalism, and other personality factors on game behaviour as a function of other player's choice. *Psychol, Beitrage,* **13**, 38–54.

Nash, M. E. (1972). "Conservatism and the fear of death." Unpublished MS., Cal. State Univ., Los Angeles.

Patterson, J. R. and Wilson, G. D. (1969). Anonymity, occupation and conservatism. *J. soc. Psychol.* **78**, 263–266.

Wilson, G. D., Ausman, J. and Mathews, T. R. (1973). Conservatism and art preferences. *J. pers. soc. Psychol.* in press.

Wilson, G. D. and Brazendale, A. H. (1973a). Social attitude correlates of Eysenck's personality dimensions. *Soc. Behav. Pers.*

Wilson, G. D. and Brazendale, A. H. (1973b). Sexual attractiveness, social attitudes and response to risqué humour. *Eur. J. soc. Psychol.*

Wilson, G. D. and Patterson, J. R. (1970). "Manual for the Conservatism Scale." N.F.E.R. Publishing Co., Windsor.

Wilson, G. D. and Richman, J. (1971). Sexual opportunity and social attitudes. *Percept. mot. Skills.* **33**, 665–666.

Author Index

Subject Index